Winning Ideas
from
Winning Schools

Winning Ideas
from
Winning Schools

Recognizing Excellence

DAWN HANSEN HELLER
with
ANN MONTGOMERY

ABC-CLIO
Santa Barbara, California
Oxford, England

Library of Congress Cataloging-in-Publication Data

Heller, Dawn Hansen.
   Winning ideas from winning schools : recognizing excellence / Dawn Hansen Heller with Ann Montgomery.
    Includes index.
    1. School improvement programs—Case studies. 2. Educational innovations—Case studies. I. Montgomery, Ann. II. Title.
   LB2822.8.H45   1989   373.12'07—dc20   89-15179

ISBN 0-87436-527-9 (alk. paper)

96 95 94 93 92 91 90 89   10 9 8 7 6 5 4 3 2 1

ABC-CLIO, Inc.
130 Cremona Drive, P.O. Box 1911
Santa Barbara, California 93116-1911

Clio Press Ltd.
55 St. Thomas' Street
Oxford, OX1 1JG, England

This book is Smyth-sewn and printed on acid-free paper ∞
Manufactured in the United States of America

For Tony,
partner in this, as in all things

Contents

Introduction, xiii

PART ONE: Planning

Chapter 1   Educational Goals and Objectives, 3
   The Planning Process, 3
   Goal Statement Content and Structure, 7
   Goal Monitoring and Revision, 12
   Communicating Goals to Students, Faculty, Parents, and the
      Community, 14
   Reflecting the Mission, 18

PART TWO: Teaching

Chapter 2   Teaching Writing, 21
   Writing and School Goals, 22
   The Writing Curriculum, 27
   Faculty Training, 32
   Resources and Support, 35
   Meeting Special Needs, 40
   Specialized Programs and Promotions, 41

Chapter 3   Teaching about Democracy, 45
   Required Courses, 45
   Elective Courses, 48
   Models and Simulations, 51
   Special Programs and Events, 52

Chapter 4   Teaching Character and Values, 59
   Policies, Procedures, and Examples, 59
   Co-curricular Programs, 63

Community Service Programs, 64
Special Programs, 71
A Continuing Challenge, 73

PART THREE: Students

Chapter 5   Students and Study Skills, 77
Required Study Skills Courses, 77
Study Skills Electives and Special Programs, 79
Across-the-Curriculum Programs, 80
Guidance by Counselors and Library Media Specialists, 81
Study Skills Materials, 81

Chapter 6   Students and Basic Skills, 83
Identifying Students with Remediation Needs, 83
Summer Programs, 84
Laboratory Programs, 85
Tutoring Programs, 86
Alternative Programs, 87

Chapter 7   Students and High Expectations, Recognition, and Rewards, 90
Clear Messages, 90
Special Honors and Incentives, 95

Chapter 8   Students and Discipline, 99
Developing Clear Rules and Policies, 99
Ensuring Understanding of Rules and Policies, 101
Clarifying Responsibilities, 102
Expectations, Consequences, and Rewards, 103
Finding the Key, 107

Chapter 9   Students and Drugs, 108
Program Elements, 109
Staff Participation and Training, 111
Parent and Student Participation, 113
Team Approaches, 114
School and Community Climate, 115

Chapter 10   Reporting Student Progress, 116
Progress Reports, 116
Special Reports, 118
Other Methods, 119

Chapter 11   Students and College and Career Information, 122
    Counseling, 122
    College and Career Days, 124
    Computer Services and College/Career Centers, 124
    Specialized College Prep Services, 125
    Information on Career Choices, 127
    Putting It All Together, 128

Chapter 12   Students at Risk, 130
    Identifying Students at Risk, 130
    Intervention and Support Services, 132
    Helping Students Who Drop Out, 137

PART FOUR: Teachers

Chapter 13   Teacher Input, 141
    Faculty Committees, 141
    Departmental Structure, 142
    Participatory Management, 143
    Other Input Methods, 144
    Encouraging Participation, 145

Chapter 14   Staff Development for Teachers, 147
    Basic Elements, 147
    Special Programs, 149
    Staffing for Development, 150
    Other Efforts, 151
    Development Incentives, 153

Chapter 15   Rewards and Incentives for Teachers, 156
    Honors and Awards, 156
    Teacher of the Month or Year Programs, 160
    Master or Mentor Teacher Programs, 161
    Monetary Rewards, 161
    The Real Rewards, 162

PART FIVE: Parents and the Community

Chapter 16   Schools and Parents, 165
    Meetings and Open Houses, 165
    Newsletters, Mailings, and Surveys, 167

Parent Committees and Advisory Groups, 167
Volunteer Programs, 169
Booster Groups, 172
Special Events, 174
Parent Education Programs, 175
Putting It All Together, 176

Chapter 17   Schools and the Community, 178
Financial Support, 178
Human Resources, 179
Jobs and Career Programs, 180
Business and University Partnerships, 181
Cooperative Efforts, 185
Outreach Activities, 188

PART SIX: In Their Own Words

Chapter 18   Success Stories, 193
Philosophy, Atmosphere, and Spirit, 193
Facilities and Services, 195
Course Offerings, 196
People, 198
Programs, 199
Special Events and Projects, 201
Alumni, 203
Special Challenges, 203

Chapter 19   Portrait of a Principal, 205
The Principal as Effective Manager, 205
The Principal as Role Model, 207
The Principal as Friend and Advocate, 208
The Principal as Teacher and Learner, 209
The Principal as Leader, 209

APPENDIXES

*Appendix A   Alphabetical List of Recognized Schools:
1987, 217*

*Appendix B   High Schools Recognized: 1986–1987
Secondary School Recognition Program, 225*

Appendix C   Junior High/Middle Schools Recognized:
1986–1987 Secondary School Recognition
Program, 245

Appendix D   Personal Viewpoints, 257
   The School Improvement Team: An Organization for Effective
      Change, 259
   Writing for Everyone, 263
   The Role of Leadership and Citizenship Education in U.S.
      Secondary Schools, 266
   The Academic Coach, 268
   Developing Self-Discipline and Self-Esteem, 271
   Empowering Teachers, 274
   Community Schools, 277

Index, 279

Introduction

The 1987 Secondary School Recognition Program marked the fifth anniversary of the United States Department of Education's program, which honors schools based on characteristics that contribute to school effectiveness and student success. That year, 271 schools were recognized at a special ceremony in the White House Rose Garden. But the recognition of excellence should and can have a lasting impact beyond those communities that have been directly affected.

The winning schools were chosen for their ability to respond to challenges faced by all American educators today. The purpose of this book is to make the practices and solutions developed by these winners available to other schools, in the belief that creative adaptation of proven solutions is more desirable than reinventing the proverbial wheel. What is offered here is a selection of approaches, programs, viewpoints, and solutions described by the 271 winners in their applications.

SELECTING THE WINNERS

The winning schools were chosen on the basis of 14 general attributes and 7 indicators of accomplishment. In addition, for 1987, special emphasis was given to creative and effective ways of teaching citizenship and the United States Constitution. The 14 attributes identified were:

1. Clear academic goals
2. High expectations for students
3. Order, discipline, and freedom from drug use
4. Rewards and incentives for students

5. Regular and frequent monitoring of student progress

6. Development of good character and values

7. Teacher input and staff development

8. Rewards and incentives for teachers

9. Concentration on academic learning

10. Positive school climate

11. Administrative leadership

12. Well-articulated curriculum

13. Evaluation for instructional improvement

14. Community support and involvement

The 7 indicators of accomplishment were:

1. Student performance on standard achievement tests

2. Student performance on minimum competency tests

3. Student success in high school or postsecondary education

4. Attendance rates for both students and teachers, and student suspensions and other exclusions

5. Dropout rates

6. Awards for outstanding school programs and teaching

7. Student awards in academic or vocational competitions

As a first step in the selection process, the chief school officer of each state was invited to nominate schools based on procedures determined within the state. Each state could nominate a number of schools equal to the total of its congressional delegation. The Council for American Private Education, an umbrella organization for private schools, was invited to nominate up to 130 schools, a figure based on the percentage of private secondary schools nationwide. Principals of the nominated schools (both public and private) then submitted written applications with detailed information about their programs, practices, and policies. All nominations were then examined by a 71-member review panel appointed by the department.

Prior to the first panel meeting, each panelist evaluated a set of applications from approximately 25 schools, using a detailed scoring sheet that included comments and questions as well as justifications for each score. In March, the panel met in Washington and convened in three-person reviewing teams to continue the evaluation process. Each team was to review its set of applications and to:

- Arrive at a consensus score

- Recommend which schools should be visited for on-site verification

- Indicate questions the panel would like the site visitors to ask during the visit

Overall the panel recommended 370 schools in 49 states for site visitations. The purpose of the site visits was to evaluate and augment the information submitted by each school by observing classroom instruction, reviewing documents, and meeting with parents, teachers, administrators, and other members of the school community. The site visits were conducted in the spring by a separate group of experts. Most of the site visitors were practicing educators, many of them principals of schools recognized by the program in previous years. Each school was visited by two site visitors for two days, after which each visitor submitted a report.

In May the 71-member review panel reconvened in Washington for a second round of scoring based on both the applications and the site visit reports. Each team again completed composite scoring forms for its assigned schools, based on both the applications and the site reports. Finally, the teams gave recommendations for or against recognition for each school, supporting their recommendations with written commentary.

A PERSONAL PERSPECTIVE

My involvement in the Recognition Program started with a phone call from Jean Narayanan of the United States Department of Education, asking me to serve as one of the 71 people on the review panel. Because I am currently a library media coordinator for a suburban Chicago high school, I saw this as an opportunity to learn about successful secondary school practices across the country and to bring those ideas back to my home district. I accepted enthusiastically and soon received copies of applications from the 27 schools assigned to my team.

I was privileged to work with an outstanding group of people on the selection panel. One-third of the panelists were educators, and two-thirds were private citizens with a keen interest in quality education. Those panelists who were not professional educators brought a special dimension to the reviewing process. Many were from organizations that have had long relationships with or interest in education. Certainly the entire group was appropriately diverse in race, religion, sex, and background—no mean task. Above all, I was impressed with the serious attitude that each panelist exhibited, and the recognition given to the efforts made by applicant schools—not just in preparing the detailed application form but in the important task of building successful and exemplary education programs for young people.

The process worked well, thanks to the hard work of the staff of the Department of Education. After seeing the process firsthand, I can certainly endorse it as a fair one, designed to limit bias and capriciousness.

I am sure nearly all of the panel participants felt that their teams were superb. I felt very fortunate to be teamed with Charlotte Locke of the Philadelphia Friends' Schools and Benjamin Ladner, executive director of the National Faculty. They were articulate, witty, caring, and serious about the task at hand. After much debate, discussion, and compromise, we were able to reach consensus on a team evaluation and score for each of our 27 schools.

IDEAS BY THE DOZENS

The 1987 winning schools represent a wide range of types—public, private, parochial, and residential. They included senior highs, junior highs, combinations of both, and middle schools. In size they ranged from very large to very small (under 60 students).

Despite the formal nature of the application form and the prescribed questions, it was amazing how the personality—the gestalt—of each school and its people came through. As I read the applications assigned to my team for the first time, I realized they contained approaches and solutions that would be both interesting and useful to the thousands of schools across the country dealing with the same daily struggles in their classrooms, administrative offices, and board of education chambers.

If there were dozens of concepts in these 27 applications, then there had to be dozens of dozens in the applications of all of the selected and recognized schools. Thus, this was a book I felt compelled to write, and write in a timely manner. The staff at the Department of Education, particularly Jean Narayanan, offered immediate and whole-hearted support. ABC-CLIO, a publisher whose reputation and professionalism I admired, expressed immediate interest. And thus the commitment was made. (Although when the six large cartons of applications and site visitation reports arrived, I had second thoughts about what I had contracted to do!)

THE FOCUS OF THIS BOOK

From the beginning it was obvious that some topics and sections of the applications offered much more potential than others for extracting ideas that other schools might borrow or adapt creatively. You will not find here any analysis of which kinds of schools won—by size, type, location, etc., and you will not find discussions on topics related to statistics, such as the number of units required for graduation or test scores. These are best left to educational researchers.

What you will find are chapters dealing with issues such as drug abuse, teaching writing, recognizing teachers, and involving the community in education. There is sufficient diversity in the approaches of the winning schools to these issues that the discussions should prove useful to others. In a few cases I had planned a chapter on a topic (for example, teacher evaluation), but found that the responses showed such uniformity (in this case, acceptance of the classic clinical supervision model) that I felt the chapter would not serve any useful purpose.

SUGGESTED USES

I hope this book will be useful in several ways. First, as a confirmation for many schools that their practices are similar to those in the winning schools. Such confirmation is professionally reassuring. I saw this firsthand when I asked my school's English department chairperson to read the chapter on teaching writing. Her response was, "This is great! This is what we're doing in so many ways, and where we're not there yet, it's on our goal list."

Second, I hope this book will serve as a resource for schools dealing with specific issues. Somewhere, someone else may have tried an approach that could work. Networking is easily arranged by a phone call or a letter, and the names of school principals, school addresses, and school phone numbers appear in the Appendixes B and C.

No inference should be made that schools cited more frequently are better than those less frequently mentioned. The number of citations can in no way be equated with the quality of a school's programs. All of these schools were found worthy of recognition in the rigorous process described above. The schools mentioned were my subjective choices (and the choices of Ann Montgomery, an able Illinois educator who contributed all of the sections related to junior highs and middle schools). The schools mentioned most often are those whose applications were written in a highly descriptive style, making it easier to understand and communicate the substance of their programs.

Every effort has been made to reflect accurately the contents of cited applications. Obviously, these were not confirmed personally, although they were validated by the site visitations to the schools.

IN THEIR OWN WORDS

Of special interest, I trust, will be the brief "Personal Viewpoint" essays in Appendix D. These were written at my request by staff members from a few of the recognized schools. Each essayist was chosen because of a vibrant thread in the fabric of a particular answer in his or her school's application. I felt these educators could share more that would be of special interest to others. I am grateful to the essayists for their thoughtful, articulate responses, and I wish to thank Randall Holdridge, Dean of Students, St. Mark's School of Texas, for suggesting the idea to me.

Finally, a special thank you to each and every one of the 271 recognized schools. These are their winning ideas.

PART ONE

Planning

CHAPTER 1

Educational Goals and Objectives

What are the overall instructional goals of your school and how were the goals identified? How are they communicated to students, teachers, and parents?

Clearly defined instructional goals provide schools with both a sense of mission and a means for measuring progress. This chapter describes the methods and approaches used by winning schools to identify and communicate their educational goals, including:

- The Planning Process
- Goal Statement Content and Structure
- Goal Monitoring and Revision
- Communicating Goals to Students, Faculty, Parents, and the Community

The Planning Process

Although the processes used by winning schools to establish and communicate instructional goals vary, they have several important factors in common:

The effort is viewed as a long-range one

The process involves groups from both the school community and the community at large

3

A number of techniques are used to guarantee a true
community effort in the planning process

Many of the schools have established planning committees
composed of parents, students, and faculty. Typical of these are the
Long-Range Planning Committee at Metairie Park Country Day
School and the Tri-Advisory Committee at Claremont High School.

Dooley School calls its goal identification methods a "team
approach to management." Georgetown Visitation Preparatory
identifies a "two-prong" process: one with faculty and staff, and
the other with parents and alumnae. Ideas from both groups are
synthesized and presented to parents and students.

At Flowing Wells High School, a School Improvement Unit
exists to examine the high school programs and to establish a formal and ongoing outcome-based process with a continued needs
assessment and educational improvement focus. A steering committee of faculty and staff and a parent advisory component ensure
the maintenance of a broad perspective.

A collaborative process, in which parents, faculty, and administration all have a part, is used to identify goals at Saint John's
School. First, a review of the relevant education literature is presented to a representative group of parents. Faculty members then
complete a series of questionnaires, which are used to determine the
school's educational goals and objectives.

The process followed at Parkway South High School when
developing its Statement of Philosophy illustrates the seriousness of
purpose and the value placed on the goal-setting process. Teachers,
students, and administrators worked together to develop seven
drafts over a six-month period. Under the leadership of the school
improvement team, the drafts were discussed in student assemblies,
reviewed at parent coffees, and displayed prominently in the entry-
way of the school. Copies were also framed and displayed in each
classroom after teachers taught a lesson concerning the meaning of
the document. After a final draft was agreed on, students were
required to write an essay explaining whether they saw Parkway
South living up to the Statement of Philosophy and offering suggestions for ways the school could better adhere to the goal statement.

INVOLVING THE COMMUNITY

The concept of a community effort is common in setting goals
for the winning schools. The community participates in a number

of different ways, either in the actual goal-setting mechanism or by providing data and input to a school committee which then formulates the actual goals. For example, at Lawton Community High School, a broad-based committee of parents, students, teachers, citizens, administrators, and school board members worked on the Statement of Philosophy and list of academic goals. Creighton Preparatory School mails a response form to all families before the start of school in order to provide information for its long-range planning committee.

Many of the schools are careful to keep a broad base for the planning process and make efforts to include various school constituencies beyond the obvious parent, student, and teacher groups. For example, at Menlo-Atherton High School the planning committee includes elementary school and community college representatives as important groups in the planning process. Brighton High School has established a committee of citizens to interact with the Business Partnership Board in the assessment and goal-setting activities.

The Novi Task Force on Excellence in Education develops the goals at Novi High School. Evidence of the interest shown by the community is the fact that the call for volunteers for the task force elicited 50 applications when only 27 could be accommodated.

Instead of establishing a separate committee, Norland Middle School uses existing groups to involve various components of the school community in goal setting. Each year the principal and the assistant principal for curriculum meet with the Curriculum Council, the Student Council, and the PTA Board to discuss goals for the next school year. The resulting information is taken to the administrative team, which identifies goals in conjunction with the overall district plan.

At Newton County High School, the existing district goals were identified by more than 400 citizens and school personnel. Woodbridge High School has held a day-long needs assessment meeting, which involved over 200 parents and students and resulted in agreement on a direction for the school. Three years later, Woodbridge used a comprehensive community survey to validate what had been established.

Narragansett High School also uses a community survey as part of its goal-setting activity. Lamphere High School planners target their surveys at specific audiences, including parents, teachers, students, recent graduates, and administrators. The Academy of Notre Dame de Namur sends queries to parents, students, and alumnae groups. These are then used by the faculty to draft the school's goal statements.

Similarly, the Academy of Mount St. Ursula uses data collected from questionnaires completed by parents and alumnae, along with teachers' assessments of student needs, to prepare goal statements. Central High School in Tennessee uses student surveys and feedback from parent organizations to develop its goals. Dobson High School employs a school climate survey in setting long-range goals.

BROADENING THE SCOPE

Many schools view goal-setting activities within a broader context. For example, accreditation agencies offer incentives and a number of tools which schools can use to develop goals and objectives. Typically, there is a relationship with the accreditation process and the documents prepared and reviewed in that system. For example, Lutheran High School West reports that statements of goals and philosophy are reviewed as part of the North Central self-study sequence. Similarly, White Plains High School reports using the Middle States process, which involves virtually all members of the school's community in creating goals for the school.

Phi Delta Kappa goals for schools are used as a basis for review by St. Louis Park High School. The goal-setting exercise developed by Phi Delta Kappa is also reported as useful by Skowhegan Area High School.

John Adams Middle School utilizes outside assistance to help in goal setting. The University of New Mexico's Education Department has led a focus session on the concept of the middle school, which now serves as an impetus for further study and goal development.

A modified Delphi Plan is used at Ridge High School to draft ongoing goals for annual growth. Joint planning by the principal and an advisory group, as well as the principal's interaction with students as the facilitator of a leadership group, are key elements in the success of the venture.

Goal setting begins at the district level at Oldham County High School, with the Board of Education setting yearly, measurable goals and performance objectives. Local schools within the district then set their own goals, as does each department, teacher, class, and school organization.

For Gladstone High School, the school board also establishes annual goals, and the high school leadership team writes specific goals for the school year. GHS reports that these goals "represent the concerns as well as the dreams of the staff." Students have input into the process, and the goal statements show that their desires and needs are carefully considered.

TARGET AND TRADITION

For schools with a long tradition and continuing role based on a clearly defined mission, there is a sense of continuity in terms of goals and objectives. For example, the Charlotte Latin School reports that its goals today are still essentially those set forth by the school's founders. The statements are reviewed periodically, but remain viable and valued.

Similarly, goals were first identified with the founding of the Philadelphia High School for Girls in 1848. While many changes have taken place in goal implementation, the administration reports that the goals themselves remain basically the same.

Many schools, like Amherst Middle School, review, revise, and refine their goals on an annual basis. Amherst developed its initial goals more than a decade ago, before the school's opening, and was thus goal-oriented from its inception.

A 45-page document called "Goals for St. Mark's" was the product of nine committees involving more than 100 parents, teachers, trustees, students, and alumni. The school has been conscientious about tying administrative policy decisions to specific items in the goals document, and its annual report is entitled "Progress on the Goals for St. Mark's." The long-range planning document and goals statements are, in a real sense, the central driving force for action at the school.

Goal Statement Content and Structure

Although the schools use similar processes to develop goals, there is much more variety in the ways they frame and structure their goal statements. Some use a central overriding statement to set the entire tone of the document. Others delineate three, four, or five core beliefs. Some organize goal statements according to the groups that will be most directly responsible for their accomplishment, such as students, teachers, or parents. Others distinguish between process and outcome statements. An examination of representative samples will illustrate the variety and breadth of approaches.

SETTING THE TONE

Several of the documents begin with an overriding view statement. For example, the staff at A. Philip Randolph Campus High School bases its goals on the core statement, "Philosophically we believe every child can learn, must learn, and will learn in our school." Geyser Public School's statement declares that the "most significant objective is the task of maintaining a strong work ethic and positive attitude that emanates from the home and the community."

The attitudes and skills to be acquired before graduation are the focus for the goals of Loyola High School of Baltimore, Inc., which mandate, "All schools are for learning, but learning is not destined to end at graduation. Skills are needed to continue beyond graduation." LHS has therefore set as student outcome goals "to think reasonably, to write and speak correctly and convincingly, and to perceive the interdependence between learning and life."

Student outcome statements form the document that sets action for Adlai E. Stevenson High School. Stevenson's Board of Education has also adopted as policy a composite description or vision of the type of school Stevenson is striving to be.

Recognizing that other elements of society have responsibility for educating and shaping the young, the goal statements developed by Burns Union High School are separated into three categories:

1. Those that are primarily the responsibility of the school

2. Those that are shared with other principal groups in society

3. Those in which the school has a supporting influence, with the primary responsibility resting with family and/or community

Sage Valley Junior High School's goals focus on instruction, primarily on the teachers' role. The four goals include teacher expertise in the Hunter instructional model; an instructional belief that all students can learn, albeit at different paces and styles; provision of successful experiences for all students; and teachable objectives in all subjects.

Each of Clear Lake High School's four goal statements focuses on students:

1. Maintain and improve an instructional program that helps students acquire the basic skills in reading, writing, and mathematics

2. Prepare students in an instructional program appropriate to their needs

3. Provide experiences that extend learning in the academic areas, thereby helping students realize the practical application of what they are learning

4. Expand vocational educational programs and related services to be realistic in terms of student needs and actual opportunities for employment

Ballard High School's four goal statements take a different approach, dealing with different groups in the community and their relationships to the school:

1. Create an atmosphere that nurtures intellectual growth and development and encourages creativity, critical thinking, and love of learning in both students and teachers

2. Offer the opportunity for each student to develop a sound mastery in basic skills and for these skills to be measured on a regular and constructive basis to ensure progress and success

3. Encourage talents of both faculty and administrators through a climate of mutual trust, confidence, clear expectations, and evaluation criteria, and conscious recognition of outstanding instructional leadership and performance

4. Inform both public and private sectors of this community of the academic, vocational, and special programs of the schools through an intensive public relations effort and impress upon the Ballard community, especially parents, the importance of their part in the education of their children

Desert Shadows Middle School has a goal list that is totally student-centered, ranging from responsible behavior to understanding of human achievement. Interestingly enough, only one goal specifically mentions academic skills.

Academy of Our Lady of Good Counsel's role as a Catholic educational community is clearly and appropriately reflected in its five overall instructional goal statements:

1. Maximize spiritual, intellectual, emotional, social, and physical development of each unique student

2. Maximize students' perception to think critically, solve problems, and communicate effectively

3. Help develop positive self-esteem and a sense of responsibility

4. Prepare students for a life-style based on Gospel values, stressing service, peace, justice, and compassion as full members of the Church

5. Develop students' ability to learn about their heritages, the heritage of the global community, and how to participate in our democratic society

Flowing Wells High School has developed a mission statement upon which its five goals and explanatory objectives are clearly based. Of special interest is the delineation of the basic beliefs upon which the overall mission of the school is founded. Teachers must believe that:

- students can learn
- teachers can teach effectively
- we must have high standards and expectations
- students need rewards, praise, and success
- students must be engaged in active instructional experiences a high percentage of the time

Students must believe that:

- they can learn and be successful in school
- they can and must get involved

A graceful statement has been adopted by Cranbrook Kingswood School as an outgrowth of the school's mission, which encompasses five elements: "to prepare students to flourish in an increasingly complex world, to move into higher education with competence and confidence, to grow physically as well as intellectually, to respect and appreciate the arts and to leave our stewardship with a strong sense of social responsibility."

A few schools have also created "profile of a graduate" documents to use as guides for annual and long-range planning. For those schools operated by Jesuits, the relevant document is called "Portrait of the Graduate of a Jesuit High School at Graduation," which was developed by the Committee on Research and Development of the Jesuit high schools in the United States. Each school is free to adapt the original document to the needs and realities of its own situation. This is what has been done at Loyola High School of Baltimore, Inc.

GOAL CATEGORIES

For many schools, goal lists are extensive and comprehensive. In order to provide a structure for such listings, the schools construct a framework of categories into which the goal statements are placed. For example, Georgetown Visitation Preparatory School has organized its goals into six areas: religious, moral, intellectual, physical, social, and psychological. Thirty different specific goals have been placed into these six broad categories.

A similar approach has been used by Poolesville Junior-Senior High School, and for all Montgomery County schools. Goals are listed under the categories of academic skills, physical development, understanding the relationship of the individual and society, scientific understanding, aesthetic expression, and career development. Each year individual schools identify specific goals for emphasis.

White Plains High School divides its goal statements among lifetime goals, community goals, and staff/instructional goals. Ridgewood High School has also identified four general goal areas— scholarship, character, citizenship, and school performance—with five to seven items under each.

Fremont Senior High School divides its goals into two discrete sets by listing student goals and board of education/staff goals separately. The lists are recognized as all-encompassing. Each year the board and staff identify and prioritize objectives in order to implement the goals. South Kingstown High School also divides its goals into two groups, those that relate to content and those that relate to process. An example of a content goal is "development of economic understanding," and an example of a process goal is "ability to adjust to change." Overall, the school has identified nine content and seven process goals.

Mesa Union School has created district goals in eight distinctive areas: student achievement, staff in-service, computer programs, physical appearance/landscaping, library skills, physical fitness, career education, and increased Hispanic family involvement. Oak Grove Junior High School, on the other hand, specifies goals in only three areas: individual, specific skills, and future learning.

When Baboquivari Junior High School wanted to develop a four-year plan to enhance student achievement, they used an assessment questionnaire with all students, paraprofessional staff, teachers, and community members participating. The resulting document has 9 goals and 69 specific objectives. Included with each of the 69 objectives is an action plan, with different segments of the community and the school having responsibility for each one. Each action plan is also assigned dates for implementation and follow-up review. It is obvious that the document is intended to be a true guide for school improvement.

South View Junior High School utilizes overall district instructional goals as a starting point. These are then refined into program goals for each subject. Each course has both terminal objectives and daily instructional objectives to guide the teacher through the content outline. In addition, the school develops its own yearly operational goals.

In a similar fashion, the goals of Parkway Central High School serve as what they call "a living organism." The product of intensive discussion, debate, and consensus, the goals have been agreed upon by faculty, students, and the larger community, and "bind us to a central purpose." The goals are set out in four separate documents: the Statement of Philosophy, which details what they are about; the Faculty Covenant, which outlines what individual teachers seek in their relationships with students; the Statement of Mission and School Goals, which draws a clear picture of the year-by-year course of action; and the Outcome Statements, which sketch a definite plan for the school for the next five years. Together, active parents, responsible students, and committed teachers agree on the priorities for the school on a yearly basis.

Goal Monitoring and Revision

Schools serious about the goal-setting process do not simply set goals and then forget about them. Progress needs to be monitored, and occasionally targets need to be changed. The winning schools follow a variety of approaches for reviewing goals and setting new ones.

The Curriculum Council at Orange Glen High School reviews its goals and discusses progress made on each one through the entire school year. Any problems encountered in achieving the stated goals are worked out by the entire council or referred to subcommittees whose specific purpose is to find solutions to any identified problems. At Proctor Hug High School, the curriculum committee and the department chairs review the established goals at least once a year to ensure consistency between the goals and what is occurring at the school.

A more formal structure for monitoring school goals is in place at James Logan High School. Elected representatives from the faculty, parents, and students meet monthly to review school programs and monitor the school plan. At Midwood High School at Brooklyn College, monthly Consultative Council meetings offer opportunities for parents and students to comment about school programs and objectives.

Feedback from parents provides the initial phase of the annual goal review and revision process at Palo Alto High School. Questionnaires are sent to every parent in January, requesting suggested goals for the upcoming school year. Then the Goal-Setting Committee is established to review the suggestions from the different groups that form the school's constituency.

In addition to monitoring progress toward goal achievement during the school year, schools committed to the goal-setting process also prepare to renew the cycle come spring. Some, like Cardinal Gibbons High School, set aside time each year to review the philosophy and objectives in order to evaluate their performance and to measure accountability. Others, like Lakeridge High School, prepare an annual school profile of student performance to identify building level improvement and progress toward goals. Another approach used by many schools, including South Salem High School, is to prepare an evaluation of the school's performance and mail it to students' homes as an annual report.

Some schools use analysis of test scores and other data to set goals and measure their attainment. At Tottenville High School, these statistics have been analyzed over a 12-year period. At S. S. Murphy High School, comprehensive faculty studies of student needs, based on diagnostic data, are used in annual goals modification.

Examining weaknesses is another approach that some schools follow. According to administrators at Saint Bernard-Elmwood

Place High School, "In order to identify goals we first identify our weaknesses. Goals are then developed as a means through which we eliminate our problem areas." At Woodbridge High School a few items are placed on a "hit list" for special emphasis, based on perceived needs. Goals are routinely "revisited" at Wayland High School, and each department looks at the Statement of Purpose and then reports to the full faculty during a structured workshop on the current relevancy of the goals.

Summer is the time that many schools use to reflect on what happened during the past school year and to plan for the next one. Shoreham-Wading River High School has "an active curriculum development program which includes bringing in a majority of the staff each summer, assessing parental and community input, and accommodating student concerns and requests as plans for the fall are completed." A summer retreat is the mechanism used by Rock Bridge Senior High School to provide faculty members with an opportunity to review the school's philosophy and goals.

A number of schools extend the planning process to include long-term goals by setting five-year plans in place. Such is the case at Crest Senior High School, where long-term goals have been identified through interviews and conferences with students, parents, teachers, and administrators. The goals are evaluated at the end of each five-year period. Central High School in South Dakota also uses a five-year cycle. Each year the objectives are reviewed and revised if necessary. Throughout, CHS aims to help all groups develop ownership of the goals and objectives of the high school program.

A more detailed five-year process is used at Chandler High School. Their Five Year Plan for Instructional Improvement includes a year-by-year timeline with a built-in monitoring process. The district administrators report on the state of the district, evaluate progress, and set goals at the end of each year. Their instructional cabinet assesses pupil progress, and departments also meet to set their individual goals.

Communicating Goals to Students, Faculty, Parents, and the Community

For many of the winning schools, communication of school goals is central to their mission. In fact, one school commented, "The goals are communicated to everyone even remotely interested in LaSalle Institute!" Goal-oriented schools use a multiplicity of methods to reach their public—printed pieces, personal contacts, orientations, workshops, open houses, newsletters, course guides, organization and club meetings, radio, and TV. And they aim to reach students, parents, alumni, faculty, and the community at large.

FOCUSING ON STUDENTS

Students at Northern Highlands Regional High School receive a list of proficiencies for each course in which they are enrolled. These represent the specific goals for the course. A similar method is followed at Lawton Community High School, where students and parents receive copies of specific learning objectives for each course in the curriculum. These objectives are used as the basis for evaluating student progress in each class.

At Centennial Senior High School, all ninth graders and their parents attend an orientation program prior to the start of school, at which the school's goals are explained. The administration at Lamphere High School conducts annual assemblies for all grade levels, setting the agenda for the school year in terms of goals and objectives.

Lincoln County High School offers an unusual approach. The school holds academic pep rallies, involving both student and community leaders, to communicate to students the significance of academic success. Archbishop Molloy High School introduced an Alumni Hall of Fame to provide role models for students. AMHS also conducts a summer orientation camp at which incoming freshmen are made aware of the school's philosophy and goals. Other methods used throughout the year to communicate the school's values to students include assemblies, retreats, club programs, and awards presentations.

Poolesville Junior-Senior High School prints copies of the local school goals on posters, which are placed prominently in all classrooms. They also distribute copies for students to keep in their notebooks for the year. Vacaville High School also uses annual posters to encourage seniors to do well on the California Assessment Program exams. The administration also includes a statement relating to self-esteem in the daily bulletin for students.

Classroom teachers are an important part of the communication system at Newburgh Free Academy. At the beginning of the year, English and social studies teachers spend three days explaining the rights and responsibilities of everyone who is a part of the school system, as well as the school's goals for the year. At

Scarborough Senior High School, regularly scheduled presentations about goals are included in orientation meetings, homerooms, tutorial classes, and guidance sessions.

Principals play important roles in goal dissemination in some schools. At Middletown High School the principal visits each English class during the first two weeks of school. At Flowing Wells High School the principal makes frequent visits to the Student Council to explain and discuss ideas and to clarify future directions. Goals developed at Boyland Central Catholic High School are taken to the entire student body via class-level meetings with the principal. The students are challenged to develop personal goals as a part of their educational experience.

Students entering Homestead High School are given PEP (Personal Educational Plan) booklets to facilitate their development of personal goals. These include copies of the school's goals and objectives and encourage students to fit their personal plans into the school's overall objectives.

FOCUSING ON FACULTY

For a school to be successful in achieving its goals, faculty members must be involved, informed, and committed to the accomplishment of those goals. Therefore, winning schools make diligent efforts to involve teachers in the goal-setting process.

Faculty in-service days serve to promote understanding of school goals at McQuaid Jesuit High School. The administration at Archbishop Molloy High School also holds presentations and workshops aimed at communicating objectives to faculty, while the principal at Haywood High School holds special orientation conferences to communicate goals and objectives to new staff members.

PARENT PARTNERS

Parents are a group critical to all schools. The winning schools make a wide variety of efforts aimed at keeping parents informed and getting them involved in the whole process of goal setting.

Private schools often establish mandatory meetings for parents, in order to ensure that home and school are working together to achieve a common goal. Jesuit High School schedules two required meetings at which parents learn about the school's philosophy, goals, and other major points of concern. Parents of freshmen at Villa Angela Academy are required to attend a Parent Night at which the school's philosophy is presented.

Public schools try different means to involve parents. Many schools mail newsletters home to parents as well as to community residents. School goals are always a part of the materials covered in the newsletters published by Gladstone High School. Metairie Park Country Day School mails copies of its Mission Statement to all students' parents and grandparents. Letters are sent home to parents via the students of Crest Senior High School, and teachers at Schenley High School Teacher Center are requested to send parents their individual class objectives.

Brief outlines (four or five pages) for all courses at Haverford Senior High School are developed and distributed to parents. These include a course outline, course goals and content, tentative timetable, course requirements, grading procedures, and teacher availability for conferences. Polk Middle School adds a personal touch to its goal communication techniques by holding seminars to teach parents how to be "Polk Parents."

Principals also work hard to keep parents informed. At Myers Park High School, the principal meets regularly with parent members of the school committee. Committee members represent the different attendance areas in the district and meet quarterly to share concerns and successes with the administration. The principal at Newburgh Free Academy conducts periodic "Coffee Tours" for parents and other members of the community, at which school goals are an inevitable topic of conversation.

Greenway Middle School apparently lets everyone know its goals—one parent states, "There is a philosophy that is real in this school—a philosophy that everyone fits into."

REACHING OUT TO THE COMMUNITY

Recognizing that schools rely on the community at large for support, many schools use mass media and a wide range of approaches to carry the message of their mission, aims, and accomplishments to this wider audience.

Local press and electronic media provide a good means for getting the message out. The assistant principal at Stephens County High School writes a weekly column for the local paper, discussing school news and the school's purpose. Local newspapers print quarterly reports on North Olmsted High School, with a list of the school's goals and a progress report on each goal and objective.

Administrators of the Philadelphia High School for Girls make frequent appearances on panels and on radio and TV talk shows, and speak to professional and civic committees about the mission and program of the school. Central High School in South Dakota has its own TV station, which the faculty uses to explain the district's educational objectives to community viewers.

Mentor Shore Junior High School uses a signboard outside the school to tell the community about its educational goals. The goals have also been translated into slogans such as "The Best I Can Achieve," which are reprinted on book covers, folders, and the like.

In an effort to reach community members, copies of the Bradley Central High School goal statement are placed in the various public and school libraries serving the area. Butte des Morts Junior High School distributes its goals through a district calendar, which is given to all residents. They also place posters throughout the district.

Reflecting the Mission

A key concept for all of the recognition schools is that everything connected with the school reflects its mission. Several winners commented on this obvious truth. For example, according to representatives from University High School, "Our goals are communicated through the instructional processes in the classroom and the values stressed in student activities and athletics." And Mother Cabrini High School might have been speaking for all of these schools when it remarked, "The goals are communicated through who we are, in words, action, and in written correspondence."

Schools may use a variety of methods to establish clear educational goals and communicate them to members of the school and community. However, there is no doubt that a clear sense of mission is critical. Only by establishing a marked route can a school know whether it is making progress toward its destination.

For a personal viewpoint on this issue, see Appendix D, page 259.

PART TWO

Teaching

CHAPTER 2

Teaching Writing

Does your school have a school-wide approach or any special programs to teach writing skills?

Every winning school in the National Secondary School Recognition Program was required to focus on its approach to the development of writing skills. When writing is viewed in the context of the total curriculum, it is evident that many schools have a clear vision of their philosophy with respect to teaching writing. They have given careful consideration to what it is they are trying to do, why they are doing it, who needs to be involved in order to accomplish their goals, and how they will measure progress.

An examination of writing programs in the winning schools shows remarkable similarity in general approach. A clear relationship exists between general school goals and writing. Many of the schools are involved with national and state writing programs, using them as a basis for local efforts. In order to implement these programs, staff in-service is generally viewed as critical. The thrust is also to incorporate "writing across the curriculum."

Individual schools employ interesting and sometimes unique avenues to improve student writing skills. In the implementation of school-wide writing programs, many different school departments are regularly included. In the area of English course curriculum as well as specialized writing courses, writing assignments, specialized materials, and the use of computers, many examples have been cited that other schools may wish to consider adapting for their own approaches to writing.

This chapter looks at teaching writing in the context of several key areas:

- Writing and School Goals
- The Writing Curriculum
- Faculty Training
- Resources and Support
- Meeting Special Needs
- Specialized Programs and Promotions

Writing and School Goals

As has already been shown, one of the hallmarks of winning schools is a commitment to developing goals and objectives in order to provide a road map to follow for school improvement. It seems evident that this is one key ingredient in the improvement of writing. Therefore, it is not surprising that writing skills often figure prominently in school-wide objectives and even in teacher evaluation plans.

The all-school writing program at Menlo-Atherton High School requires that all teachers under evaluation submit a writing framework as one of their goals for the year. All other teachers file their plans for implementing the writing goal with the administrator in charge of instruction.

Because improvement of writing is a school-wide objective at South Kingstown High School, each teacher is required to develop a personal goal related to writing. In recent years, system goals at Newton County High School have directed teachers to include the teaching of reading, writing, and speaking skills in all content areas.

The philosophical framework for teachers at Wenatchee High School is that "writing is thinking." They are committed to providing both formal instruction and frequent practice appropriate to each grade level. And the University of Chicago Laboratory School has a straightforward target goal for all students: emphasis on development of a clear, well-developed writing style.

WRITING ACROSS THE CURRICULUM

Many of the specific strategies and objectives developed by the recognized schools are directed toward "writing across the curriculum." In other words, all teachers are expected to emphasize writing skills—as well as reading, listening, and speaking skills—in their classes.

In some schools, such as East High School, this expectation is translated into a requirement that student grades in all courses be partially based on writing proficiency. At Southwest High School all teachers assign at least one writing assignment per week as part of their course work. At Dover High School, a special writing-across-the-curriculum pilot project has established standard criteria of acceptability for all written work done in all subjects.

Holy Trinity Diocesan High School actively participates in the Every Teacher Is a Teacher of Writing Program. Through in-service, staff members are presented with the theory as well as the practical aspect of this approach. As a result, teachers in every subject area are expected to assist in the development of writing skills. And at Ferndale High School, "writing instruction is viewed as the responsibility of all teachers," and specific writing objectives are to be accomplished by the end of each school year.

An award-winning writing-across-the-curriculum program promotes active, involved, and creative learning. The staff at Gretchen Whitney High School believes that when writing is no longer viewed as the exclusive territory of the English department, the payoff is a rise in student achievement. Furthermore, they believe that literacy, knowledge, and conceptual thinking must be objectives of all courses, in all departments. Therefore, writing competency is required and assessed in all classes.

The English department at Westbury Senior High School has spearheaded the development of a school-wide writing program. In summer workshops, staff members create model writing lessons and assignments. In this way, teachers are able to give students organizational patterns appropriate for different modes of composition.

Several years ago Lakeridge High School began systematic efforts to improve student writing. A Writing Committee was established to provide direction to the school staff and to monitor and support implementation efforts. Believing that higher levels could be achieved, the committee designed a school-wide improvement strategy that stressed the development of writing skills in all curriculum areas. Included in the strategy were teacher in-service programs on methods and techniques, a style guide to unify expectations, and the establishment of standards for work in all classrooms.

The approach at Myers Park High School includes a school-based writing team of seven faculty members. The team provides 15 hours of in-service for the entire staff during the first year of the program and an additional 10 hours during the second year. Their special focus is an emphasis on peer coaching and applications for writing.

An effective writing-across-the-curriculum approach demands careful preparation. For example, Mother McAuley Liberal Arts High School began by advising department chairpersons about the proposed writing program in detail. Information, including methods of evaluation, was distributed and discussed. Then all teachers received questionnaires eliciting their comments and questions as a way to prepare for in-service. The subsequent in-service sessions dealt with types of assignments, expectations, methods of evaluating student writing, and suggestions for improving student writing through faculty cooperation.

A departmental approach is also used at O'Fallon Township High School. First they held an in-service program, which began by considering the rationale for having students write in all disciplines. This was followed by discussions on using various types of writing to promote learning and applying guidelines for writing tasks in content areas. The program concluded with samples of both formative and summative writing tasks for those content areas. Following the in-service, each department assessed the current level of student writing in its courses and set goals for improving and expanding the skills of students. Members of each department now meet quarterly with an administrator to discuss their progress in implementing new and better writing methods and tasks.

It is clear to the staff at Boyland Central Catholic High School that the school-wide approach used to teach writing is based on a specific policy for teachers: each teacher is expected to incorporate essay-type responses in assignments and tests. Their goal is to help students in every discipline on every level become proficient in written thought.

ASSESSING WRITING COMPETENCY

How can schools assess student writing ability? The obvious answer is that students must write in order to be evaluated. In some districts, students must pass a writing competency test in order to graduate.

At the beginning of each year, Denbigh High School staff members analyze student writing samples in order to develop a sequential writing program designed to meet the needs of students at all levels. Then teachers meet by levels to determine specific writing skills to be taught in each grade, taking into consideration the writing skills necessary for success in other content areas at each level. At the end of the year, teachers grade final compositions by each student, applying the same analytical scoring scale used nine months earlier at the start of the process.

Collecting writing samples is the first activity of every teacher in every discipline each semester at Scarborough Senior High School. Weaknesses are categorized by class so that an action plan can be developed to improve writing skills semester by semester.

Baboquivari Junior High School implements Arizona-mandated testing by requiring students at each level to submit two papers demonstrating essential writing skills in addition to regular writing assignments. Language arts department members score the papers, and results are reported to the district. Students must meet competency requirements in order to pass English.

Homestead High School sends a clear message about the importance of writing by requiring students to pass a writing competency exam and demonstrate an ability to communicate clearly in written work. Writing competency is required of all students who want a diploma from Brighton High School. South Kingstown High School also requires its graduates to demonstrate mastery of writing skills—to be eligible for a "college-prep" diploma, students must pass two one-semester writing courses beyond the basic level. Basic skills and/or remedial courses are offered through the senior year for students having difficulty with writing skills.

Chandler High School presents solid evidence that its writing-across-the-curriculum objective has been met. Since the program was initiated, all eligible seniors ready for graduation have passed the writing competency test. Valued—required—mastered!

PROGRAM EXAMPLES

How does the writing-across-the-curriculum philosophy translate into specific programs in specific departments? Award-winning schools can provide some helpful concrete examples.

Upper-level mathematics classes at Skowhegan Area High School write critiques of articles in mathematics journals. Literary research and writing about geometric shapes provide an opportunity to focus attention on the special vocabulary of mathematics. Science teachers demand properly written laboratory reports, and the social science department requires all classes to have some essay tests as well as written research essays. The development of essay writing skills is also considered important in advanced foreign language classes. Finally, the guidance department provides instruction in writing job and school admissions applications.

At Westbury Senior High School, the physical education department includes writing as part of its curriculum, and the business department has revamped the word-processing curriculum to include original writing by students. Office education classes in Haywood High School also include an emphasis on writing. Students learn to write the most common types of business letters, resumes, and letters of application. Business writing is also emphasized in the school's Jobs for Tennessee Graduates Program, which involves students who may need some remedial help in basic writing.

Every department at Blue Springs Junior High School has been infused with enthusiasm for writing. Students come to understand mathematical word problems by creating their own. A narrative style is used to record scientific observations in lab experiments. To gain perspective on various historical periods and practice their synthesis, analysis, and evaluation writing skills, students imagine themselves living in other times and create "I was there" essays. Students even write in foreign language classes, learning more about their own language in the process.

These are not isolated examples. Metairie Park Country Day School counts social science, science, foreign language, and computer science classes as important components of its approach to writing. At Blind Brook High School, science, foreign language, and health education courses are cited. At Cate School there is a partnership between the science and English departments, with science papers being graded by English as well as science teachers. At Clear Lake High School, work-study students in health occupations education keep daily journals, homemaking students prepare written menus and meal preparation descriptions, and art students write reports and essays on art topics.

An arresting special events approach has been developed at Garger High School. One March, for example, was declared Writing-across-the-Curriculum Month, with the theme "Words March On!" During March each department planned a special writing activity for one specific day during the month. The obvious message sent to students, parents, community, and faculty is that writing is critical and part of every course.

A prime example of a writing-across-the-curriculum attitude comes from Woodbridge High School. Having set school-wide goals for achievement in writing, they have a standard and significant response to students who bemoan writing assignments in psychology, biology, political science, or chemistry. When the young people cry, "But this isn't my English class!" teachers counter, "Oh, yes, it is!"

The Writing Curriculum

Despite the importance of a writing-across-the-curriculum approach, winning schools recognize that it is the English curriculum that must form the organized structure for developing writing skills, with skills learned one year laying the foundation for the next. A good example is the sequence described by Villa Angela Academy:

> By the end of ninth grade, students should be able to write a simple thesis statement, develop three points of proof, and be able to write an effective introduction and conclusion. The students will also have had practice in writing a five-point sentence outline that will be developed into a five-paragraph essay once the outline is approved.
>
> By the end of tenth grade, students will have had more practice writing five-paragraph essays with controlling thesis statements. These are usually done in a more in-depth manner with more emphasis on content and style.
>
> By the end of eleventh grade, students will be able to write a thesis theme on some literary work, using the literary work as a basis of proof for their position. Eleventh-grade students are also taught the skills of writing a research/term paper, and write on some aspect of American literature.
>
> In the twelfth grade, elective courses are offered, each with its own writing objectives.

A similar approach is used at the Marist School in Georgia. The ninth-grade emphasis is on five-paragraph essays, including outlining, editing, and rewriting. Tenth graders take a Writing the Essay course in which they learn to refine the outlining and editing process; those in American literature courses are also required to submit critical literary essays. Eleventh graders are required to take a course in writing research papers, and students in English literature classes continue to do critical literary writing. Twelfth graders are required to take Senior Composition and World Literature, which also involve in-class literary analysis.

Efforts to improve writing usually include special attention to scope and sequence, with specific writing skills to be taught at each grade level. At St. Louis Park High School this means identification of the skill level as well. In other words, the curriculum specifies when each skill is to be introduced, when it is to be emphasized, and when it should be mastered. It also indicates the number, length, and kinds of papers required for each level.

Junior high school English courses often focus on a three-step process of prewriting, writing, and revising. Others, such as Van Hise Middle School, pay attention to the depth of writing for each level. For example, sixth graders at Van Hise concentrate on topic sentences and paragraphs. Seventh graders develop paragraphs through expository, descriptive, and creative writing. In eighth grade emphasis is on five-paragraph compare-and-contrast papers on literature.

The Pittsford Middle School addresses a concern that teaching thinking skills is a vital aspect of writing, and that thinking, organizing, drafting, and revising should be conscious parts of each piece of writing. Students produce opinion essays, literary analysis, personal essays, business letters, and research-based reports. They are alerted to the need for expository/informative writing for everyday living and the importance of creative writing for expression of personal, affective needs. The program is a cycle of readiness, teaching, and extending, since the district specifies types of writing to be taught at specific grade levels while extending others at higher levels.

A very focused approach is evident in the English program at Cardinal Gibbons High School. Besides the writing done in all required literature classes, students must also take additional one-semester composition classes during their sophomore, junior, and senior years.

SPECIALIZED COURSES

Specialized, required one-semester courses devoted to writing seem to be an increasing trend. These allow a singular focus on the act of writing and take a variety of forms.

At Edgewood High School of the Sacred Heart, all juniors are enrolled in Competence in Writing, which focuses specifically on writing skills. Students are provided with opportunities to explain and organize their ideas in the following forms: the paragraph; descriptive, narrative, and persuasive essays; and the argumentative research paper. In addition, the course emphasizes usage, correct mechanics, and vocabulary building.

Students at Adlai E. Stevenson High School have the option of taking a required composition course in either their junior or senior year. They must pass a composition proficiency test at the conclusion of the course.

Teachers of a required one-semester junior-level course at Londonderry High School approach writing as a process, giving emphasis to prewriting, drafting, peer editing, and revising. Juniors at Brother Martin High School are also required to take a one-semester course focusing on essay and term-paper writing. At Dwight-Englewood School, students participate in a special writing program in their sophomore year. During the first semester, three class sessions per week are devoted to working with students on composing and revising skills, and students write papers weekly.

At Torrey Pines High School, students take a writing screening test at the end of ninth grade. As tenth graders they are then placed either in a composition course emphasizing intensive writing skill development or in a course including both literature study and writing.

Some schools provide a required composition course at the freshman level. This is the case at Alexander Hamilton High School. At the end of the one-semester course students must meet a system-wide competency requirement. Students who do not meet the requirement by the end of their freshman year continue their studies in a competency-based curriculum until the standards are met.

At Episcopal High School, freshmen must enroll in both the regular year-long English I course and a one-semester composition course emphasizing thinking and rhetorical skills. The school also requires seniors not enrolled in Advanced Placement English either to take a one-semester collegiate rhetoric and composition course or to complete a four week, four-hour-per-day intensive summer seminar in composition.

A different approach has been adopted at West Bloomfield High School, which is currently phasing in a writing-based curriculum. At the end of the second year all ninth- and tenth-grade students will be expected to have a minimum of 20 complete writing experiences per year. All grade levels will be included in this writing-based curriculum by the time the second phase-in period is completed.

In addition to required courses, many of the recognized schools offer electives to improve student writing. Most typically, these are provided as senior electives. For example, four different electives are offered to seniors at McQuaid Jesuit High School: Creative Writing, Exposition, Journalism, and Mechanics and Sentence Construction.

Centennial Senior High School offers two options for seniors—a course for college-bound students and one for those not planning to attend college. College-bound students study advanced writing processes, culminating in the writing of a major research paper. The course for those planning to enter the job market emphasizes skills needed in today's work world, including typical business communications. The single senior composition course at Darien High School emphasizes writing skills that are important in nonliterary content areas, such as critiquing works of art and analyzing scientific research.

Six different one-semester electives in writing have been developed for students of Alfred Bonnabel High School. These include Basic Writing, Technical Writing, Creative Writing, Advanced Creative Writing, Intermediate Composition, and Advanced Composition. The required English classes at Bonnabel, however, also incorporate a sequential writing program designed to enhance the improvement of writing skills.

WRITING ASSIGNMENTS

Of particular interest are the special kinds of assignments students must complete in schools that emphasize writing. These can be contest entries, literary efforts, or traditional research paper assignments.

At Oldham County High School, many teachers incorporate journal writing as an instructional tool. Students are required to make journal entries on specific topics as well as to write thoughts or opinions on specific problems or their own individual concerns. Teachers review journals on a regular basis and provide feedback and encouragement to pupils. At the Episcopal School of Acadiana, journals are also required in two courses: Geometry (an interesting choice) and ninth-grade English.

Petoskey Middle School utilizes journals, a student newspaper, and a book of student writings to encourage writing. They also sponsor a Writers' Round Table, where students interested in writing meet once a week to share ideas.

Another typical writing assignment is the senior research paper. Seniors at Blind Brook High School must produce a 2,500-word paper as part of their course work, and the school reports that substantial teacher time is devoted to tutorial sessions aimed at helping students to develop their papers.

The writing of original children's books, complete with illustrations, has become a tradition in the sophomore English classes at Shulamith High School for Girls. A nearby branch of the public library arranges an exhibition of these original works each year. This school also makes extensive use of journal writing, requiring both freshmen and juniors to keep journals.

Evergreen Junior High School is even more insistent. While emphasizing different genres of writing at different grade levels, the school requires that all students in the last grade (ninth) send a final draft of a writing project to a publishing house to be considered for publication.

WRITING CONTESTS

Many schools encourage or require students to enter various kinds of writing contests. Sometimes it is a local contest, such as the one sponsored each year by the English department at Edgewood High School of the Sacred Heart. This competition sparks the writing of essays, poems, short stories, and one-act plays. A literary magazine is developed from the entries submitted to the contest.

A monthly writing contest is conducted by the English department at Yarmouth Junior-Senior High School, "to give students an opportunity to gain recognition for their writing efforts and to give them an audience for what they write." Each month the contest features a different genre—informal essay, short story, haiku, narrative. The best submissions then appear in an annual publication.

All English honor students at Alfred Bonnabel High School are required to enter local, state, and national essay competitions. The same requirement is made of students at Marion Heights Academy and Stanton College Preparatory School. Students are noted for their successful participation in local, state, and national contests, including the Daughters of the American Revolution Essay Contest and the Scholastic Magazine Writing Competition. Since S. S. Murphy High School instituted a program to encourage competitive writing, nearly 50 percent of the school's students have won prizes at local, state, and national levels. The publication of a literary journal has also created heightened student interest.

Faculty Training

In order to implement a successful curriculum, staff members must be fully informed of current practices, research, and methods in teaching writing. They must also be aware of and committed to the specific program and goals outlined by their individual schools. This is accomplished through teacher participation in local, state, and national writing projects, and through in-service sessions held by the schools themselves.

LOCAL, STATE, AND NATIONAL WRITING PROJECTS

Local, state, and national writing projects are having a major impact across the country, from Maine to Alaska. Primarily an outgrowth of the Bay Area Writing Project (now called the National Writing Project), these spin-offs are viewed by school administrators as significant sources of training for English teachers and other staff members.

For English teachers at Greely High School, the Bay Area Writing Project offered at a nearby state university provides opportunities to refine their own and their students' writing. All English teachers at GHS have participated in either a one-semester or summer-session workshop based on the Bay Area Project.

The Bay Area writing model is also used at Garden City Senior High School and at the Bonn American High School, where the methods propounded by the project "help students gain insight into subtle issues of syntactic variety and precise use of language." Similarly, key staff members at Maryhurst High School receive training in the Louisville Writing Project, which was inspired by the Bay Area program.

State writing projects are important to a number of the winning schools. At University High School, methods emphasized in the California Writing Project are used by the entire English department. The Alaska Writing Consortium Project is the basis for in-servicing Petersburg High School teachers in content-area writing. The Vermont Writing Project provides the framework used by the English department at Woodstock Union High School to incorporate a school-wide writing process into the curriculum.

Nether Providence Middle School utilizes the Wallingford-Swarthmore Writing Project (an outgrowth of the Pennsylvania Writing Project) as a teacher support group. Graduate-level courses and in-service programs, as well as informal seminars on the nature of the writing process, help teachers think and act effectively when teaching writing. Several staff members are also enrolled in the Literacy Network, a cooperative seminar which views writing as a natural expansion of reading comprehension. The network offers teachers an opportunity to explore current research and techniques under the leadership of the University of Pennsylvania staff.

A district-wide commitment to effective writing instruction has led administrators at Haverford Senior High School to enlist staff from the Pennsylvania Writing Project to train teachers. Saint Bernard-Elmwood Place High School joined the Miami University-sponsored Ohio Writing Project, a program that trains teachers in writing skills and how to teach them in the classroom. And North Olmsted High School sought affiliation with Cleveland State University in order to participate in the University's National Writing Project.

The program followed at Chandler High School illustrates a typical approach to promoting a school-wide emphasis on writing using national or state models. For the past several years, one of the goals developed by CHS' instructional cabinet has been to teach writing across the curriculum. Consequently, several teachers, including one in mathematics and one in graphic arts, have attended the Greater Phoenix Area Writing Project, which provides intensive training in using writing to teach in all subject areas. Since then, these teachers have trained other CHS teachers through semester courses. In addition, all faculty members have been in-serviced on using writing as a means to enhance and enrich their particular subject areas. Because of the in-service program and because the originally trained teachers continue to be available to assist other content-area teachers, writing at Chandler High School is used as a tool in every classroom.

THE IMPORTANCE OF IN-SERVICE

Faculty in-service appears to hold the key to a successful writing curriculum. However, several districts describe important initial steps to be taken before starting an in-service writing program—steps that prove central to the subsequent success of in-service offerings.

Leadership is of paramount concern to the administrators of Charlotte Latin School, who are committed to a "writing as process" approach. When searching for an English department chairperson, they looked for someone who was experienced in writing programs and who could train other faculty in the approach. For its ten-session faculty course on writing, CLS also utilizes a staff member who has received university training in the process and who has served as a trainer in many schools throughout the state.

Before beginning a system-wide writing program, staff from Garger High School spent a year studying and visiting other schools. The year's study allowed them to feel confident about the comprehensive in-service workshops offered; the specific goals, objectives, and minimum assignments required; and the evaluation standards established.

Dr. Roland N. Patterson Intermediate School 229 also spent some time deciding how to proceed with its writing program. Led by their principal, the staff carefully studied materials submitted by consultants and publishers before selecting Dr. Evelyn Rothstein and the Write Track program. Dr. Rothstein visited the school once a week to train all staff involved in writing. She used a variety of techniques, including demonstration lessons in classes of various subject areas and at assorted grade levels. She also evaluated teachers' lessons by sitting in on their classroom presentations, following up with a critiquing session.

Providence Day School has also used an interesting approach to in-service. Most of their upper school instructors have spent five weeks as Teaching Fellows in the University of North Carolina's Charlotte Writing Project, an affiliate of the National Writing Project.

When a school district makes a commitment to the value of writing as both process and product and to using writing as a tool for learning, it will generally translate that commitment into special programs for faculty. Dobson High School has offered a one-semester graduate-level course, the Dobson High Writing Project, for representatives of content areas other than English. The course serves a twofold purpose: to teach teachers how writing can be used in all subject areas, and to foster the theory that writing enhances learning. In addition, Dobson held a school-wide in-service day to disseminate information about the importance of writing for college entrance and for use outside of school, and to allow departments to apply writing techniques for classes across the curriculum.

Once they have a writing program in place, many schools continue with in-service activities geared toward more specific strategies and objectives. Newton County High School, for example, has provided its language arts department with a two-year in-service program devoted to ways to teach writing in order to improve student scores on the Georgia State Writing Sample, on college placement exams, and in college freshman writing classes.

Resources and Support

Winning schools draw on a number of internal and outside resources to support their writing programs. These include sourcing or developing materials and guides, establishing writing laboratories and computer labs, employing peer tutors, making special administrative arrangements, and hiring support staff.

MATERIALS AND GUIDES

Many schools prepare special materials to use in implementing their writing programs. These are typically handbooks, style manuals, and guides which provide a common set of instructions for both students and staff.

Proctor Hug High School's participation in the Northern Nevada Writing Project has led to its extensive use of the project's High School Writing Guide. Cibola High School developed its own writing skills handbook for all teachers and students. A locally produced Writing Process Handbook is also important to the program at Crest Senior High School.

An English teacher at Wheeling High School has produced a Guide to Written Work, which provides a common approach to writing on a school-wide basis. Three English teachers at Woodstock Union High School have published a style manual that is used by all teachers and students. These kinds of publications are common in many of the winning schools.

Scranton Preparatory School has published four books, each volume geared to a particular grade level, to support its own comprehensive four-year plan to teach writing skills. The system, inspired by a faculty member, is called the "Core" system because each sentence is organized by using a particular base, or core, to determine its structure. For example, if a certain phrase is used as the "core," the sentence structure can be varied by using the phrase in different positions in the sentence. Scranton Preparatory School reports, "By teaching the students the many different kinds of phrases and the many different positions in which they may use

them in a sentence, we have begun to teach them how to vary their
sentence structure, and, therefore, how to create writing style. Writing is a craft and the students are taught how to 'craft a sentence'
in a multitude of ways."

James Logan High School produced its handbook, Project
Write, through a school-funded summer curriculum project which
included representatives from all academic departments. The book
describes the total school approach to writing and illustrates its use
across the curriculum.

WRITING LABS AND COMPUTER LABS

Many schools mention writing laboratories as an important
component of their writing curriculum. Two elements are common
in these laboratory settings: staffing for the lab (both student and
professional), and computer equipment that allows young people
to take advantage of word processing for writing and revising.

The central purpose of a writing lab at some schools is to
assist students who are performing below grade level. Such is the
case at Dobson High School, where the emphasis is on individualized learning based on each student's needs. Students come to the
writing lab, which has a workshop atmosphere, for practice and
individual help. Valley High School students who require more
intensive training than the regular course curriculum provides are
placed in Developmental Writing Lab, a year-long course designed
to remediate serious writing problems.

D. Russell Parks Junior High School has a Writing Center
staffed by a full-time teacher. Each student spends three weeks in
the center during the year, receiving intensive training and practice
in different modes of writing. The program provides for individual
differences and allows additional time for students who need it.

The Language Arts Laboratory at Wayland High School has
a full-time teacher available to support students having difficulty
with the writing curriculum. Lamphere High School's writing lab is
staffed throughout the day to provide tutorial help to students.

A dual-purpose writing lab is being developed at William
Fremd High School. Students with writing problems can receive
remedial help, while more proficient writers can polish their skills.
Appropriate computer software is available for independent work.

Many schools demonstrate a belief that computers, along with
appropriate staffing and word-processing programs, are important
tools for writing labs. One approach is to place the computer
laboratory in the school's library/media center. The West Bloom-

field High School Writing Center, located in the Media Center and staffed each period by English teachers, houses software for students to use in prewriting, word processing, and revising. Oldham County High School has hired an additional librarian to work with students and teachers in its writing lab, which is open from 7:30 A.M. to 6:00 P.M.

The Parkway South High School Reading/Writing Lab is also located in the library. The lab is staffed each period by a writing or reading teacher and a student "cadet teacher" who provide assistance to students in all subject areas. At the Writing Place in Lakeridge High School, specially trained teachers and parent volunteers offer advice, encouragement, and support to all students on a daily basis.

Many schools have special computer centers dedicated solely to the improvement of writing skills. In Louisville, Kentucky, parents and community members joined together to raise money to purchase computers for such a center at Ballard High School.

The special education department at Yarmouth Junior-Senior High School recently received a grant to establish a computer-based writing program geared to learning-disabled students. In this program, Project Write, students use word processing to become actively engaged in the process of creating, editing, and rewriting their compositions. They also learn to be comfortable using a computer.

Several schools require all students to learn to use word processing programs in writing labs, in order to make the most of the programs' potential for easy document revision. Cate School, for example, offers a course in word processing and requires students to become proficient in it, so that all departments may expect students to be able to generate, edit, and revise papers easily.

At Marist High School in Illinois, a highly specialized and computerized writing skills program, Writer's Workbench, is used at all levels. This program provides detailed analysis of each student's writing, including sentence structure and patterns, length of sentence, amount of development, and even a reading level score. This frees up teachers to work with students on content and development of ideas.

Palo Alto High School is trying a special experimental computer-assisted writing program. One-half of the average-ability tenth-grade English classes are participating, and the other half are serving as a control group. The experimental groups are working with the computer to develop fluent writing and to increase interest in writing. The English Department at Moanalua High School, using a $20,000 Developmental Grant from the Educational Consolidation and Improvement Act (ECIA), Chapter Two, has developed and incorporated a creative writing approach via computer to motivate underachieving students in grades 9 through 12.

PEER TUTORING

A number of schools have found that peer tutoring programs work especially well in writing labs. At Torrey Pines High School, students needing help at any stage of the writing process can take advantage of the Composition Conference Center, a special writing skills facility initiated by the School Improvement Program. Open all day, the center is staffed by at least three trained peer tutors and one adult each period. On request, tutors will also go into classrooms. An additional goal of the Composition Conference Center is to stress writing across the curriculum to all faculty. Accordingly, the center serves as the site for a workshop series on teaching writing skills, which is connected to the San Diego Area Writing Project.

Larson Middle School utilizes peer conferencing to help students analyze their writing strengths and correct their weaknesses. Student editors are trained to make thoughtful revision and editing suggestions. The peer conferencing sessions focus on specific correction areas in order to give writers and editors a common base and to serve as a guide to reaching a final draft stage.

Peer coaching figures prominently in the school-wide writing plans at both Myers Park and Darien High Schools. At Darien, one of the first high schools to establish a peer tutoring writing center, selected students take an evening course, Advanced Composition/ Peer Tutoring in order to become trained writing tutors. The tutors staff the Writing Center during their unscheduled periods, helping other students with the writing process.

ADMINISTRATIVE ARRANGEMENTS

Many of the winning schools demonstrate their commitment to successful writing programs by instituting special administrative arrangements. Often the arrangements involve allocation of additional funds, which may take the form of support for reduced class loads for writing teachers or a reduction in overall class size.

At Newton County High School, all writing classes are limited to a maximum of 25 students. The same limit of 25 students per English class applies at Stanton College Preparatory School. Further, each teacher at Stanton has a maximum load of 100 pupils per day.

To encourage greater attention to student writing, English teachers at Loyola High School of Baltimore teach one less period per day than teachers in other subjects. The same staffing pattern has been adapted at McQuaid Jesuit High School, "so that additional time can be devoted to reading and evaluating frequent student writing assignments."

So that they may do a thorough job of teaching writing skills, English teachers at Ridgewood High School carry a load of four classes each day, with an average of 21 students per class. In addition, teachers are required to spend five periods each week giving writing tutorials to individual students. English teachers also have a four-course load for all writing classes at Darien High School, where similar arrangements have been extended to the social science department. Each social science teacher has a reduced schedule of four classes one semester of each year to help ease the load in grading papers and assignments.

At some schools, reductions in teaching loads are accompanied by other special arrangements to enhance the writing program. Teachers of English courses at Milton High School have a four-class load with an average class size of 19. Each teacher's fifth instructional period is devoted to individual tutorial conferences on writing. Every student is scheduled for these conferences at least once per term, in addition to short in-class conferences that may occur during writing workshops.

SUPPORT STAFF

A second kind of administrative arrangement effected to improve writing is the hiring of support staff to assist writing teachers. Menlo-Atherton High School employs a full-time writing aide to read papers and tutor students on social science assignments. A different plan is used at University High School, where substitute English teachers are hired in order to give classroom teachers additional time to grade student compositions.

Sheboygan South High School budgets money to support a lay reader program for language arts and other selected instructors. Lay readers assist in correcting language usage and make it possible for teachers to give more writing assignments. The readers use selective correction to isolate and highlight specific errors. This practice allows students to zero in on specific problem areas and greatly enhances their opportunities for improvement. The writing program at North Salem Middle School has received administrative support through the hiring of two additional staff members— a writing coordinator to develop and direct the program and an outside consultant to monitor the program.

Other winning schools have established a variety of different special and often creative arrangements. At William Fremd High School, sophomore classes are split for one school quarter, with half of each class going to the Reading Lab for a mini-reading course while others stay with their classroom teacher to work on individual writing assignments. Split classes are also the chosen strategy at A. Philip Randolph Campus High School, where ninth-grade students are offered a Writing Workshop program. Classes are divided in half for two periods per week. The Writing Workshop teacher takes half the class to use word processors to improve composing and revising skills. The regular teacher uses a process-oriented curriculum with the other group. After eight weeks, the teachers switch groups so that all students participate in both approaches.

At Archbishop Molloy High School, a special composition program for sophomores includes a team teaching approach. English teachers are parallel-scheduled and team teach during the first quarter. During each succeeding quarter, the resulting large class is reduced by 15 students, who meet with one of the teachers in a separate composition class. The selected students work on writing skills through close interaction with both the teacher and their peers.

One teacher is freed up each hour of the school day at Jackson Hole High School to consult on a referral basis with individual students or groups of students about writing problems. These teachers also serve as supervisors in the school's computer laboratory and oversee the writing done there.

Meeting Special Needs

For students with writing problems, the formula used by a number of schools is to catch them early and provide immediate intervention, as well as intensive course follow-up. Before entering ninth grade, freshmen at Xavier Preparatory School are tested in basic writing skills. Any student needing remedial work must attend a summer school session. The Northfield Mount Hermon School has established a three-day writing workshop during orientation for all entering freshmen and sophomores. McQuaid Jesuit

High School also requires a pre-prep program for entering freshmen who need work in reading and writing skills.

Oneida Middle School has instituted a DEX (Double Exposure) class to help students who have writing difficulties. Two teachers work together in this non-pullout remedial program, which has received recognition for its effectiveness.

Diagnostic essays are used to monitor student progress and achievement at Parkway South High School. The diagnostic essays are written each fall by all freshmen and sophomores, and are followed by a mastery essay in the spring. The compositions are graded by a special panel of six English teachers over three-day periods. The purpose is to assess students' instructional needs as well as to measure individual progress over the course of the year.

Many schools follow a practice similar to one used at the Madeira School, where students who have reached the junior level and still show weak writing skills are required to take a special course, Structured Writing.

Specialized Programs and Promotions

Many of the recognized schools have instituted specialized approaches, events, and programs to enhance their overall approach to writing. A number of the ideas outlined here offer potential for creative adaptations by other schools across the country.

Schenley High School Teacher Center

Through Schenley's Critical Thinking project, 36 teachers from English, social studies, science, and special education received ten hours of in-service training to become familiar with the writing process, to practice writing, and to develop writing assignments for their classes. As a result, teachers have become more comfortable using writing as an instructional tool, have increased the variety of writing activities in instruction, and have developed skills for use in the Monitoring Achievement in Pittsburgh (MAP) program. MAP requires students to write a variety of compositions in both English and social studies classes. The compositions are evaluated using a criterion-based rating scale. All students at Schenley write such compositions and receive feedback on them at least eight times per year through the MAP program and the Critical Thinking project.

Vacaville High School

The school-wide Mode-of-the-Month program was conceived several years ago by two VHS mentor teachers. The program requires all English students to write a monthly essay, using a different writing mode each month. The eight modes used during the school year include narrative, definition, process (analysis), classification, cause and effect, comparison and contrast, pros and cons, and argumentation. To improve spelling, lists of ten words appear each Monday in the daily bulletin, and teachers in each class test students on the words during the week. Student writing and spelling appear to be improving as a result of the emphasis placed on both processes.

Brookwood High School

Fostering the development of communications skills is not merely a school-wide concern, but a community goal. One recent year, in the belief that reading and writing are interrelated skills, all feeder elementary and middle schools participated with Brookwood to promote reading for learning and pleasure through the Community of Readers program. To correlate with American Education Week and the school's reading program, a reading rally called "A Family Affair" was held. The next year the project was entitled "Taking Charge: Strategies for Success." This project fosters development of all kinds of communications skills as well as organizational and study strategies.

Tottenville High School

Tottenville students are introduced to the Read to Write program as entering freshmen, and this writing program is reinforced in all succeeding terms. It is a structured reading/writing program predicated on the symbiotic relationship between reading and writing. The writing program features a core of four specially trained teachers who instruct all other members of the English department. In addition, there is a close correlation with other departments in a writing-across-the-curriculum approach.

Ballard High School

Implementation of a $30,000 state-funded grant allows Ballard teachers from major academic areas to create writing assignments that will encourage improved writing and critical thinking skills. The plan includes the creation of a broadcast studio to operate in conjunction with the writing lab. Students will be able to write scripts in the lab and "publish" their writing via broadcasting.

St. Thomas More Catholic High School

This school regularly arranges for specialists to present programs about writing. For example, Robert Cormier, a noted author of young adult fiction, spent a day with students in their English classes discussing writing as a process. The school also brought in John Cutsinger, a national authority on school publications, to consult with students about the necessity of strong writing in their own publications.

Great Valley High School

Great Valley's Artist-in-Residence program has brought Edward Albee, Richard Reeves, Ralph Keyes, and Mark Medoff to the school to teach student groups about writing, using a laboratory setting.

McQuaid Jesuit High School

An annual alumni award is given each year to an outstanding McQuaid senior on the basis of his or her creative writing ability.

Miller Junior High School

A unique friendship essay project indicates Miller's willingness to encourage and share in students' writing. Students wrote essays and poems on friendship, which were attached to helium balloons and launched on Friendship Day. People from surrounding states found the balloons and wrote back to the students.

Haverford Senior High School

At Haverford, as at many other schools, writing folders are maintained for each student. However, at Haverford the staff goes one step farther. All folders are sent home to parents before the end of the school year, so they can see the progress made by their children and the quantity of work produced during the school term.

Midwood High School at Brooklyn College

Every major academic department at Midwood has at least one publication to which students aspire for membership. The social science department alone has developed two new publications during the past two years: *Law Review* and *Journal of Asian, African, and Latin Studies.* Opportunities for writing thus abound at this school.

Scotia-Glenville High School

In order to teach critical thinking and problem-solving skills, science and English teachers use written learning logs to enable students to synthesize their learning and relate it to their own experiences. Students respond to reading and films by recording in journals not only their understanding of the subject matter but also their personal reactions to it.

Gladstone High School

Here formal and informal writing assignments in courses such as biology, physiology, history, psychology, global studies, and advanced foreign languages are the rule rather than the exception. Specific writing assignments are designated for English classes throughout the four years. Hundreds of pieces of writing are on display during the Writing Fair held in conjunction with the school's spring drama production and art show. Periodically, samples are also posted in the Board of Education room at the district office.

In other words, as reported by the staff at Gladstone High School, "Students cannot escape writing!" This seems to be the practice at secondary schools throughout the country that attain recognition status.

For a personal viewpoint on this issue, see Appendix D, page 263.

CHAPTER 3

Teaching about Democracy

Does your school have a school-wide approach or any special programs that foster understanding and appreciation of democracy as a form of government and a way of life and of the United States Constitution as the framework for American democracy?

American schools place a major emphasis on courses and programs that teach our country's history, promote good citizenship, and foster the principles on which our democratic republic is based. Virtually all states require that high school students earn at least one credit in American history and one in American government. Beyond this basic core, winning schools take a variety of approaches to teaching students about democracy.

This chapter describes how schools teach about and help incorporate democratic values through various combinations of the following:

- Required Courses
- Elective Courses
- Models and Simulations
- Special Programs and Events

Required Courses

Many of the recognition schools require students to take related courses beyond the basics of American history and government. A number of these classes are aimed at expanding students' world views and giving them a context in which to understand their own system of government. Others focus closer to home, on local and state governments.

GAINING A WORLD VIEW

An understanding of the larger, global view—the interdependence and significance of events throughout the world—is part of the graduation course requirements in a number of schools. Flowing Wells High School requires freshmen to take a course in World Areas, and all Woodbridge High School freshmen must take a year-long course in World Regional Studies. While a major focus of the Woodbridge course is world geography, history, and culture, students also examine the relationships and role of the United States in regions of the world. Current issues such as poverty, the arms race, and international trade are explored, along with the future of the United States in creating, shaping, and resolving these issues. The goal? To inform future voters and to encourage them to become active in the debate over world affairs.

At the Academy of Our Lady of Good Counsel, students take World Areas as freshmen and European Culture as sophomores. In both courses, other cultures and governments are explored using the American system of democracy as a reference point. At Proctor Hug High School, all sophomores enroll in World History. Juniors take U.S. History, and seniors take U.S. Government. This approach ensures that, as the staff notes, "the student is exposed to a broad field of human experiences first (other cultures, systems, ideas); then the field is narrowed to American history, and finally the seniors study political ideas."

Modern World History, including U.S. involvement, is required for all ninth-grade students at Geyser Public School. Students at West Bloomfield High School take a World History course that concentrates on the study of Western institutions and the foundations of democracy.

Four years of social studies are required for graduation at Palo Alto High School, with classes including U.S. History, U.S. Government, Economics, and three semesters of World History. Throughout these courses there is "a strong emphasis on the rights and responsibilities of citizenship, and the nature and importance of political participation."

Blind Brook High School recently expanded its graduation requirements to include the Origins of Democratic Thought and Western Civilization in ninth grade and a class examining non-Western societies in tenth grade. Eleventh graders study Democratic Processes from Colonial Times to the Present, and seniors select from a variety of electives to complete the four-year requirement.

In addition to requiring a formal social science course emphasizing democracy, Martin Kellogg Middle School strives to place other subjects within a historical and social context. Novels in language arts classes are selected for historical as well as literary significance, and the required general music program teaches music history in relation to other historic events.

LEARNING ABOUT THE COMMUNITY

Many schools, such as Oak Grove High School, require freshmen to take a one-semester course on the concepts of state government. For many schools, such courses, along with state history courses, are state requirements.

Courses in local history and government are required at a number of schools. The sophomore-level course at Londonderry High School includes a community service unit in which students must do an eight-hour project to benefit the local community. Many other schools have begun to include a community service component in their graduation requirements, providing students with opportunities to contribute to, as well as learn about, their own communities.

As part of their political science requirements, students at Woodbridge High School may observe a democratic meeting in process or volunteer to work for either a candidate for public office or a current office holder. In addition, they must research a local issue, exploring all sides of the problem and suggesting possible solutions.

FIRSTHAND EXPERIENCE

Many junior high schools, like Millard North Junior High School, require social studies students to take a trip, usually to Washington, D.C. In the capital, Millard's students visit, observe, and meet with their congressional representatives.

King Philip Middle School has extended its field trip program to an organized, year-round effort concentrating on specific historical events. For example, on one trip students travel to Salem to learn about the witch trials and the relation of geography to growth and decline of population centers. Other trips acquaint students with mill life, Jewish settlements, industry, and their heritage.

A generous Parent-Teacher Organization offers scholarships to help defray costs. Students who cannot make the trips participate in a program of related activities.

Elective Courses

Social studies electives offer a wide variety of opportunities for students in many of the recognition schools. A survey of social studies electives offered by these schools shows an extensive range of choices.

LEARNING ABOUT LAW

Elective courses dealing with law and justice are offered at many schools. For example, a Police and Crime course is especially popular with students at Tottenville High School. More than 300 students a year sign up for the class, which is team taught by two social studies teachers and a police officer. Tottenville officials report that the course does an outstanding job of linking civic concerns with the curriculum, and that its success has led to its adoption by more than 75 other high schools. Another course at Tottenville, Crime and War, provides a study of the Bill of Rights and individual liberties.

Legal Systems in the United States, a senior-level elective at Scotia-Glenville High School, gives students the opportunity to study criminal and civil law while working closely with local government and law enforcement agencies. A second course, Street Law, covers basic legal issues on both a national and local level.

Some courses are aimed at relating law to everyday life. Garger High School requires students to take a semester course, Practical Law, along with the traditional government and history courses. A relatively new elective at Lutheran High School North is Introductory Law. The course is designed "to provide students with excellent additional opportunities to understand and practice their roles as informed, active citizens." And Broadmoor Middle Laboratory School offers Living Law as an elective course. One semester concentrates on civil law, the other on criminal.

Constitutional law is also a popular basis for a number of electives. Dwight-Englewood School offers Issues in American Law, a senior-level elective covering such issues as First Amendment rights, due process, and the roots of affirmative action. The course is taught by faculty members who have had special graduate work related to the Constitution. At Haverford High School, a one-semester course, The Constitution and the Process of Federalism, is offered at the freshman level. Midwood High School at Brooklyn College offers as an elective Constitutional Law, which surveys U.S. Supreme Court cases.

At Newburgh Free Academy, students in a Constitution course do more than study the functioning of American democratic ideas in theory—they also have the opportunity to participate in special programs such as Youth in Government. Delegates from each social studies class are elected to represent their class and school in a county-wide mock government.

The Constitutional Law course at A. Philip Randolph Campus High School emphasizes the rights and responsibilities of citizens as well as their constitutional and civil liberties. A police officer participates in the development of the curriculum and its instruction, which makes use of case studies and mock trials. In addition, the course involves student contact with government officials of various ethnic backgrounds.

ECONOMICS COURSES

Courses related to economic issues are offered at a number of schools, and in some cases are required. The content and approach of these classes vary widely, as indicated by the following examples.

Charlotte Latin School
Charlotte Latin School's Free Enterprise course relates relevant events in American history to the nation's economic development, as well as providing an introduction to our economic system.

Myers Park High School
One of the most popular courses at Myers Park is Applied Economics. Students in the course operate a small business in the classroom as part of their study of general economics. The students also use a classroom microcomputer to publish company financial statements, conduct management games, and create economic simulations in order to gain a greater understanding of our free enterprise system.

A COURSE SAMPLER

A survey of related electives at the winning schools shows a wide variety of offerings in areas other than economics.

Shoreham-Wading River High School
Shoreham-Wading River offers some unusual electives in addition to The Law and All of Us, which focuses on constitutional rights as they are defined in the legal system. Computer Research and the Social Sciences examines the role of data in the decision-making process of government. And a Futures course considers how the democratic community can affect changes within itself and plan for its future.

A. Philip Randolph Campus High School
A. Philip Randolph offers Urban Studies, which actually involves the students in issues and resolutions designed to improve the quality of life in the inner city.

Lutheran High School West
Lutheran has the elective U.S. War and Peace for seniors.

Northfield Mount Hermon School
Northfield Mount Hermon provides a diverse selection of social studies electives, including Minorities in America, Use and Abuse of Power, Government and Civil Liberties, and the United States and East Asia.

Central Catholic High School
Central Catholic High School's equally diverse selection includes History of Political Ideas, American Foreign Policy, and The American Presidency.

Academy of Notre Dame de Namur
Academy of Notre Dame de Namur students can choose from courses like Women's History, International Relations, and Supreme Court Decisions.

Parkway South High School
Parkway South offers Minorities as an elective course; it focuses on the study of the Civil Rights movement throughout history, with an emphasis on the Thirteenth, Fourteenth, and Fifteenth Amendments as well as other relevant legislation and court cases.

South Kingstown High School
South Kingstown reports that two courses, Youth and Law and American Citizens in a Changing World, "were added to the curriculum to provide students with increased awareness of democracy and its importance in our society."

Garden City Senior High School
Garden City offers a course on The Media as a Social Force. It looks at the constitutional guarantees and limitations under which all of the media operate. Special topics include the FCC Fairness Doctrine, freedom of the press versus a fair trial, the role of the media as formulators of public policy, and national security versus the people's right to know.

Several schools offer truly unique social studies electives. East High School, for example, offers an elective in American Military History. Perhaps most unusual is Scotia-Glenville High School's Sports in American Society, which presents sports as a microcosm of American society, with emphasis on the politics, economics, racism, and feminism involved in American sports.

Models and Simulations

Many schools have discovered that the principles of democracy are best promoted by offering students opportunities to observe the functioning of our republic up close, by involving them in simulations such as a model United Nations, a model Congress, or a model city council, and by providing mock trial experiences and other special events. Simulations of all kinds are incorporated in studies of government in these schools.

NATIONAL AND INTERNATIONAL MODELS

Fifteen students from Shulamith High School for Girls participated in the National High School United Nations held in April, 1987, representing a delegation from a foreign country. Delegates were also sent to a regional mock United Nations held at the University of Dayton by Mount Notre Dame High School. The student delegates were selected by the school's Junior Council on World Affairs, an active co-curricular organization on campus.

Tottenville High School created a unique model Congress, inviting more than 60 students from various schools in New York City to participate in the three-day program. Midwood High School at Brooklyn College also created a model Congress where students simulated the roles of congressional representatives by writing, debating, and enacting legislation. Each year Midwood also invites a member of the U.S. House of Representatives to meet with the student delegates.

At St. Louise de Marillac High School, a special project involving 20 area elementary schools provided a framework for teaching participants the principles of legislative action. Each elementary school sent four representatives from their "school state" to consider ten bills for passage. The day began with opening remarks by a local congressman, after which students were divided into committees for discussion on proposed bills. They then met in political party caucuses to discuss strategies for the General Session which followed. High school students assisted as facilitators during the full-day session. Because of its success the first year, this has become an annual event.

LOCAL SIMULATIONS

Local city governments are also used as models for simulations at a number of schools. One of the most effective simulations, at Petersburg High School, involves the creation of a real local decision-making situation.

Another program featuring local government takes place at Pompton Lakes High School, where the entire student body participates in a program called Change of Town Officers. In this activity students run for election and form political parties to field candidates for mayor, city council, and a slate of borough officials. The winners plan and run a borough council meeting. An interesting aspect of the program is that all students must register to vote in the Change of Town Officers elections. Just as in real life, only those registered can vote.

A different approach to learning about community politics is used in Kentucky, where the governor and the Kentucky Department of Education have endorsed an activity called Local Government Week. As part of the week's activities, more than 50 students from Oldham County High School are matched with local elected officials from all three branches of government. The students spend a school day with the county officials, learning their roles and functions. The officials reciprocate by visiting with students at the school later in the year.

Special Programs and Events

A number of schools have made a major commitment to promoting democracy by scheduling a variety of special activities, such as participation in the national Close-Up program, mock trials, field trips, and marking significant dates.

CLOSE-UP

Many schools report major involvement with the national program Close-Up. In this two-part United States government study program, state-level student caucuses are followed by a week-long Close-Up program in Washington, D.C.

Typical is Edgewood High School of the Sacred Heart, which has participated in the program for more than five years. Other schools reporting active participation include Wayland High School, Garger High School, Oak Grove High School, St. Louis Park High School, and Geyser Public School.

Geyser's participation is especially noteworthy. In a school with an enrollment of 53, five students and a teacher went to Washington, D.C., for the Close-Up week, and the school set a goal to send ten students the next year. The community of Geyser raised over $4,000 to send the group to Washington. The school reports, "This major sacrifice by the community was undertaken because both parents and community members expressed a strong belief in the need for students to be exposed to the larger world outside of Geyser."

LAW AND THE LEGAL SYSTEM

Some schools hold special events to build student understanding of the American legal system. Newburgh Free Academy reports, "The importance of a fair and impartial trial is brought to life for our students through the use of a mock trial conducted by the Constitution class as part of the curriculum." This activity involves the entire school. The school computer is used to select and summon potential jurors. With local attorneys serving as resource guides, student lawyers select a jury, and the Constitution class prepares and presents the case. The trial proceeds, and culminates with the jury rendering a verdict. School officials report, "This exercise enhances student interest and increases participation in a Youth Court conducted in cooperation with the city's juvenile authorities."

While many schools utilize law studies to help students understand democracy, Los Altos Intermediate School takes students to visit both a county courthouse and a federal district court. A judge visits with the students, as do a public defender and a prosecutor.

Later the students watch an actual trial and write papers about their experiences.

Each year the Academy of Our Lady of Good Counsel participates in the New York State Mock Trial Competition. Students from area high schools serve as lawyers, prosecutors, and witnesses, thus learning through a hands-on approach the intricacies of the court system.

The observation of Law Day is also a frequent event at many schools. Typical is the program at Stephens County High School each May, when prominent figures in local, state, or national government are invited to talk to the assembled student body.

HISTORICAL ANNIVERSARIES

The anniversaries of historical events provide an ideal framework for schools to celebrate and to inculcate an appreciation of democracy at the same time. The Bicentennial of the United States Constitution provided a special opportunity for such observances. In special recognition of the event, Wayland High School participated in the "Sign On to the Constitution" campaign sponsored by the National Council of Christians and Jews.

Franklin High School provided the leadership for a structured program that involved the entire community as well as parents and students in a Bicentennial celebration in Franklin, Wisconsin. The program, funded through a $15,000 federal grant, helped to improve student understanding and appreciation of the American form of government and political institutions.

Perhaps the most extensive Bicentennial program described by any school was the one conducted by Londonderry High School. In 1984, the school started a three-year program to mark the occasion. As part of the program, several students and faculty members were involved in making a videotape presentation for the opening ceremony of the Bicentennial celebration at the Annapolis Naval Academy.

MORE IDEAS

Many other kinds of special events held at the winning schools foster an understanding and appreciation of democracy. Many schools, for example, encourage their pupils to enter essay contests as a regular part of the social studies program. The following examples demonstrate some of the additional ways schools have found to promote democratic ideas.

Miller Junior High School

Each year, Miller holds a special Patriotic Program honoring heroes. Throughout the year, there are flag raisings and retreat ceremonies led by military or veterans groups. The school also has periodic red, white, and blue days when students are encouraged to dress in the colors of the flag.

Benjamin Elijah Mays High School

School-wide social science fairs are an annual event at Benjamin Elijah Mays.

Mother McAuley Liberal Arts High School

Students prepare displays and productions to enter in the annual Chicago Metro History Fair, which draws contestants from throughout the greater Chicago area.

Palms Junior High School

Students at Palms can join Junior State, a debating society meeting weekly during lunch to discuss current issues. The group has frequent miniconferences with groups from other schools in an effort to promote understanding of contemporary society and its issues.

West Bloomfield High School

West Bloomfield hosted the first Michigan Social Studies Olympiad, in honor of both the state's Sesquicentennial and the Constitution's Bicentennial. The half-day Olympiad was open to all grade levels and featured events such as a library research "college bowl," drama skits, essay and poster contests, and historical model building.

Middletown High School

A computer modem connects this school's computer lab to other schools throughout the country, enabling social studies students to carry on long-distance debates on contemporary issues.

Skowhegan Area High School

Skowhegan has set aside money for a speakers' program that brings a wide variety of individuals to its campus, including the chief constable of the Central Scotland police, an editor from *National Geographic,* and a Drug Enforcement Agency official.

Providence Day School
The social studies department sponsors an annual Great Decisions program for students, parents, and faculty.

Palmer Junior High School
A unique opportunity awaits students at Palmer. Because of the school's proximity to the Truman Historic District, students have met every U.S. president since Truman, as well as other assorted historical figures. The school district has also published its own textbook about the community's history, with students assisting in the book's production.

White Plains High School
White Plains is involved in a consortium of nearby schools, colleges, and corporations to focus on major foreign policy issues. Students, teachers, and administrators attend monthly forums sponsored by the consortium and the Foreign Policy Association. The school also has a social studies newspaper, which publishes special issues on topics such as civil liberties and the Constitution.

St. Mark's School of Texas
An annual sophomore class project, Issues Day, consists of planning a day-long program for all St. Mark's students during which a varied program of speakers, panel discussions, films, and simulation activities is used to examine a single national problem. The program's purpose is to help prepare students to meet their adult roles as citizens in a participatory democracy.

Yarmouth Junior-Senior High School
Eighth-grade students at Yarmouth take part in a simulated debate over the ratification of the Constitution, complete with costumes and historical roles. Throughout the year, the students are immersed in the election process, and in November the school holds a mock election using voting booths borrowed from the town and copies of actual ballots. Part of the election process includes bringing major candidates into the school to discuss issues.

S. S. Murphy High School
Graduation at S. S. Murphy is organized by student clubs, always around a patriotic theme. Only student speakers are permitted. Officials report that the spectacle has brought visitors from many other school systems.

South Winnishiek Senior High School

Each month the Student Council and faculty choose two students as Citizens of the Month. Those selected are recognized for being good citizens and for personal accomplishments. They are recognized in local newspapers and given special pins and certificates.

Centennial Senior High School

A unique program at Centennial brings visiting teachers from places like the People's Republic of China, Chile, and France to the campus. These teachers collaborate in presenting a unit on American history as taught to high school students in their native countries. The guests are also asked to analyze American traditions and institutions from their unique viewpoints, thus giving Centennial students a special perspective on American history.

Southside Junior High School

Advanced social studies students at Southside have worked with drama students to create a commercial about the Constitution. The commercial is available for viewing at the school's media center.

Bonn American High School

A location in a foreign country and a student body including many international students provide Bonn American students with special opportunities for comparing the American form of democracy with systems in other countries. Students visit the *Bundestag* (parliament) and meet with a variety of foreign ambassadors during the course of the year.

The Madeira School

An intern program at Madeira places every junior as a congressional intern for one full day a week throughout the year. In a recent year, juniors were placed in 98 different congressional offices. To support the internship program, each junior takes a non-credit Public Affairs course covering the basic principles of American government and politics. In addition, each participant writes a paper on the internship experience, which is used to help evaluate their internship performance. The program is also supported by monthly Capitol Hill seminars, including talks by journalists, policy activists, and political figures.

As a follow-up to the junior program, seniors at Madeira serve internships in organizations involved in the political process or the promotion of democratic values. Through their internships, students work directly to support their personal visions of a just democratic society.

American schools choose a whole spectrum of methods to teach American youth about democracy and democratic values: required courses and electives, special events and simulations, essay contests, debates, visits to historic sites, and internships in local, state, and national government. Communities often take an active part in these efforts to transmit to the nation's youth the values that we place on our democratic form of government.

For a personal viewpoint on this issue, see Appendix D, page 266.

CHAPTER 4

Teaching Character and Values

How do school programs, practices, and policies, as well as individual teachers and administrators, foster the development of sound character, democratic values, ethical judgment, good behavior, and the ability to work in a self-disciplined and purposeful manner?

Whether they intend to or not, schools have a major influence on students' character and value development. Although specific programs and practices are important for fostering sound values and judgment among students, even more instrumental is the prevailing attitude of administrators and teachers.

This chapter describes how winning schools foster character development and teach values through:

- Policies, Procedures, and Examples
- Co-curricular Programs
- Community Service Programs
- Special Progams

Policies, Procedures, and Examples

How schools treat students, the policies they choose to adopt and enforce, the methods of enforcement, and the role models provided by teachers and administrators—all of these contribute to the messages students receive about character and values.

SENDING THE RIGHT MESSAGE

Schools that are serious about qualities like honesty, ethical judgment, and dedication to worthwhile causes recognize that they cannot pay mere lip service to values. They must practice what they preach. And they do, in many different and creative ways.

The attitude expressed by many of the schools is exemplified by these comments from the Clear Lake High School teachers' manual:

> Most young people want guidance and good images to learn from. Some even appear starved for this. We must give them all we have and give it with generosity. These young people will be running this world some day and they will be what we make of them. School is practice for real life. Our goal as educators is to impart our training, experience and personalities to students to get them ready for real life. It is not fair to show them a life that is false or unreal. Our own experience should show us that readiness to accept responsibilities is a mark of maturity and readiness for real life.

Similarly, the application from St. Mark's School of Texas stresses the importance of the school's effort "to empower students themselves to be the voices of school standards, and to some extent its arbiters, guiding them while also assigning to them significant responsibility to demonstrate and practice good judgment, and expecting that they be accountable."

CLEAR POLICIES

Clearly defined rules and responsibilities let students know what is expected of them and provide common standards of behavior. The kinds of rules adopted and the way they are created and imposed strongly affect student attitudes toward the concepts and principles schools are trying to convey.

Poolesville Junior-Senior High School distributes a Student Rights and Responsibilities Handbook to all students. Student leaders and teachers go over the rules and responsibilities with students, who are expected to use the handbook as a guide for their behavior.

Students at Kirby-Smith Junior High School, which has a greater than 64 percent mobility factor in its community, are taught responsibility through deadlines and processes. Students who feel they have been wronged are encouraged to report the misbehavior rather than fighting it out. The school tries to instill a strong sense of right and wrong and reports that its diligent efforts are paying off.

The School Community Governance Program at Stone Ridge Country Day School of the Sacred Heart is viewed as critical to the school's mission. The program requires that all faculty and students actively participate and contribute to the good of the school community.

Administrators at Blind Brook High School apparently believe that growing maturity must bring with it growing opportunities to exercise choices and self-discipline. A campus policy prohibits ninth and tenth graders from leaving the school grounds during the school day. Eleventh graders, however, are permitted to leave the campus at lunch time by signing out and in. By the senior year, students may leave the campus during any unassigned period without explicit permission.

At Ridgewood High School, "people demand the best from each other." Students demand the best from their teachers, and teachers from their students. This attitude is supported by several specific policies:

An attendance policy that spells out the risks of excessive absenteeism

A behavior policy that is clear on the consequences of misbehavior

A policy on plagiarism that takes the subject seriously

A drugs and drinking policy that includes preventive measures

In addition, report cards at Ridgewood include notations on industry and attitude as well as grades.

Dalton Junior High School uses a school motto to encourage character: "If It's to Be, It's Up to Me." Teachers have high expectations, and students are taught to analyze what they do and how it affects others. The school follows up with a Time-for-Self room and a self-referral policy for students.

The development of a cheating policy at Myers Park High School grew out of combined student, faculty, and parental concern and interest in developing sound character and values among the student population. Well-defined expectations are communicated to students at James Logan High School, where a school-wide cheating policy addresses the issues of academic honesty and defines consequences for students who cheat on homework or exams.

Woodmere Middle School has a strict policy supporting citizenship. No student may be on the honor roll unless she or he has perfect citizenship in all classes. Parents have been very supportive of this stance.

Valley View Junior High developed its code of conduct using input from all levels. The final document was approved by the school board and clearly defines what acceptable behavior is and how misbehavior will be handled.

ROLE MODELS

The school motto at Los Gatos High School is "Honesty of Purpose and Intensity of Effort." School officials believe they can best live up to the motto through fair enforcement of clearly stated rules and regulations, coupled with high expectations. Most important, however, are the daily examples set by responsible, caring adults who demonstrate honesty of purpose and intensity of effort in everything they do.

The school philosophy for Lawton Community High School includes this statement: "It is the school personnel's responsibility to serve as supplementary role models for our students. Therefore, we strive to maintain high standards of personal and professional conduct through which we provide positive examples of citizenship, morals, and social responsibility."

Faculty members at Charlotte Latin School are clearly expected to act as role models. Similarly, every older student is expected to act as a model for younger students. Standards for behavior include courtesy, concern for others, group spirit, and a sense of teamwork.

The Teachers as Advisors Project affords faculty and students at Stanton College Preparatory School the opportunity to develop more personal relationships. The project encourages the free exchange of ideas and the open discussion of student concerns. Advisors care and listen. This enhances the effectiveness of teachers as positive role models. Daily meetings allow for the discussion of far-ranging topics about student concerns, current events, and many other issues.

The importance of the principal's role is clearly demonstrated at Mooresville Junior High School, where the principal advocates saying nothing if you can't say something positive. And the principal at Tredyffrin/Easttown Junior High School holds regular grade-level lunches with students to foster a good atmosphere for dialogue and to encourage students to think and function effectively.

Co-curricular Programs

Opportunities for participation in clubs and sports are an important aspect of high school life. Students frequently attest to the fact that they learn more from these experiences than from some of the more formal academic programs offered in their schools.

CLUBS AND ORGANIZATIONS

Many schools try to guarantee that each student can find at least one activity in which to participate and feel at home. This includes making sure students know about the available options. Students at Dobson High School, for example, are made aware of all available co-curricular opportunities during the regular class registration process. This ensures that all students are informed of the wide variety of programs offered through the school's 58 different clubs and organizations.

To guarantee opportunities for participation, schools employ a variety of scheduling procedures. Some, such as Shulamith High School for Girls, provide a weekly activity period in which groups can meet. Others, like Shoreham-Wading River High School, have a daily activity period.

Most schools offer a central core of traditional and typical activities. A few, however, describe some more unusual offerings. Students at Proctor Hug High School, for example, can join "Little Willy's Gang," a Shakespeare group, while students at Tottenville High School can hone their skills with the fencing team, the magic club, or the karate group. West Bloomfield High School's up-to-the-minute offerings include a racquetball club, a video club, an investment video club, and a marketing club. And students at Mount Vernon High School can add their voices to the barbershop quartet program or explore medical careers in the medical opportunity club. Playful students at Koda Junior High School can choose from options as diverse as juggling and board games. Clubs at Koda meet before school, which doesn't start until 9 A.M.

Faculty sponsors at Dwight-Englewood School write comments on the quality and extent of participation of all students in their sponsored activities. These comments are mailed to parents— evidence of the importance and value the school places on co-curricular activities.

ATHLETICS

Athletic programs offer schools the opportunity to enforce the concept that athletics involve more than winning—how one plays the game is also vitally important. One way that message comes across is through a "no cut" policy for athletic teams. This is the policy on many Wayland High School teams. As a result, the teams are quite large and many students have an opportunity to participate.

Coaches at Crest Senior High School place great emphasis on sportsmanship, and try to create an aura where students strive to do their own personal best. To this end they have established a special Team before Self award.

The same sense of character building was commented on by a coach from Miramonte High School at a fall football team banquet. He measured the success of the season by the development and improvement of each player's ability to perform as part of a team effort, to improve himself physically and mentally, to build discipline and responsibility, and to become a better person.

Community Service Programs

A major trend at many of the winning schools is the inclusion of programs of service to the school, to the community, and to other causes and programs that benefit others. These take many forms: some are included in course work required for graduation; some are part of extra-curricular service and volunteer programs; some are independent programs; and a few are part of larger community programs.

COMMUNITY SERVICE REQUIREMENTS FOR GRADUATION

An increasing number of schools are instituting a community service requirement for all students. The requirements range from a single-semester program or a minimum number of hours to four-year programs.

Creighton Preparatory School

All sophomores have a one-quarter required community service component as part of their theology course. As juniors or seniors, students can enroll in an awareness workshop that carries the service orientation to greater depth. The entire student body also takes an active role in various school efforts to help needy families and to support various missions in the United States and abroad.

Stone Ridge Country Day School of the Sacred Heart
The required community service program at Stone Ridge teaches volunteerism as citizenship in action and fosters an awareness of issues and agencies in the context of public policy. The program, Social Action, requires all students to contribute in some way to the needy in their area. Teachers also participate, providing role modeling for students. Stone Ridge reports that "young alumnae frequently comment on the value they derived from Social Action."

Villa Angela Academy
A required part of the sophomore religion curriculum is the student service program. This is a released time activity in which each student volunteers 90 minutes of assistance each week in an area elementary school, nursing home, senior citizen residence, or hospital. The experience is integrated into class discussion and reflection exercises, and each student keeps a journal of her experiences. An additional required program at the senior level is the Senior Community Experience Program (SCEP). For two weeks in May, each senior is required to report each regular working day to a sponsor in a business or career of her choice.

Scranton Preparatory School
The senior program at Scranton Preparatory includes a graduation requirement of 50 hours of service in the community. Seniors are given opportunities to reflect on this experience—which can include work in day-care centers, Boys Clubs, hospitals, nursing homes, and soup kitchens—during twice-a-week sessions in their theology classes. In addition, incoming seniors may participate in special service projects coordinated by the school during the summer months, such as traveling to Mexico City to work in an orphanage.

Georgetown Visitation Preparatory
Seniors at Georgetown are required to make a commitment of weekly volunteer service in the local community. The student government also sponsors an all-day "Service-a-thon," through which students support 15 different community organizations.

Fairfield College Preparatory School
Fairfield students must fulfill a four-year service requirement.
Freshmen participate in an inner city field day. Sophomores participate in Special Olympics. Juniors contribute 15 hours of service to
the school or to their local parish. Seniors must perform 40 hours
of service in an approved community service project. All of these
requirements are closely monitored by the Director of Community
Service, in conjunction with other staff. Students reflect on their
experiences through planned lessons in their theology classes, and
seniors meet in special reflection groups once a week.

The Madeira School
A sophomore-level program, Ethics and the Community, supports the school's program of community service. In addition, all
sophomores work every Wednesday in a community service organization such as a hospital, day-care center, nursing home, or
center for the mentally or physically handicapped. Students are
evaluated twice a year by their on-site supervisors. Seniors, who
may choose from a variety of options for their senior internships,
often choose community service placements.

SERVICE COMPONENTS IN COURSES

A number of schools offer specialized courses incorporating a
service component in the curriculum. Again, the winning schools
offer a wide variety of approaches.

Flowing Wells High School
The Skills for Living classes at Flowing Wells include a minimum of 16 hours of community service work for each student.
Projects are selected to provide a wide range of community assistance.

Harwood Junior High School
Each home economics class at Harwood selects an annual
project to help the community. One class chose adopting a grand-
parent from a local nursing home, and each student visited a "grand-
parent" twice a month. Another class gave a Halloween party for
children and grandchildren of the staff. One group helped at a
carnival for students in a school for the severely mentally retarded,
and another became involved in school beautification. Not to be
outdone, the small engine class repairs mowers, edgers, and chain
saws free for senior citizens every year.

Midwood High School at Brooklyn College
The social studies department at Midwood offers a Community Service course in which students become involved in community organizations such as hospitals and medical centers, youth centers, senior citizen homes, and offices of elected officials at the federal, state, and local levels.

Brighton High School
A Brighton course, School and Community Service, provides organized opportunities for students to serve the community. One interesting special project involved the Building Trades class, which worked with the Historical Society to restore an old school.

Lamphere High School
The social studies department at Lamphere has just instituted a community service course whose objective is to encourage students to volunteer their time to nonprofit organizations.

Poolesville Junior-Senior High School
Poolesville woodworking students have refurbished the town hall and recently built a community band stand. The students in social studies classes once adopted a school class of West Virginia flood victims and collected school supplies for them.

Kinston High School
Class-related service projects are strongly encouraged at Kinston. Psychology students volunteer in nursing homes. Marine technology students conduct an annual clambake for senior citizens. The sophomore class sponsors an annual "Litter-a-thon." The health department sponsors a peer tutoring program at a local elementary school. The home economics classes provide a play-school program for nursery school children. And the National Honor Society is involved with a Neighborhood Guild's Halloween party for youngsters.

SCHOOL-WIDE PROGRAMS

Many schools offer a range of opportunities for students to contribute community service under school sponsorship.

Tottenville High School
The Key Club Programs involve many Tottenville students in community projects. Some students serve as teacher assistants in

elementary and intermediate schools. Others help at a local hospital, at senior citizen centers, and at homes for the handicapped.

Shoreham-Wading River High School
NEXUS is the name of the active school-sponsored community service program at Shoreham-Wading. More than 400 students are involved in ongoing monthly volunteer service to nursing homes and nursery schools as well as one-time projects such as blood drives or senior citizen health screenings.

McQuaid Jesuit High School
Students from McQuaid help seven different agencies in the community. Perhaps most unusual is the annual cooperative effort with the local Chamber of Commerce to clean trash and litter from area expressways.

Lakeridge High School
Two interesting facets of service are evident in this Oregon school. Through the Lakeridge Service Club, students are able to volunteer to assist less fortunate people in their community. Service Club members have also participated in the annual day-long cleanup of Oregon beaches. Another Lakeridge program, developed and run by students, is Saferide. On weekends, student volunteers staff phones and provide transportation for students who call in concerned about their own or someone else's ability to drive after consuming alcohol.

Seth Low Intermediate School 96
Seth Low regularly offers service to its community. The orchestra plays on an ongoing basis at a nursing home. A group of students makes regular visits to a senior center. The learning disabled students run the school store. A volunteer corps serves as readers to the blind. And a special neighborhood beautification project has given the community flowers, fences, and a clean park.

Greely High School
A majority of Greely students are involved in special services to others, both in and out of school. Project Pride is a special service program within the school, incorporating the use of student volunteers in many departments and programs.

Archbishop Molloy High School
Student participation in school-related community activities is handled through the Religious Activities Office. Currently, 375 students are involved, and 275 more are waiting to be assigned to

voluntary activities such as hospital work and Special Olympics. Students commit themselves to these activities on a weekly basis. The school reports that over the four years of a student's enrollment, the amount of volunteer activity increases dramatically, so that by the senior year community service has become part of the fabric of each student's life.

Henderson High School
The staff at Henderson reports 16 different kinds of projects in which students are involved, including entertaining at local retirement homes, hospitals, and churches; serving as volunteer aides in hospitals, fire companies, and rescue squads; raising funds for a wide variety of worthy causes; and even researching and publishing biographies of prominent community citizens.

Gretchen Whitney High School
Many students at Gretchen Whitney participate in a Big Brother/Big Sister program. Each student is assigned to an elementary school child who is having difficulty and is in need of special attention and assistance.

Academy of Notre Dame de Namur
Students at Notre Dame give service on an individual basis through the Social Service Organization. Girls are encouraged to be involved on a weekly basis, with each student taking the responsibility for her own transportation and work times. Every student in the school is personally interviewed by one of the social service moderators, who helps guide her in choosing the most appropriate place to do her service work.

Saint John's School
Students at Saint John's are strongly encouraged to participate in school-related community activities. The high school also offers a course in volunteerism for a selected number of juniors and seniors, and the Interact Club is a community service organization open to all students.

Charlotte Latin School
The Dean of Students at Charlotte Latin maintains a continuously updated list of volunteer activities students can perform for a minimum of 40 to 50 hours per one-quarter credit hour. In addition, four major service clubs in the school are active in a wide range of special programs.

Cardinal Gibbons High School
The diversity of service projects at Cardinal Gibbons provides a picture of the range of programs available at the recognition schools. Students at this community-conscious school have contributed many hours of service to such projects as the Haitian Center, SADD (Students Against Driving Drunk), the International Students' Service Club, individual class projects to help families in need, blood drives, a Jump Rope for Heart program, Special Olympics, walkathons, and providing Bibles for missions, as well as providing service and performances at hospitals, churches, schools, and homes for the elderly.

CLUB SERVICE PROJECTS

At many schools, one or more clubs participate in community service projects. At some schools clubs are required to participate in such projects at least once each year.

At Parkway Central High School, school policy requires groups to perform some service project during the school year. This service requirement is also part of the interscholastic athletics program. Sports teams provide services as do organizations like the music, art, and drama groups.

Similarly, the clubs at Cardinal Gibbons High School must perform service projects to justify their existence. At North Bend High School, clubs provide vital manpower for the diverse service activities in which students engage. The Food Club puts on many banquets for community activities, the Business Club wraps Christmas gifts at the local mall, and Student Council members assist in preparing for special community celebrations.

The Science Club at Granby Memorial Middle School is an active outreach group, trying to share scientific knowledge while fostering enjoyment and rapport. The group has sponsored a Halley's Comet Watch for more than a thousand people, stocked local lakes and ponds, offered scientific slide shows on assorted topics, and had an Appreciation Night recognizing two community members for their science awareness.

OUTREACH PROGRAMS

In a sense, all of the volunteer programs are a type of outreach effort, but some programs go beyond the usual service actions to reach out to a particular segment of the community, as shown by the following examples.

White Plains High School

Two new physical education courses, Recreational Leadership and Sports Officiating, encourage students to take an outreach approach. The teenagers use their new skills and knowledge to help out at the local handicapped children's hospital and the local psychiatric hospital, at the Wheelchair and Special Olympics, and at Recreation Department programs by working with disabled children.

Gladstone High School

A special program of outreach to elementary school students is a feature of the service program at Gladstone High School. High school students tutor pupils in reading and special education classes at the elementary school. They also teach classes in Spanish, art, and first aid to third and fourth graders. Through these and and many other service activities, students at Gladstone are taught that the fourth "R" is responsibility.

Franklin High School

Through a cooperative program with the local police department, Franklin High School students present an antivandalism program aimed at impressing middle-school students with the wrongness of such destructive acts.

A. Philip Randolph Campus High School

A special outreach program at this school involves the adoption of a local senior citizen home. As part of the program, Randolph students plan parties and musical events for the residents. The spirit of cooperation and volunteering extends to the staff at Randolph. Faculty members serve as team leaders from 7 A.M. to 6 P.M., encouraging maximum student participation in school programs.

Northfield Mount Hermon School

Through Northfield's Outreach program, students volunteer service to children, the elderly, the mentally handicapped, and to court-referred adolescents. Throughout the school program, responsible student activism is encouraged.

Special Programs

In addition to policies, co-curricular programs, and community service, schools employ a variety of other ways to foster the development of sound student values.

Claremont High School is especially concerned with helping students develop high self-esteem. Many staff development programs have addressed this issue. In addition, the school holds special school-wide multimedia assemblies on specific topics designed to examine values such as responsibility for one's self, respect for others, and self-esteem.

The staff and administrators at Shulamith High School for Girls recognize that issues of morality exist everywhere, including on the pages of the daily newspaper. Consequently, they make special efforts in their programs and retreats to use trigger films, videocassettes, and television programs to heighten every student's sense of moral awareness.

William H. Farquhar Middle School offers a special program called Sensitivity Awareness Symposium (SAS) to sensitize staff and students to the existence of hate groups and prejudices. Students participate in role playing, watch videotapes, and read articles to help them understand the contributions of racial, religious, and ethnic groups to our society.

PEER COUNSELING PROGRAMS

Peer counseling programs are especially effective at fostering student cooperation, concern, and understanding, as well as helping students to solve problems and build self-esteem.

The peer counseling program at Mount Notre Dame High School provides interested students with specialized training, helping them to understand themselves at the same time as they learn techniques for working with both their peers and elementary school children. The peer counseling program at Palo Alto High School has served as a national model for many other schools. In addition, the school has an extensive Friendship Project—a kind of buddy system wherein older students help transfer students, handicapped youngsters, and newer students during their first year in high school.

Cibola High School

The desire felt by many of these schools to develop good character and ethical values in their students has been codified into a year-round program at Cibola High School. Born out of a perceived need to build a cohesive, active student body from the diverse populations served by the school, the Cougar Challenge Program is a student motivational program built on the following principles:

1. People tend to support that which they help to create

2. What you reward you get more of

3. What you emphasize, you maximize

4. Every human action is either tension-relieving or goal-achieving

One staff person, the activities director, is in charge of the overall program, which is broken down into three primary areas of responsibility: spiritual, social, and scholastic. A key element of the program's success is that the staff members at Cibola serve as role models, demonstrating the qualities they hope to foster in students. Staff members also give many hours of additional support to help students with studies and personal problems.

A Continuing Challenge

The same kind of dedication shown by the winning schools is evident in school districts across the country, wherever schools recognize that values education is a responsibility they cannot ignore. In these schools, citizenship is taught by example as well as in required courses about American government; values are learned on the playing fields and in nursing homes and hospitals; and students come to understand that who their teachers are is just as important as what they teach. The attitude common to these winning schools is aptly summarized on the application submitted by Middletown High School:

Our faculty puts into everyday practice the belief that the best teacher of sound character is a total school environment built on the principles of fairness and consistency and focused on encouragement rather than punishment. We believe that when an individual's problems are handled fairly—in the eyes of the student as well as the staff member—students learn the value of an equitable democratic system. Further, we seize errors in judgment as an opportunity to teach alternative thought processes which mirror established moral and democratic principles and try to give students an appreciation of the parallels between school community and the democracy in which we live. By consistently enforcing well articulated discipline policies and by encouraging and modeling appropriate social and academic behaviors, our staff demonstrates a commitment to the development of the whole child.

PART
THREE

Students

CHAPTER 5

Students and Study Skills

Does your school have any programs that concentrate on developing student study skills?

The process of learning is an important element of education. Students who acquire skills that help them learn are equipped to make the most of their abilities. This chapter describes how winning schools help students develop study skills through:

- Required Study Skills Courses
- Study Skills Electives and Special Programs
- Across-the-Curriculum Programs
- Guidance by Counselors and/or Library Media Specialists
- Study Skills Materials

Required Study Skills Courses

Many of the winning schools require students to take concentrated units related to study skills. These units can take many forms and vary considerably in approach and content. They are usually taught as part of freshman English classes, but some schools take a different approach.

At Stanton College Preparatory School, improvement of study skills is a priority. Therefore, all seventh-grade students are required to take a laboratory class including units in outlining, reading comprehension, note taking, test taking, and vocabulary development. Additionally, all eighth- and eleventh-grade students receive instruction in specific study and library skills in their research classes. Students and teachers also work on activities related to study and test-taking skills during the daily advisor class periods.

At Archbishop Molloy High School, teachers of freshmen have devised a study skills program with guidelines to be followed in every subject area. Throughout the year, special days are devoted to emphasizing a significant skill in each subject.

All freshmen at Ridge High School are required to take a course in thinking skills that is also designed to help improve study skills. A required course in study skills is also part of the program for freshmen at Blind Brook High School. This course is designed to help students assess and, where necessary, alter their study habits and attitudes. Included are materials on learning how to learn, independent study techniques, flexible reading rates, main idea and paragraph organization, listening and note taking, outlining, vocabulary, library skills, report writing, and test taking. Similar programs are offered to freshmen at Jesuit High School New Orleans and Northfield Mount Hermon School.

Orange Glen High School has received a grant to provide materials that would enable teachers to incorporate study skills into freshman social studies classes. The school developed a booklet of specific lesson plans designed to improve skill proficiency. All departments are responsible for incorporating these study skills into their content instruction. A study skills unit is built into the four core subjects in ninth-grade academic classes at Dover High School. The unit was devised as part of a ninth-grade orientation committee recommendation.

Valley High School offers a four-year sequential study skills program which is administered to students in all English classes during the first two weeks of school. The ninth-grade program focuses on suitable study methods while making students aware of their own learning styles. It also includes a reading comprehension unit with emphasis on outlining, drawing inferences, skim reading, and reading for the main idea. The final lesson involves time management. The tenth-grade program reinforces the ninth-grade unit, with an additional focus on writing skills. All lessons include pre- and posttests to enhance student interest. The eleventh-grade program is administered in conjunction with the local community college. All students take the standard entrance test for the college, in order to learn both where they are strong and where they are in need of remediation. The second part of the program deals with test-taking skills in preparation for college tests such as the SAT. Finally, the twelfth-grade lessons deal with skills important to job seekers and college-bound students: pressure, test taking, writing under a tight deadline, and prioritizing work.

SHORT COURSES

Specialized minicourses are another approach sometimes used to spotlight survival study skills for high school. Sometimes these are required of every student; other times they are targeted toward students identified as needing a strong start to increase their odds for success in high school.

Deer Path Junior High School has a type of minicourse focusing on formal study skills such as memorization, note taking and outlining, organizing work, and keeping records of assignments. Computers are also used to reinforce study skills. A short course approach is also used at St. Mark's School of Texas. Every entering freshman must complete a two-day program prior to the start of school in the fall. Topics in this study skills program include how to use time productively, how to be a demanding reader, how to take effective notes, and how to be a great student in science, language, math, and other fields.

Study Skills Electives and Special Programs

Some of the winning schools offer special electives geared toward specific kinds of study skills. Others have study skills courses focusing on students with identified special needs or aiming to improve skills in test taking, particularly for college admissions tests. Other schools hold special study skills programs outside of regular school classes.

Wilbur Rowe Junior High School takes a rather unique approach to study skills. In addition to learning to read better, remember facts, and manage time, students also learn that to "get smarter" they need positive attitudes and good habits. Consequently, they work on self-understanding, stress management, and decision making in this upbeat course.

College preparatory skills courses are very common. Some are offered in early morning or evening sessions. Others take place during the summer. At a few schools these courses are available during the regular school day. Such is the case at Pompton Lakes High School, where juniors and seniors may enroll in the course College Prep Skills.

Occasionally parents are invited to become involved in programs aimed at helping them aid their children in improving study skills. This is the approach taken by the Philadelphia High School for Girls, which holds special evening sessions to work with parents of students new to the school.

Lynnhaven Junior High School has a Study Skills Center. Students who have problems with the nine-week study skills curriculum are referred to the center, where staff and parent volunteers assist them.

Across-the-Curriculum Programs

The trend toward writing and reading across the curriculum is echoed in programs that provide study skills lessons in all of a school's classes. Each department at Ridgewood High School has determined the study skills students need to master the objectives in its particular discipline. These study skills are incorporated into the course work. To establish their knowledge of the skills, all students are tested periodically. The tests are item-analyzed by the computer services department, with the results broken down by study skills for each department. The results are then reviewed with both teachers and students.

The faculty at Metairie Park Country Day School believes that study skills are best developed within the regular curriculum. Therefore, all assignments require that students apply the skills stressed by teachers.

Meany Middle School also teaches study skills across the curriculum. Writing is taught in the language arts program and reinforced in other departments. Outlining is part of the social studies curriculum. Graphing and charting are covered in science and math, and evaluating and critical thinking are taught in all subject areas.

After having tried separate study skills sessions, the Episcopal School of Acadiana now presents these skills by department within the regular curriculum. The same approach is used at Georgetown Visitation Preparatory School, where all teachers—particularly those with classes in the ninth and tenth grades—integrate the development of study skills into the content of their courses.

Because of Wheeling High School's strong belief in the importance of an integrated study skills program, one staff member is given released time to coordinate a school-wide study skills program. One feature of the program is a monthly publication providing valuable study skills information for all staff members to use in their teaching. A different study skill is emphasized each month.

Ferndale High School has implemented an across-the-curriculum study skills program that serves every student. A unique feature of the program is "Conspiracy Days," when all faculty members "conspire" to teach and reinforce the same study skill within the context of their courses. Since the skill is taught for six consecutive classes and within the context of all disciplines, retention and generalization are very high. Some of the skills taught are writing a bibliography, locating information using all parts of a textbook, following written directions, listening skills, time management, and note taking.

Guidance by Counselors and Library Media Specialists

Another common approach to study skills instruction involves school guidance programs. In some schools this consists of one or two sessions dealing with central issues such as the importance of doing homework and how to study for tests. In other schools, study skills sessions have become significant parts of ongoing group guidance, with formal curriculum guides and year-long efforts.

An example of the latter is the program at Scotia-Glenville High School, where the guidance department chairperson teaches a ten-hour study skills minicourse. He wrote the student and teacher texts based on the Cambridge Study Skill System. Groups of 12 to 15 students may enroll in this specialized course, which is offered three times a year.

Counselors are vital to Parcells Middle School's study skills program. After each grading period, counselors meet with students whose grade point average is below 2.0, to begin a study skills program and set goals for the next quarter.

Another partnership frequently used to build student study skills is the one between classroom teachers and the school's library media staff. Traditional lessons in the use of the library and its various materials are expanded to included broader topics related to improving general study skills.

Study Skills Materials

Popular commercial study skills materials are used by most of the recognition schools. Most often mentioned by recognition high schools is the Harvard Milton Academy Study Skills program, which has been endorsed by the National Association of Secondary School Principals. Among the specific schools that mention using these materials are North Bend High School, Mount Vernon High School, and Newburgh Free Academy. Also mentioned is the Ohio Study Skills Program. North Olmsted High School, for example, uses the Ohio program as a guide for the development of a K–12 study skills continuum.

Other schools prepare their own materials. At Clovis High School a Study Skills Curriculum committee has been established to develop a curriculum guide for teaching study skills at all grade levels. Harold S. Vincent High School has published a study skills book explaining how to study in each subject area. The book also emphasizes general skills such as test taking, note taking, and general study habits. Vincent held an all-school Studying across the Curriculum Day, during which teachers reinforced the skills in their disciplines. The school also holds a Preparing for Exams Day before final exams. Adlai E. Stevenson High School has published the Stevenson Study Guidelines pamphlet, which is sent out each summer to students as part of fall registration materials.

In addition to being used in courses, study skills materials are also occasionally distributed to parents. This is the case at Lakeridge High School, which produces and distributes an annual brochure describing how parents can support good study habits at home.

Another trend is that of providing computer programs that students can use to improve at their own pace. These are most commonly used in conjunction with reviewing for ACT and SAT exams.

Although programs may differ in administrative detail, types of course offerings, and choice of focus or across-the-curriculum approaches, it is obvious that outstanding schools consider teaching students *how* to learn of critical importance.

CHAPTER 6

Students and Basic Skills

Does your school have any programs that provide remediation in basic skills or other areas?

Helping students who are deficient in basic skills is a standard practice for junior and senior high schools. Such deficiencies cannot be ignored; vigorous efforts are necessary to help bridge the academic gap.

The establishment of special programs through federal funding (Chapter I) and ESL (English as a Second Language) classes are central in many schools. These are targeted programs designed to assist remediation in basic skills.

This chapter describes how schools identify and assist students with special needs through the following types of programs:

- Summer Programs

- Laboratory Programs

- Tutoring Programs

- Alternative Programs

Identifying Students with Remediation Needs

Many high schools couple eighth- or ninth-grade testing with remedial classes in reading and mathematics for those who need them. Many schools also use ongoing testing to pinpoint students who need work in basic skills.

At North Olmsted High School, all ninth-grade students take the Iowa Test of Basic Skills. Students scoring below competency level are required to take a one-semester remedial reading course in their sophomore year. Tenth-grade students at North Olmsted take the Test of Academic Progress (TAP). Again, those scoring below competency level in reading must take one semester of remedial reading in eleventh grade. In addition, mathematics students in grade-level courses take a state norm-referenced test designed to predict success in college mathematics. A senior review course is available to help low-scoring students increase their probability of success in college math.

Students at Deer Path Junior High School are tested to determine if they are eligible for a special program, Unmotivated Underachiever. Teachers design specific academic goals for each student who is not achieving his or her grade potential.

Summer Programs

A number of schools, especially private ones, require students whose entrance scores demonstrate marked weaknesses to attend special pre-entrance programs. The approach taken by Marist High School in Illinois is typical. Students are identified for the remediation program based on the results of a January entrance examination and on consultation with the appropriate junior high school official. Each student spends six weeks in a special summer program emphasizing reading, language arts, and mathematics. Students are tracked in these areas for a period of one to four years, using special textbooks and prescribed student programs. Computer-managed instruction is also available. Students who succeed in these basic programs, which cover the areas of mathematics, sciences, languages, social studies, and English, then transfer to academic level courses.

A similar structure exists at Creighton Preparatory School. Based on entrance exam results, students are recommended or required to take pre-entrance summer school courses in as many as two or three academic areas. During the school year, individual and group tutoring is provided for students identified by teachers as needing additional help. In addition, the Creighton summer school provides yearly remedial courses to keep students on track for graduation.

The staff at Central High School in South Dakota takes an aggressive approach to basic skills development. First, the 100 lowest-scoring students are identified and brought in during the summer for a week of instruction. These students are then homogeneously grouped into world history/study skills classes taught by a certified history teacher who is also a reading specialist, so that basic skills can continue to be stressed.

Laboratory Programs

Los Gatos High School

Many schools have established special laboratories to provide remediation in basic skills. An excellent example is the structured lab program at Los Gatos High School. For example, the Writing Lab and the Mastery Math Program accept students on the basis of teacher recommendations, previous grades, and test scores. In both programs, efforts are made to keep classes small. This ensures that students receive more individual attention than is available in regular classes, and that they receive the training necessary to improve their skills and move to a higher level.

Freshmen entering Los Gatos are initially placed in mathematics classes on the basis of entrance test scores. Students must place at the 80th percentile or higher on the mathematics section of the test to qualify for beginning algebra. This is because experience has shown that most students scoring below this level will have great difficulty in algebra and need to develop their math skills further before attempting it. The school strongly believes in the importance of placing all students in classes where they can experience success.

For students experiencing difficulty in beginning foreign languages, the Los Gatos foreign language department has a series of teacher-developed, computer-assisted drills to be used in remediation sessions. Rather than being forced to drop their foreign language courses, struggling students are quickly identified and recommended for participation in remediation sessions. If a student is reluctant to take advantage of this service, a phone call to parents often helps change his or her mind and leads to success in the classroom.

Kesling Middle School

Kesling Middle School has a Diagnostic/Prescriptive Reading Skills Lab for students who score below recommended levels. A reading specialist, a full-time assistant and a wealth of hardware and software are available to students working in the lab.

Claremont High School

A unique feature at Claremont is the Learning Center. This program "provides a strong human support system for all students but particularly for students needing support in basic skills." In addition to tutoring and helping with homework, the center provides specific instruction in the basic skills to enable students to successfully complete the district's proficiency tests. In fact, the school reports, "Through this support, workshops, and summer programs, we have had no student fail to graduate because of failure on the basic skills proficiency test."

Southwest High School

Southwest High School operates a Study Center, which is heavily used by students before and after school. Thirty computer stations with materials on eight core subject areas are available for student practice. Southwest also features a highly developed testing and referral system, parent volunteers, support from community organizations, and a local library tutoring program, all of which have resulted in "a tremendous rise in achievement scores in the last several years."

Fremont Senior High School

Staff development is important for helping teachers learn how to aid students. At Fremont, faculty forums provide information to help faculty members. Students having academic difficulties are scheduled into Resource Labs, where teachers trained in the forums help them to develop study skills as well as work on content.

Tutoring Programs

Special tutoring is another common approach used to assist students experiencing difficulties with basic skills. Typical is the program at Jesuit High School in Florida, where the school makes individual tutoring available to students who need to sharpen their skills in a particular academic area.

A learning resources teacher has been added to the staff at Mars Hill Bible School to assist students with learning difficulties. Students are referred by parents, faculty, and counselors, and their needs are determined through grade reviews and individual diagnostic testing.

The Tutoring Room at Lynnhaven Junior High School provides a place for students to receive help in any subject with which they are experiencing problems. Students report to the Tutoring Room during lunch hour, and may receive tutoring either from faculty members assigned to the room or from National Junior Honor Society students who have volunteered to serve as peer tutors.

One of the teachers at Ballard High School voluntarily initiated a Math Tutoring Center after school one day per week. The center was so popular (and successful) that the school system expanded the program to two teachers who are employed to provide after-school math tutoring every weekday.

At many schools tutoring is provided by members of the National Honor Society or by specially trained peer tutors. Student tutoring at Dwight-Englewood School is available through the school organization Helping Hands. In addition, students experiencing difficulty in any subject are encouraged to seek extra help from their teachers. Each Monday a period at the end of the day is specifically designated for extra help. All teachers are available and no school activities or athletics are scheduled.

Three times each week, a tutorial period at Moanalua High School provides all students an opportunity to obtain help on an individual basis. A. Philip Randolph Campus High School features a mentoring program in which college students work one-on-one with high school students. Another service provided by Randolph is a Homework Hotline, which students are encouraged to call for help in completing assignments.

Alternative Programs

A number of schools offer alternative programs within or outside of the standard curriculum for students needing extra help. The innovative Second Chance program at South Winnishiek Senior High School allows students to schedule themselves into an additional section of a class in which they are having difficulty. This gives the students extra time for remediation, review, and reinforcement. The approach has the additional advantage of being easily implemented on a day-to-day basis by students or teachers.

An alternative program for students who have not done well in school and have a low self-image has been created at St. Louis Park High School. Students in the Mini-School program receive credit in English and social studies. The Mini-School staff includes English, social studies, and learning disabilities teachers.

An English-reading block of three periods a day has been established at Alfred Bonnabel High School for students who score below the eighth-grade level on the Comprehensive Test of Basic Skills in reading and who have failed the first year of English. The classes employ a team-teaching approach—while an English teacher concentrates on writing and communication skills, a reading teacher assists students in all subject areas.

Lincoln High School has set up a required small group study hall for sophomores, juniors, and seniors with low academic standing. The study hall helps emphasize the school's focus on academic expectations.

Horace Mann Academic Middle School has a volunteer Homework Lab and a community-based tutorial program, as well as a students-at-risk program that operates on special contracts. Benjamin Elijah Mays School also relies on community support for its Adopt-a-Student program. Students identified as having special needs are "adopted" by individuals from the private sector who work with them for a year or longer to improve their skills.

A Teacher Advisor program at Saint Bernard-Elmwood Place High School provides a structure for teachers to work briefly with small groups of students (an average of 15) on a daily basis. The teachers also meet with the students in 50-minute bi-weekly sessions to reinforce needed skills.

Each freshman at the University of Chicago Laboratory School is scheduled into the Freshman Center for two periods per week. The center provides intensive instruction in study skills development as well as tutorial help and individual counseling.

The LaSalle Institute mathematics department has set up a self-pacing program for students having difficulty keeping up with the curriculum. These students use the same text as other students but take four years to complete what is usually a three-year sequence. Students are selected for the classes on the basis of department recommendations, parent or student requests, lack of success in previous years, or standardized testing. Students who show strong improvement may also choose or be recommended to move into a more challenging course.

If they are willing to contract for regular attendance and other specific course objectives, low-ability students at Vacaville High School may voluntarily enroll in School-within-a-School core courses to obtain basic skills remediation. At Middletown High School, academic detention has proven helpful. Students who are not completing homework or who are not achieving in class work are detained after school to ensure that they apply themselves to courses.

For each of the science offerings at Wayland High School (physical science, biology, chemistry, and physics) students may choose from non-college, college preparatory, honors, and Advanced Placement levels. Wayland thus provides a science program to meet the needs of all students.

Some schools offer remedial programs in physical education. Haverford Senior High School uses its excellent fitness facility to provide an adaptive physical education program tailored to meet each student's needs and remediate both temporary injuries and permanent disabilities. At Wheeling High School, physical education students are grouped by ability according to health-related fitness. Students undergo extensive fitness tests and are placed in classes best suited to their abilities.

In fact, the phrase "best suited to their abilities" could be applied to many of the efforts expended by the winning schools to assist students with deficiencies. Successful programs are designed to help eliminate or at least reduce deficiencies, through such means as change in content, change in pace, and change in organization of the school day, as well as through additional support services and tutorial opportunities.

CHAPTER 7

Students and High Expectations, Recognition, and Rewards

Please describe strategies used in your school to communicate high expectations for achievement and behavior to all students.

Aside from grades, does your school have procedures for recognizing outstanding student accomplishments in course work as well as other school activities?

High expectations and rewards go hand in hand. Schools that set high standards are also quick to reward accomplishments of all kinds. This chapter describes how recognition schools communicate high expectations and recognize and reward student accomplishments through:

- Clear Messages
- Special Honors and Incentives

Clear Messages

High expectations are reflected in many school mottoes, as shown by these examples:

Excellence Plus—St. Louise de Marillac High School

High Expectations Pay Off—Henderson High School

Pride—Excellence—Lawton Community High School

The Excellence Continues—Rock Bridge Senior High School

Additionally, many of the school applications express philosophies grounded in high expectations. Scranton Preparatory School comments, "If you expect good behavior from students and positive attitudes, that is what you will get."

THE RIGHT START

Many schools set the tone for high expectations on the first day of school. At Wheeling High School, for example, "opening day assemblies for each class are held for the purpose of communicating achievement and behavioral expectations." Each student receives a folder printed with student rules and regulations, and a flip-chart covering rules and expectations is also mailed to each family at the beginning of the school year.

Gladstone High School makes special efforts to communicate expectations to freshmen and new students. Within the first two weeks of school, the principal, vice-principal, and counselors meet with new students for two class periods of orientation. The discussions focus on behavior and academic expectations, school procedures and regulations, goal setting, discipline, and attendance.

Chandler High School wants to convey the message that students rise to the level of expectations set by the community, administrators, parents, and teachers. The principal at Chandler meets with each sophomore English class to discuss school traditions, rules, and expectations for achievement and involvement. Additionally, all students receive a school competency handbook and a conduct code handbook for themselves and their parents.

A similar approach is followed at Vacaville High School, where one of the four administrators speaks to each of the English 10 classes during the first week of school. The administrators discuss school expectations for achievement and behavior and encourage questions and student feedback on regulations, procedures, and programs.

The first day of each year at Oak Grove High School is devoted entirely to communicating school rules and expectations, with a different rule discussed each class period. Students take a short quiz at the end of the period to show how well they understand what is expected of them. On the second day of school, teachers explain their specific expectations with respect to students' academic achievement and classroom behavior.

At South Kingstown High School, the report of the school's Standards Committee is reviewed with all students at the beginning of the year, and expectations are enumerated during class meetings and study halls throughout the first week. Items from a recent report included:

1. Requirement of up-to-date notebooks in all classes

2. Requirement that reading and writing assignments be given and completed in all subject areas

3. All-school emphasis on improvement and evaluation of student writing

BROADCASTING THE MESSAGE

Brown Middle School encourages individual success through posters and bulletin boards emphasizing high expectations, with themes such as "We can stay under a cloud or get busy and find our rainbow." Brown also recognizes outstanding scholars by posting honor rolls. Van Hise Middle School also uses posters to proclaim the "Van Hise Way," emphasizing punctuality, staying on task, being prepared, and respect. Wenatchee High School's Improvement Team communicates its message, "All Students Can Learn," in newspapers, signs, and through personal contact with teachers and students.

Central High School in Pennsylvania uses student-organized public relations to highlight individual academic achievements. Central's 300-page handbook showcases the history and programs of the school. And at Alfred Bonnabel High School, all students and faculty attend a "state of the school" address once each nine weeks. The speeches help keep everyone focused on the goals for the year.

Sometimes expectations are communicated more subtly. Students at St. Louise de Marillac High School do not have passing bells and have no supervised study hall. The message is that students are responsible for controlling their own behavior and that they are expected to be self-disciplined.

Tradition plays an important part in maintaining high expectations. When representatives of Midwood High School at Brooklyn College attend school fairs or speak before groups, they stress that their school is in many ways old-fashioned—no gimmicks, no easy way to earn a diploma.

Several strategies for communicating high expectations are cited by Yankton Senior High School, including:

Examples and expectations set by faculty

Stringent grading scales established by the district

Grade requirements established for extra-curricular participation

A tradition of excellence in education in the community

FACULTY AND ADMINISTRATION

The way a school is operated has a big impact on how students perceive school values. Many schools have adopted specific policies or established specific programs to foster high expectations. The importance of a stable faculty has also often been mentioned. Some cite a low student-counselor ratio as being helpful. Others point to weighted grades, honors, and Advanced Placement courses as significant. Academic teams in such subjects as mathematics and chemistry have also been mentioned as important.

Faculty and administration members play critical roles in communicating expectations to students. The principal at Scotia-Glenville High School, for example, plays a major role in

> communicating high expectations for achievement and behavior to all students. During the summer he mails a letter to parents outlining school procedures and defining the discipline code. In the fall he acts as a freshman homeroom teacher in each section for a week in an effort to become acquainted with students and to communicate expectations regarding behavior and achievement. . . . On a regular basis he provides appropriate reprimands and rewards to keep students on task.

Each teacher at Homestead High School produces a list of rules, regulations, and class expectations and distributes them to all students. Students are required to have parents sign these sheets to be certain the communication cycle is complete.

The various departments at William Fremd High School present their expectations in different ways. The foreign language department distributes a pamphlet called "How to Succeed in a Foreign Language." The art department has a collection of 3,000 slides of former students' art work to use as examples. And special education teachers maintain weekly contact with parents.

The guidance program at Mother Cabrini High School is designed to help all students through a unified cooperative effort with faculty, parents, and administration, and focuses on communicating high academic standards along with high behavior standards. Each student is also assigned a faculty mentor each year, and the mentor takes an active role as a supportive person to the student.

The faculty at Middletown High School is committed to 80 percent of all students achieving at an 80 percent or higher level on all summative measurements. As a result, teachers have implemented several techniques for motivating—and in some cases one might say "forcing"—students to reach their maximum potential. It is not uncommon to find a number of students after school each day of the week serving academic detentions for not completing written homework, reading assignments, or test reviews.

PARENT INVOLVEMENT

Virtually all of the winning schools expressed the belief that parental involvement is a key to setting and attaining high achievement goals. Evening Open House programs, during which parents follow their child's schedule in miniature, and teachers outline expectations and standards for their courses, are universal. So is the mailing of publications describing the guidelines and rules all students are expected to follow.

Some schools set up spring visitation for eighth- or ninth-grade parents prior to their children's entry into high school. These programs provide an opportunity to set the tone for the coming years. A few schools also prepare reading lists of titles students are expected to read during the summer prior to entering high school.

As the staff at Oldham County High School has remarked, "We communicate high goals and expectations through collaborative goal setting, by modeling, and by encouraging mutual respect and support." With parental support, the goals are much easier to reach.

Audubon Junior High School provides each student with a contract indicating behavior and grooming standards. The contract is thoroughly reviewed at school, then sent home to be read and signed by parents and students, and then returned to the school. The monthly school newsletter indicates to parents ways to aid their children in achievement.

Special Honors and Incentives

Winning schools use a myriad of honors and rewards to inspire achievement and stimulate effort. One frequently used technique includes naming a Student of the Week and/or a Student of the Month. Often civic organizations will participate in these recognitions.

At the Academy of Our Lady of Good Counsel, the monthly award is designed to recognize unsung heroes—those who are compassionate, provide service, possess a positive school spirit, and behave responsibly. And at the Episcopal School of Acadiana, the monthly recognition is for students who have contributed to the community in a spirit of citizenship. Kate Griffin Junior High School takes the Student of the Month concept and shares it with the entire community. The students' photos are posted on an outside bulletin board so everyone knows who they are.

Other typical ways that schools showcase student achievements include exhibitions, science and art fairs, and exhibits in nearby malls. Some schools maintain a Wall of Fame featuring outstanding graduates. Parkway South High School has expanded this concept—inside the school's front doors are posted honor rolls and the names of students with the most improved grades for the past quarter, along with information on students, parents, and staff being highlighted for special contributions to the school. In addition there is an entire wall displaying current newspaper clippings about Parkway South.

Blue Springs Junior High School has established a citizenship honor roll to reward good behavior and proper study skills, regardless of academic standing. The citizenship honor roll receives the same status as the academic honor roll. Those who excel in academics, citizenship, or school projects are treated to coke and pizza parties with the principal. Perfect attendance is rewarded with a pizza party at a local restaurant. Blue Springs also features student work on CAT-LINE, a special phone line for district information.

At Evergreen Junior High School, classes compete for honors and special treats. The principal compiles data from each grade report and shares the student performance information with the entire school. Graphs of performance by grade level are posted in each class. Statistics are shared about the honor roll, citizenship and attendance. The class with the highest percentage of honor roll students receives a luncheon each quarter, and a breakfast is awarded to the class with the highest percentage of good citizenship.

Other frequently cited recognition techniques include use of an electronic message board to highlight students' achievements, distribution of press releases, posting of honor rolls and college acceptances, inclusion of articles in parent and student newsletters, and sending personal letters by the principal to deserving young people.

More formal methods include traditional awards banquets and ceremonies, including undergraduate honors and awards as well as those for seniors; bestowing local scholarships; induction into honor societies for academic, musical, and other achievements; recognition of accomplishments at school board meetings; and designation of special honors at commencement through the colors of robes or tassels, special certificates, or honors diplomas.

EXTRA CREDIT

A number of schools offer ways for outstanding students to participate in special projects or even earn college credit for their work. For example, students at Northern Highlands Regional High School may take certain courses and receive dual credit, for both high school and college.

Seniors at A. Philip Randolph Campus High School may take college classes. On non-class days, they may participate in senior research seminars, where they work with teachers in small groups to learn procedures for following up on college assignments. Randolph students are encouraged to take the Preliminary Scholastic Aptitude Test (PSAT) in the ninth as well as the tenth and eleventh grades. In the eleventh grade students are also given a regularly scheduled scholastic aptitude course in both mathematics and English to help improve their scores.

The senior project at Garden City Senior High School encourages research and interdependence in a variety of courses. A climate of demanding standards within the school is supported by very high parental expectations. Dobson High School is known as a "Challenge School." Ten percent of the student body participates in the Challenge or accelerated curriculum. In addition to established advanced or honors courses, 30 other courses may be "challenged" by students with faculty approval.

UNIQUE APPROACHES

In addition to these widespread recognition practices, a number of less common approaches have been reported. Some schools use cable television to showcase students. Others give gift certificates from the school supply store for student accomplishments. A few give a "Gold Card," which provides free admission to school events for teenagers having perfect attendance or a qualifying grade point average.

Proctor Hug High School has instituted an incentive program, Caught Being Good, which brings recognition and rewards to those who are "caught." Apples for Excellence is a program at Saint Bernard-Elmwood Place High School recognizing outstanding achievements of students, staff, and citizens.

Audubon Junior High School has begun a Young Black Scholars program to recognize and encourage those students in their 92 percent black population who make a B average. For each student selected, a dollar amount is deposited in a college scholarship account each year the student maintains the average. McDonald's also awards coupons for every A on report cards.

Edgar Martin Middle School awards a positive free period to all students who have no failures on their report cards. The activities for the free periods are decided jointly by the Parent-Teacher Organization, Student Council, students, and staff. Oneida Middle School provides a rare treat for its straight-A students. On Recognition Day, a limousine arrives at their homes to take them to school.

A special program at Orange Glen High School, the Champion's Circle, outlines rewards, rights, responsibilities, and rules for students. The program attempts to link school, home, and community in support of students. It provides rewards and incentives for outstanding citizenship, attendance, and special service to school and community. It draws upon the business and professional community for leadership, financial support, and experience in providing motivation and incentives. The school hopes, through the Champion's Circle effort, to emphasize that good citizenship is important and worthy of recognition.

Baboquivari Junior High School's cross-age tutors (students who tutor others) participate in a monthly drawing for five dollars. This is considered their chance for a paycheck for their skills in tutoring. The students are also advised to mention tutoring experience when applying for jobs.

Both Garger High School and McQuaid Jesuit High School award academic letters to emphasize that academic accomplishment is valued as highly as athletic prowess. Similarly, Darien High School gives a special award at the end of each athletic season, honoring the team that had the highest cumulative grade point average during that season.

Perhaps the most unusual and interesting approach was cited by Lincoln County High School, where an academic coach has been employed to coordinate recognition for academic achievement. The academic coach is responsible for academic assemblies, competitions, honor roll recognition, academic banquets, awards, bulletin boards, and many other items. Lincoln County also has an Academic Booster Club, whose primary purpose is to advance and encourage high standards of achievement in all academic areas. These boosters work closely with the academic coach to develop a program of recognition and incentives.

What schools expect in terms of behavior and achievement, they are likely to get. Those setting high standards and rewarding achievement, as do virtually all of the winning schools, obtain their goals and enjoy many student achievements worthy of recognition.

For a personal viewpoint on this issue, see Appendix D, page 268.

CHAPTER 8

Students and Discipline

Summarize your school's overall approach to discipline. Are there any special procedures or programs to maintain order and discipline? What factors contribute most to order in your school?

> Good discipline starts in the classroom, where students can be taught appropriate behavior through the educative process.
> —Harold S. Vincent High School

This philosophy, expressed by Vincent High School, represents a common thread in the applications submitted by many of the recognition schools. Such an overriding philosophical framework seems to be an essential factor in maintaining order in a school. Additionally, it helps school personnel keep a sense of perspective regarding discipline, and allows them to focus on long-range goals despite short-term difficulties.

This chapter describes how winning schools maintain discipline through:

- Developing Clear Rules and Policies
- Ensuring Understanding of Rules and Policies
- Clarifying Responsibilities
- Expectations, Consequences, and Rewards

Developing Clear Rules and Policies

School discipline policies may be developed by individual teachers, administrations, or even students. Some schools involve the entire school community in policy development. One such school is Parkway South High School, whose discipline policy was established by a committee of parents, teachers, students, and administrators to reflect community standards. For St. Louis Park High School, a tradition of good discipline reflecting both parental and community standards is the key element in ensuring all students the right to a productive educational environment.

TEACHER-DEVELOPED POLICIES

Teachers at Crest Senior High School develop their own sets of rules, along with the consequences and rewards associated with each rule. Copies of each set of rules are posted in the respective classrooms and filed with the administration. Crest has also developed an assertive discipline plan specifying proper behavior on buses, during assemblies, and for any total school activity.

Teachers at Burns Union High School are also required to submit discipline plans in writing, outlining their philosophy and methods for managing their classes. The teachers also spend time at the beginning of the year discussing rules and procedures.

The disciplinary focus at Shiloh Middle School is on helping students "develop self-control, self-respect and respect for others and their property." Teacher teams work to develop a Discipline Management Plan to apply to all classrooms, thus establishing continuity. In addition, Shiloh has two special programs under way. One is a model program designed to bring administrative supervision to smaller groups of people. The other is First Fight Offenders, a counseling program allowing students involved in first-time fights to examine feelings about and alternatives to fighting.

Rules of classroom management are also published and posted by each teacher at Mars Hills Bible School. In addition, at the end of each year, parents and students are asked to evaluate the disciplinary methods used by classroom teachers.

STUDENT PARTICIPATION

A number of schools have involved students in the policy development process. At Blind Brook High School, for example, every student submitted a written analysis of the discipline code. The student analyses were used as part of the modification process prior to the plan's final adoption. And at Episcopal High School the discipline code was voted into existence by 83 percent of the student body after an extensive series of meetings.

One factor that has helped maintain a positive approach to discipline at the University of Chicago Laboratory School is the student handbook, which was written by the students themselves. Thus the school's specific rules and disciplinary procedures have been developed by those who will be governed by them. The handbook, which is updated yearly, outlines expected behavior and the resulting disciplinary actions if infractions occur.

Ensuring Understanding of Rules and Policies

Schools use various methods to ensure that students and parents have a clear understanding of rules and policies. These range from posting and/or distributing copies of individual classroom or school-wide discipline policies to holding special assemblies.

Haywood High School prints its code of conduct on cards to be given to every student. Similarly, all students at Flowing Wells High School receive a school-wide discipline plan based on the school's policy: "Students have a right to learn; teachers have a right to teach; and no one has a right to prevent this from happening." Students are required to show the plan to their parents, who sign an affidavit indicating they have received and read it.

At Bradley Central High School, each student receives a copy of the discipline policy during registration. After a discussion of the policy by homeroom teachers, each student signs a form indicating that he or she has read and understood it. These signed forms are placed on file in the school office, thus ensuring that no student can plead ignorance of a rule. Another focus at Bradley is appropriate behavior at school assemblies. Because of the large size of the student body, the gymnasium is the only indoor facility spacious enough to hold everyone. As a result the gym is used for serious and formal occasions as well as athletic events and pep rallies. Therefore the principal and teachers work to reinforce the awareness that, regardless of the setting, some activities require students' silent attention and respect.

Scarborough High School requires both students and parents to attend discipline management training sessions during the first month of school. And Adlai E. Stevenson High School makes certain that all students are aware of school rules by requiring them to pass a test on the student guidebook.

Clarifying Responsibilities

Successful schools require that every person involved be aware of his or her responsibility in maintaining school discipline. The responsibilities of students, parents, and staff must be clearly defined, along with consequences for violations and rewards for compliance.

STUDENT AND PARENT RESPONSIBILITIES

Los Gatos High School places the responsibility for student behavior and regular attendance with students and parents, not the school staff. A few simple rules relating to attendance, behavior, and cheating have been adopted. Students are expected to live by these rules, and if they cannot, parents are expected to effect whatever changes are necessary.

Two contrasting approaches to student responsibility are evident at Mother Cabrini High School and McQuaid Jesuit High School. Mother Cabrini provides students with "unscheduled time"— no bells ring to signal the start and end of classes, and therefore students must be disciplined and exercise responsible use of freedom to be successful at Cabrini. At McQuaid Jesuit High School students have no free time, and no study halls are scheduled. Students are accounted for every minute of the day, and attendance is taken at the beginning of each class.

STAFF RESPONSIBILITIES

Order is maintained at North Olmsted High School because faculty members are visible in hallways, restrooms, and on various duties. The faculty abides by the basic behavior theory that "proximity to authority alters behavior."

High visibility on the part of administrators and staff, discipline with dignity, quick response, and consistency characterize the approach to maintaining order at Poolesville Junior-Senior High School. Poolesville also has several special programs and procedures. A safety/security assistant, whose responsibilities include questioning strangers, ensuring that students arrive at class promptly, and curtailing mischief, monitors the grounds and hallways. An in-school suspension program and an administrative detention hall after school are supervised by a behavioral assistant.

Believing that no disciplinary action is effective without home contact, individual counseling, and a concerted effort to understand the reason for a certain behavior, Shoreham-Wading River High School has instituted a house group system to provide such attention. Each teacher at Shoreham is responsible for 12 to 14 students and deals with them individually for discipline and for personal and academic reasons. Each teacher has one full period each day for meeting with his/her hour group advisees on an individual basis.

At Westbury Senior High School meetings are held throughout the year to develop commitment on the part of the entire staff—teachers, aides, secretaries, and custodians—to maintaining a climate conducive not only to expected behavior but also to the development of positive interpersonal relationships.

STUDENT DISCIPLINE RECORDS

Several schools maintain special discipline-related records. The system at Garger High School keeps an individual file on each student. This file, which the student may review, shows all official contacts with the office and requires a student signature on all forms to be mailed home.

The administration of Lincoln County High School believes that good discipline is necessary for learning to occur and thus maintains a disciplinary record on every student. Teachers submit a daily disciplinary report listing the name and problem of any student who caused a class disturbance. All information is transferred to the central file, which is reviewed periodically by the administration so that habitual offenders can be called in for corrective action.

Expectations, Consequences, and Rewards

Most schools use a detailed sequential plan in their overall approach to discipline. The process generally starts with detentions and continues through parent conferences, appeals, in-school suspension, and finally out-of-school suspension or even expulsion. The responsibility for maintaining order is a shared one, with teamwork viewed as essential. Teachers take a vital role in handling the majority of disciplinary problems, based on guidelines established for classroom deportment.

At Central High School in Tennessee, major discipline problems are handled by a process of progressive referrals. Two programs used at Central to help deter continual problems are ISS (in-school suspension) and ASW (after-school work). These are used in lieu of regular suspension. In the ISS program, students are placed in a supervised room with their regular classroom assignments. These must be completed along with a checklist of mandatory requirements. The ASW program is used to handle tardies and other minor disciplinary problems. Students in ASW are given work assignments, usually involving campus beautification.

A detailed sequential unexcused attendance policy at Central High School in South Dakota spells out the consequences for each violation. A student's first unexcused absence results in detention. The second leads to in-school suspension, which involves meeting with a guidance counselor to complete self-assessment forms along with regular student assignments for the missed day. Students absent three times without excuses must come with their parents to a meeting where they sign a contract regarding their continued attendance at Central High School. At each step of the process, parents are notified by telephone. Out-of-school suspension is rarely used at Central, and only when attendance or serving in-school suspension is deemed of no value to the student.

OTHER APPROACHES

Schools use a variety of approaches to encourage good discipline and deal with infractions. Following are some representative examples.

Newburgh Free Academy
The Student Assistance Center (SAC) at Newburgh is used as a "cooling off" place for minor disciplinary infractions. Students stay in SAC anywhere from one period to three days, during which time they do classwork assigned by instructors. Personal tutoring is also available from the professional SAC staff. Once a student is placed in SAC, the parents are contacted and the staff begins to assess attitudes that would influence his or her future behavior.

Shulamith High School for Girls
A citizenship grade accompanies scholastic grades on every report card issued at Shulamith. An unsatisfactory mark can eliminate a girl from eligibility for the honor society or student government office. It also prohibits a student from receiving honors at graduation. In this way the attitude of the school toward order and discipline is made crystal clear.

Maryhurst High School

At Maryhurst, a residential school for girls with special problems, a behavioral management levels program is in place "to identify the successful behaviors students are expected to master and to provide incentives for achievement. Behavioral objectives are identified at six different levels of ability in the following categories: dependability, perseverance, cooperation with authority, cooperation with peers, emotional control, and study skills."

Washington Middle School in New Mexico

At Washington, student-run judicial boards review student behavior problems and prescribe possible solutions and methods for encouraging student success. Students thus learn to resolve conflicts in a nonviolent manner.

Ridgewood High School

At Ridgewood, four grade administrators are specifically charged with maintaining discipline. Each administrator is responsible for the behavior of a particular class and stays with that class for its entire four years at the school. Students become well known to the grade administrator, who can thus consider individual differences and special needs. This structure has the advantage of facilitating personal contacts in a large school, as well as guaranteeing quick response in case of emergency.

Myers Park High School

Self-discipline is Myers Park's overall goal for its students. In the belief that discipline is a learned behavior, the school has set up a series of consequences and/or educational opportunities for students needing help. For example, an after-school time management seminar is a component of the tardy policy, and a tobacco education program is the counseling component for smoking offenders.

South Burlington Middle School

South Burlington helps students think through their discipline problems by requiring all students referred to the office to describe in writing both the problem that caused the referral and their plans for resolving the situation.

Lawton Community High School

Lawton staff members feel that the school building itself helps foster the excellent discipline the school enjoys. The carpeted open-space design features class areas clustered around an open media center. Students pass between classes with music instead of with bells, which creates a more quiet, comfortable, and orderly atmosphere than is found in traditional buildings. Reportedly, "Visitors routinely comment on the mature, orderly conduct of our students in a building which doesn't 'feel' like a school."

Dublin Middle School

A demerit system deals uniformly with infractions, helping Dublin students recognize a consistent, defined set of rules. Demerits accumulate through the year and may result in a Saturday School assignment or a suspension. Detentions are given for misconduct in the classroom. Dublin students have consistently improved their behavior under this program.

Petersburg High School

The sense of belonging and school pride that has been developed among Petersburg students over the past years ensures that discipline and order are not major problems. One factor helping Petersburg maintain its new facility in excellent condition is the establishment of a $1,000 fund for repairing damage caused by vandalism. Any money left unused at the end of the year reverts to Student Council use. Many years the entire $1,000 is turned over to the council.

Oldham County High School

Seven factors have been identified as contributing to order at Oldham County:

1. Expectations of parents for standards of excellence

2. The Board of Education's commitment to establishing and maintaining an orderly environment

3. An administrative staff that deals with discipline consistently, firmly, and fairly

4. High expectations for teachers in their professional conduct

5. High student expectations regarding interpersonal relationships

6. Uniform enforcement of established policies and procedures in both discipline and attendance

7. Holding students accountable for their actions

Finding the Key

A key factor in successful school discipline is the one expressed by the staff at Mahomet-Seymour High School: "The most important component is the fact that almost all of our students see value in what is going on in the classrooms, shops, studios, and gyms."

The other key component is a recognition of the rights and responsibilities of all concerned, as expressed in this passage from the application submitted by Xavier Preparatory School:

> We recognize that on this journey to become peaceful citizens of the Kingdom, there will be some setbacks. There will be some behavior patterns that must be unlearned. Because of this, we established guidelines that will enable us to create a nonviolent environment in which all have rights and all have responsibilities in respecting the rights of others.

For a personal viewpoint on this issue, see Appendix D, page 271.

CHAPTER 9

Students and Drugs

By what means does the school discourage the sale, possession, purchase, and use of drugs by its students and on its premises?

The winning schools agree overwhelmingly with officials at Mahomet-Seymour High School that "any school must do all in its power to reduce the sale, use, and possession of drugs, both on the school premises and in the community in general." Among the schools, the following three factors were considered significant in the fight against drugs:

A firm, clear, and strict policy regarding the use of drugs by students

Strong support for such policies by faculty and administration

An important role for parents and students themselves in combatting drugs

Schools have addressed these factors by various combinations of formal and informal programs and policies involving staff, students, parents, and the community. This chapter covers aspects of successful anti-drug programs at the recognition schools, including:

- Program Elements
- Staff Participation and Training
- Parent and Student Participation
- School and Community Climate

Program Elements

The best drug and alcohol abuse prevention programs seem to include the following elements, gleaned from the program descriptions provided by Skowhegan Area High School, West Bloomfield High School, and William Fremd High School:

1. Threefold goals of education, intervention, and prevention

2. Well-defined and stringent board policies, focusing on intervention at the time of a first offense

3. Education for students, to provide information and designed for prevention

4. Mandatory programs for drug/alcohol abusers

5. Evening programs for parents and athletes

6. Thorough staff in-service programs

7. Healthy school climates with programs that emphasize raising student self-esteem

8. Support groups for affected and recovering students

9. Community education programs to build understanding

10. Efforts to discourage substance abuse prior to prom and graduation, and plans for positive alternatives for weekend activities

An overview of the steps taken by Ridgewood High School shows how the basic elements can be combined into a total program:

1. Take a leadership position in a community effort to discourage drug and alcohol abuse among young people

2. Participate actively with community agencies

3. Provide informational programs for parents

4. Provide ongoing cooperation with local and county police

5. Provide a regular staff development program emphasizing awareness and responsibility

6. Provide, as part of the curriculum, a health program teaching all aspects of the problem

7. Establish a student assistance program headed by a certified drug and alcohol abuse counselor

8. Introduce additional policies regarding drug and alcohol use for students participating in athletics and activities

9. Ensure that specific policies addressing possession, use, and sale are clear, well-publicized, and consistently enforced

10. Ensure that early identification and intervention lead to counseling and other services for students and their families

EDUCATION AND INTERVENTION

Many schools follow a multifaceted approach similar to Chandler High School's, which includes three aspects: education; strict enforcement of rules against possession, sale, or use of illegal substances; and intervention. Any student found guilty of a drug-related offense has the option of either a ten-day suspension or a five-day suspension with a full-session enrollment in the counseling intervention program. In this program, a counselor and a teacher meet with small groups throughout the year to help them refrain from further use.

A similar first offender effort is applied at Brookwood High School. Students who are first offenders receive a mandatory nine-day suspension. However, if both parent(s) and student opt for attendance at all sessions of the Alternative Drug and Alcohol Abuse program, the suspension is reduced to three days.

"The Challenge" at Garden City Senior High School is a five-part alcohol education program designed for high school students. The program focuses on students' attitudes toward alcohol use and heightens their awareness of the consequences. All juniors participate in a series of staged events simulating a teenage social evening.

The students move from a simulated party to another area where they view an automobile accident vividly portrayed in a movie clip and experience a dramatic arrest for driving while intoxicated, conducted by village police officers. They then proceed to a consciousness-raising segment and conclude with a "rap session" in which students and a social worker discuss the issues raised.

At Central High School in South Dakota, the drama teacher and a group of 12 students were trained to present extemporaneous dramatic episodes focusing on prevention of drug and alcohol abuse. These vignettes have been presented not only to parent and student groups at the high school but also to junior high and elementary school parents.

Bradley Middle School was the kick-off school for the presidential Just Say No to Drugs campaign in its area. A community rally involving students and staff, an all-school assembly, and a school district rally focused attention on efforts to combat drug abuse. The Student Council also sponsors a drug awareness program.

The substance abuse program at the Santa Fe Indian School has been cited as exemplary. The program emphasizes education, counseling, and alternative activities, including community service.

Staff Participation and Training

The expectations of faculties and administrations are critical elements in keeping schools drug-free. For example, the high visibility of four administrators and three campus proctors, coupled with the clear expectation by all staff members that drugs are not to be sold, purchased, possessed, or used on campus, is a primary deterrent to substance abuse at University High School.

Olympus Junior High School, like most junior highs, has a closed campus. The safety of the students is further ensured by a policy wherein all staff members are alert for visitors. Even neighbors watch and call the school if they see any suspicious person in the area.

In cooperation with the local Lions Club, the staff at Centennial Senior High School has produced a handbook for parents on chemical use/abuse/dependency that was adopted in its entirety by the Lions International as part of their drug prevention education efforts. The handbook has enjoyed worldwide distribution.

SPECIALIZED TRAINING

Staff training is critical if school programs are to be successful. Twelve members of the secondary faculty at North Bend High School volunteered for a week of Impact Training one recent summer. Objectives included:

1. Heightening awareness about chemical dependency

2. Understanding the impact of drugs in the school setting

3. Identifying the role of school personnel

4. Stimulating action planning for school program implementation

The group has continued to meet since the one-week seminar and has encouraged others to join them. Group projects have included an all-school assembly, a school-wide survey on the use of chemicals, an in-service for all faculty and staff, and an evening presentation attended by more than 200 parents.

Northern Highlands Regional High School has developed a detailed substance abuse policy built around a staff Chemical Awareness Team. The policy includes team guidelines and procedures, a referral and follow-up plan, a school secure-grounds program, and parental consent for student urine and blood analyses. The team is serious about communicating to the community and to the students the message of "no use."

SPECIAL STAFF MEMBERS

Many schools have added staff members who specialize in leading the fight against drugs. Ferndale High School was one of the first schools in the state of Washington to employ a state-certified drug and alcohol counselor. The counselor provides faculty in-service, parent information, and crisis and short-term intervention with students.

Londonderry High School also has a staff person available to help students and their families deal with drug problems. Any disciplinary action involving the use of drugs automatically involves a referral to this counselor.

A "suspension diversion" program at Holy Trinity Diocesan High School places any student found to be in possession of or under the influence of drugs or alcohol in a counseling program for a minimum of 16 weeks. Holy Trinity also has an outreach counselor who, together with interns she supervises, is available to students two days a week.

Parent and Student Participation

Many schools have made special efforts to involve parents in the fight against drugs. The strong support of a parent group, Circles of Concern, is important at St. Mark's School of Texas. This program, which has served as a national model for school-parent cooperation on substance abuse issues, aids the school in taking a family approach to stopping drug abuse.

The Caring Parents organization at the Academy of Notre Dame de Namur provides a way for the school to work with parents in confronting drug and alcohol issues. One of the group's most significant projects is the publication of the Caring Parents Directory, a form of parent peer pressure aimed at creating a network of homes supporting the prevention of substance abuse.

At Wheeling High School, parents take an active role to reduce and eliminate substance abuse. Each year several mailings go out to student homes, stressing the need for parents to be on the alert. Prior to the holiday season parents receive a special Teacher-Parent Council booklet entitled *Let's Have a Party*, which provides tips on making teenage social gatherings both fun and drug-free.

To guarantee parent support and commitment, the Wenatchee High School policy is that each dance, event, or party must be chaperoned by twelve parents, along with three administrators and two security guards.

Worthingway Middle School sponsors a mixer for parents to discuss characteristics and concerns about their middle school children. WMS also offers a support group—By Parents, For Parents—to deal with specific adjustment issues, which may include drugs. The school has also sponsored two highly successful community programs. Get High on Life involved 24 community members discussing happiness without drugs. CARE (Cancel Alcohol Related Emergencies) was offered by a local hospital and highlighted the dangers of drinking and driving.

Milton High School was one of the first high schools in Massachusetts to adopt a chemical abuse program for student athletes. The school requires all athletes and their parents to attend a Chemical Awareness Night before the students can participate in the athletic program. In addition to hearing a guest speaker, parents and students meet in small groups to facilitate dialogue.

STUDENT PARTICIPATION

The Milton High School SADD (Students Against Driving Drunk) chapter annually sponsors a rally at prom time to enlist peer support against alcohol and drug abuse. (The first chapter of SADD was founded at MHS.) Lakeridge High School holds monthly student discussion sessions. These open forums provide opportunities for students to raise and comment on issues related to drug and alcohol use. A recent session involved more than 350 students.

Rock Bridge Senior High School has taken a positive approach to improve student self-concepts and feelings of self-worth. Rather than taking a negative approach of "that's wrong," the program aims to help students feel better about themselves and to show them ways to cope without drugs and alcohol. An important component is the positive peer support group, Kids Listening to Kids, which has been very successful in helping students to relate to others and to deal with problems without turning to drugs.

Gatesville Elementary School has a relevant and flexible curriculum geared to early adolescent stages of development. Students learn about drugs against a background of self-concept, decision making, and goal setting. Seventh graders participate in Pushing Back, a special program that gives students the methods to deal with stress and saying no.

A refusal skills program at Clovis High School trains high school students to make presentations to elementary school students regarding drug use and peer pressure. Obviously, this program is of value to both high school and elementary school students.

Teenagers at Yarmouth Junior-Senior High School participate in off-campus workshops as part of the school's chemical awareness program. Each class—freshmen, sophomores, juniors, and seniors—goes off campus for the two-day seminars on chemical use and abuse. Workshop organizers use improvisational theater, guest speakers, testimonials of former drug abusers, and small-group discussions to explore the issues.

Team Approaches

At South Salem High School, a broad-based awareness and prevention program includes a nationally recognized Drug/Alcohol

Awareness Week, a "how to" drug/alcohol awareness workshop, parent and student sobriety support group meetings, a published directory of parents who have pledged to sponsor only drug-free social events in their homes, and a yearly drug/alcohol-free graduation party. A committee of parents, teachers, administrators, and students coordinate education and awareness efforts.

Fort Couch Middle School also uses a team approach. Five faculty members and ten parents have been trained to develop a drug/alcohol task force targeting self-esteem and better communication. The school also has support groups, self-assessment programs, peer counseling, and a drug prevention curriculum.

School and Community Climate

The importance of school climate was mentioned in several applications as a significant factor in discouraging drug abuse. For example, Blind Brook High School wrote, "our overall milieu, characterized by openness, intimacy, and high expectations, provides a powerful antidote to student involvement in the drug scene."

The community and home, of course, have a profound influence on both schools and students. As noted by the administration of Geyser Public School, "A sound set of personal values originating in the home, and demonstrated good judgment on the part of students has made Geyser a 'drug-free' school. In Geyser, families are intact, and not only do parents attend to where their children are and what they are doing, they also look out for their neighbors' children." That's an unbeatable combination.

CHAPTER 10

Reporting Student Progress

Other than report cards, does your school have regular procedures for notifying students and parents of student progress in class?

Most schools have standard procedures in addition to report cards for monitoring student academic accomplishment. These include:

- Progress Reports
- Special Reports
- Other Methods

Progress Reports

Probably the most common method of monitoring student progress is the use of periodic progress reports. At Greely High School, for example, progress reports are issued during the fifth week of each marking period. Every student receives a report from all of his or her teachers during the first quarter. Reports indicating failure or danger of failure must be signed by parents and returned to the school; otherwise the principal or assistant principal telephones the parents. In addition to issuing progress reports, teachers also call or write to parents, and in some cases request conferences. Also, all freshmen who receive progress reports indicating failure or danger of failure are contacted personally by a guidance counselor.

South Salem High School reports, "We insist on ongoing communication with the student and parent." Teachers give students immediate feedback on assignments and provide frequent grade summaries between grading periods. All students receive complete progress reports at the end of each six weeks. Four times a year they also receive a report showing grades, cumulative GPA, credits and competencies completed, and credits needed for graduation. South Salem believes its progress reporting system "provides positive reinforcement, objective reporting, an early warning of problems, and a thorough review of achievement."

Scarborough Senior High School sends home progress reports similar in format to report cards at the midpoint of each six-week grading period. Teachers use microcomputers in the computer lab or at home to record the three-weeks grade and to request parent conferences as needed. Teachers also mail home notices for any students who have been absent from their classes four times during the semester, as a caution against the accumulation of excessive absences. As a positive note, the last Wednesday of the month is designated Happy Gram Day. Every month each teacher mails at least ten Happy Grams—brief positive notes to parents.

Larson Middle School teachers recognize that students have different needs in terms of monitoring. All parents receive progress reports at the midpoint of each ten-week grading period, and parents whose children require closer monitoring receive reports every two weeks. For some students, a daily assignment sheet is shuttled back and forth between parent and teacher to keep everyone abreast of the student's progress.

Lutheran High School West has instituted a Friday Traveling Card for parents desiring more frequent monitoring of their child's achievements. The card provides a progress report to parents every two weeks.

MID-TERM REPORTS

Nearly every school sends mid-term progress reports to the homes of students who are in danger of failing or who have a D average. Lakeridge High School takes an unusual approach by sending home mid-quarter progress reports that recognize three levels of student performance:

1. Unusually high achievement

2. Strong improvement from previous levels

3. Performance that is falling below expectations

Approximately 50 percent of the students receive these reports each quarter. Lakeridge also has a special program for keeping parents who are difficult to reach during the day informed about student attendance problems. Each quarter, five different faculty members are responsible for making evening phone calls to parents of students who had unexcused absences during the day.

Special Reports

A few schools use specialized reports to help keep parents and school personnel up-to-date and informed. For example, the foreign language department at Cardinal Gibbons High School sends notices to parents each quarter regarding students' academic improvement in language classes. In addition to the school-wide reporting procedure used at Yarmouth Junior-Senior High School, individual departments also have reporting systems, such as weekly computer-generated reports in math and science and individual student conferences in English.

To provide structure for selected students, Pittsford Middle School uses homework pads that must be signed by both teachers and parents. At Lamphere High School, a math department aide calls the homes of students who have failed to complete homework.

School policy at Lincoln County High School dictates that every club or activity sponsor receive a report naming participants who have received deficiency notices. Sponsors are asked to initiate contact with these students to try to help them improve their school performance.

KEEPING STUDENTS INFORMED

Students at Dr. Roland N. Patterson Intermediate School 229 are always aware of their progress, since charts indicating student progress are posted in all classes. Oneida Middle School encourages self-esteem and facilitates progress reports through self-assessment reports, which are part of the national Cornell Life Skills Training Program.

At "forecasting time" each semester, all students at North Bend High School receive unofficial computer printouts of their complete transcripts. Each printout indicates the classes being taken, grades received, grade point average, rank in class, attendance, and an evaluation of the student's progress toward graduation. Because students must meet specific credit and course requirements to advance to the next grade level, counselors meet individually with all students experiencing academic progress troubles. Together the counselor and student map out a plan that will allow the student to make up deficiencies as efficiently as possible. The plan is given to the student and a copy is mailed home to the parents.

Interim notices have been computerized at Novi High School. The school's administration has also scheduled a late bus so that students needing help can take advantage of after-school assistance provided by faculty.

MONITORING ATTENDANCE

Many schools have installed computerized telephone attendance systems that make it possible to monitor absences much more efficiently, resulting in more effective reduction of absenteeism. Mount Vernon High School's computer telephone attendance system (BEN) is supplemented by Attendance Alerts, which are mailed to parents when warranted.

Under the new school-based attendance program at Middletown High School, parents are contacted whenever their children are absent five or more days in any term. If parents request it, the school will contact them every time their child is absent.

Other Methods

Other common methods schools use to keep parents apprised of student achievements include mailing discipline and attendance reports, calling parent-teacher-counselor conferences, and issuing more frequent written status reports at the request of the parents. This is most common prior to and during the student's senior year, when parents want to be kept informed about graduation requirements, the student's current status in terms of graduation, and units and specific courses he or she still needs in order to receive a diploma.

Teachers at Burns Union High School telephone parents or mail home school postcards regarding issues like absenteeism, tardiness, classroom behavior, study habits, tests and exams, and daily assignments. Washington Middle School in New Mexico holds Weekly Family Plan meetings to discuss student progress and analyze possible solutions for deficiencies. These meetings generate many weekly parent-teacher conferences.

Students who fail a class or earn three or more D grades are placed on academic probation for the next quarter at the University of Chicago Laboratory High School. During this probationary period the principal maintains frequent contact with parents regarding the student's progress, with student progress reports, letters, phone calls, and conferences. Class attendance for all probationary students is monitored period by period, and any unexplained absence is dealt with by a direct call from the attendance office to the home. Student progress is also monitored by assigned counselors. If there appears to be a general drop in grades or effort, the student's counselor will schedule a meeting with teachers, students, parents, and the principal in an attempt to remedy the situation.

Counselors also play an important part in the efforts at Middletown High School. They communicate frequently with parents by:

Asking parents to sign a written record of every counselor-student conference

Calling parents when a counselor-student conference indicates that a student is experiencing problems

Monitoring student progress through semi-weekly progress reports

Monitoring student progress through daily homework cards

Notifying parents about potential failures that may prevent a senior from graduating

Notifying parents of underclassmen about academic failure and its impact on grade advancement

Schools encourage all types of methods for contacting parents to ensure that they are kept abreast of their children's progress or problems. In fact, teachers at Franklin High School are required to maintain parent/guardian contact regarding a student's poor progress or they cannot fail that student. Teachers are also encouraged to call home to praise student progress and to inform parents of ways to help students succeed.

An excellent overview of the many and varied procedures used by schools to keep parents informed and involved can be provided by summarizing the efforts of just one school, Lincoln County High School. The official notification to parents is the deficiency report, which is mailed the fifth week of the nine-week grading period. Teacher-created forms are also used, along with telephone conferences, parent conferences, parent-teacher meetings, counselor conferences, group sessions, study hall peer tutoring, and letters from teachers, the academic coach, or the principal. Many teachers also send home graded work to be signed and returned.

With these kinds of efforts in place, it seems unlikely that parents of any student at these schools would feel isolated or uninvolved in their child's education.

CHAPTER 11

Students and College and Career Information

What programs exist to provide information and advice to students about career and postsecondary educational opportunities available to them?

Three factors affect how schools advise students regarding career and additional educational opportunities: the school's mission, the school's goals, and student and parent aspirations. At winning schools, these three factors complement and boost one another, enabling the schools to offer programs, counseling, and information services that meet the actual planning needs of students. These services include:

- Counseling
- College and Career Days
- Computer Services and College/Career Centers
- Specialized College Prep Services
- Information on Career Choices

Counseling

Winning schools emphasize a four-year comprehensive plan matching student interests and activities with both the high school educational program and potential careers. Central to this planning, as expressed by the Cate School, is "the genuine concern,

122

expertise, and tireless individual attention which the counselors provide." Virtually all of the schools have staff members who provide group and individual counseling aimed at helping students and their parents explore various options.

University of Chicago Laboratory High School

A good example of an intensive counseling program is that described by the University of Chicago Laboratory High School. At the beginning of the freshman year, each student is assigned to the freshman counselor, meeting with the counselor two times per week for the entire year, either individually or in small groups. During these meetings, the counselor gives course selection and college advice and helps students find information about specific career options.

Sophomore, junior, and senior students are assigned to one of two additional counselors. In addition to receiving individual direction, juniors and seniors participate in a series of counselor workshops held once a week for a full quarter as part of the regular school schedule. Workshop topics include the college admission process, scholarships, career choices, SAT and ACT testing, and personal advice.

In addition to their assigned counselors, senior students have a second counselor who is responsible only for the college admission process. This college counselor helps students prepare letters for admission, complete college applications, and arrange site visitations. The counselor also arranges school presentations by college placement people. Seniors may attend as many of these presentations as they like; juniors may attend with advance permission.

TESTING

A common service provided for students is specialized testing, which helps students, parents, and counselors explore postsecondary options based on a student's identified interests and talents. One of the most frequently used tests is the ASVAB (Armed Services Vocational Aptitude Battery), which measures aptitudes for general academic and career areas that encompass most civilian and military work options.

EIGHTH-GRADE ORIENTATION

A number of schools offer orientation to eighth graders so students may begin planning early for a successful high school experience. The program offered at Milton High School is typical of such information/orientation programs. The orientation is the beginning of a four-year career exploration program encompassing decision-making skills, goal setting, course selection, and future planning. In keeping with the comprehensive guidance model, Milton has developed a guidance curriculum for use as a planning guide for grades 8–12.

College and Career Days

Most of the winning schools participate in some form of career day in which speakers from the community talk about their jobs. College days are also common, with admission representatives present to answer questions. Some schools with large college-bound student populations are able to host these on their own. Other schools cooperate with local community colleges or establish district- or area-wide programs in order to attract a large number of participating colleges.

Many schools also invite career and college speakers to address student groups throughout the school year. Specific school departments often arrange for vocational speakers to give presentations in conjunction with specific courses. For example, a draftsman might be asked to speak to a drafting class; an entrepreneur to a seminar in business issues; or a newspaper editor to a journalism class. College representatives and alumni, on the other hand, are more likely to speak to small groups of students who sign up to meet with them on the basis of college application plans.

Computer Services and College/Career Centers

Many schools offer computerized college and career search programs. The best ones provide interest inventories as well as information on occupations, programs, schools, and financial aid resources. The programs offer students the ability to research college or career options based on multiple variables. For example, a student could call up a list of highly selective, small Midwestern colleges with strong geology departments and opportunities to participate in intercollegiate tennis. In addition to computer decision-making systems, students at schools like McQuaid Jesuit High School also have access to relevant materials on videotape or laser disk.

Many schools house the computers and software for college and career searches, along with an array of print and audiovisual resources, in specialized career/college centers located in their library media centers. An example is the excellent Career Center at Claremont High School. The center's program and operation are planned and conducted by a full-time career guidance teacher who works closely with counselors and teachers. She is also assisted by a career technician.

Other schools rely on volunteer help. Miramonte High School has a Career Center coordinator who works with the more than 40 parents who voluntarily staff the career college information service for students. Parent volunteers also manage the College and Career Center at Darien High School. Since the Darien Career Center also serves as the location for counselor-student appointments, specific materials and information are right at hand.

Specialized College Prep Services

In today's highly competitive college admissions environment, many parents expect schools to offer specialized assistance to young people. Schools provide these services in a variety of ways.

Some schools use newsletters to keep families apprised of college and career information. At Poolesville Junior-Senior High School, for example, the guidance department sends home a monthly newsletter full of timely tips. Guidance newsletters are also published monthly by Stanton College Preparatory School, which also holds monthly meetings with all twelfth graders to keep them up-to-date on current information. And during the spring, Stanton counselors teach a one-week course to all eleventh-grade classes regarding the college application process.

Eleventh graders also get a head start at Gretchen Whitney High School, where guidance administrators hold biweekly "early bird" group sessions during the second semester to help juniors prepare and organize for the college admissions process. In the summer before their senior year, students at Blind Brook High School receive copies of the Common Application and the school's Senior College Planning Guide, along with updates of their evaluations from teachers and copies of their transcripts to date.

A monthly calendar showing scheduled visits by college rep-resentatives is issued by the Ridgewood High School guidance de-partment. In addition, the department also sponsors a guidance information telephone hot line, which students can call to receive messages about college visits and testing deadlines.

O'Fallon Township High School

A College Think-In is held each year on the last day before Christmas vacation at O'Fallon Township High School. Graduates from the previous year who are now in college are invited to return to the school for the event, which is held in the auditorium. Any senior who has applied to at least one college is invited to attend the session, at which the returning college freshmen share their experiences and answer questions from the seniors. School officials report that question topics range from coed housing to numbers of hours spent studying to the actual cost of schooling.

Another unique service at O'Fallon is the publication of a Senior Scholarship Sources (SSS) bulletin, which includes informa-tion about every scholarship opportunity that arrives in the guid-ance office. Approximately three to four scholarship descriptions fit on a page. Each description includes eligibility requirements, whether the scholarship is based on need, the date the application is due, and how to apply. As each page is published, an announce-ment is made on the morning public address system and printed in the daily school announcements. Seniors simply pick up a copy of the SSS in the guidance office, check the criteria, and, if interested in a particular scholarship, follow instructions on how to apply.

Many schools prepare and distribute print materials to help students and their parents understand the college application pro-cess and other options. Middletown High School, for example, publishes information on scholarship opportunities, in the form of a Cash for College booklet. At Myers Park High School, the college guidance counselor has compiled the Senior Handbook, a how-to book about applying for college. Similarly, the guidance office at Narragansett High School has developed a College Book detailing the process, the time involved, and the planning necessary for after graduation. Copies of the book are mailed each summer to stu-dents entering their senior year.

The staff at Ridge High School has designed a Self-Concept Portfolio to be used by all students to facilitate their planning. And the guidance department at Cardinal Gibbons High School has developed a 30-page College Guide to help students through the college decision process.

Information on Career Choices

Schools use many different approaches to help students consider career options. Most use an integrated approach incorporating career information into regular and special high school courses.

Thompkins Middle School uses an after-school academy program to introduce students to initial career experiences. Other institutions run specialized career awareness workshops and seminars or hold career days (or nights) to bring information to students.

A few schools require pupils to enroll in a special career education course. At Gladstone High School, for example, all sophomores are required to take a one-semester career education class that provides information and advice concerning vocational opportunities.

John Adams Middle School has a World of Business course to meet the needs of students today and anticipate their needs of tomorrow. Students use computers and typewriters while being introduced to various career opportunities. The program and the teachers are highly organized to help students learn to function both in school and in business.

A series of freshman, sophomore, and junior weekly seminars at Creighton Preparatory School is devoted to career awareness, decision making, life-styles, and the world of work as well as postsecondary educational planning.

Guidance counselors at Garden City Senior High School have developed a special career/college program for juniors. On each of five consecutive days, one period is dedicated to the instruction, assessment, and implementation of career goals. Students participate in interest testing, vocational aptitude testing, career counseling, and discussions on college interviews and visits. They also receive advice on researching schools, financial considerations, and application techniques.

Washington Middle School in Montana emphasizes the three Cs for career success: communication, cooperation, and coping. Students learn resume writing, filling out job applications, and interviewing. Girls also participate in a special program, Expanding Your Horizons, which stresses nontraditional fields for women.

Jefferson Junior High School uses a varied approach. They have a computerized information program, field trips, a career fair, and a parent/community "teach in" that emphasizes careers and offers trips to colleges.

USING COMMUNITY RESOURCES

Some schools make excellent use of community resources by inviting speakers to share their expertise and experiences in the workplace with students. Each year, Benjamin Elijah Mays High School holds a Youth Motivation Day featuring classroom presentations by parents, former students, and other persons invited from throughout the Atlanta metropolitan area. The event's purpose is to present information regarding postsecondary educational and career opportunities.

At Ben Davis Junior High School, six consultants from major businesses are assigned to individual classes. Each week the consultants provide instruction aimed at helping students understand the economic system of business. Ben Davis students also take field trips to local businesses.

In addition to regular visits by business and industry representatives (as well as college representatives and military recruiters), students at Lincoln High School can use the services of the local Job Services office in Wisconsin Rapids. The office holds regular hours at the school two days a week, to provide career information and assist students in finding employment. Lincoln also has a Designated Vocational Instructor (DVI) program, which provides a trained instructor to assist students and teachers in planning post-high school career opportunities for students with special needs.

Putting It All Together

Brookwood High School
Brookwood High School offers an excellent example of a four-year program that ties together both college- and career-oriented services. Brookwood's counseling department provides classroom guidance for each grade level, on topics such as:

Why make good grades (ninth grade)

Four-year plans (ninth grade)

Choosing a career and setting goals (tenth grade)

Postsecondary educational choices (eleventh grade)

Senior checklist (twelfth grade)

At the beginning of each year, a senior counselor-coordinator meets with all seniors whose grades average 85 or above to discuss additional choices related to scholarships, selective colleges, honors programs, etc. Parents receive information through a newsletter that lists testing dates and specialized information. Individual counseling appointments are also scheduled for all seniors and their parents, as well as for anyone else who requests them.

Brookwood also offers parent meetings, which are well attended. For example, parents of freshmen meet to learn about course choices and four-year plans. Parents of sophomores and juniors meet to organize planning for the senior year, for careers, and for postsecondary education. And parents of seniors meet early in the fall to learn about procedures for post–high school planning, financial aid, and college admissions.

Sequences, specific topics, and particular services vary from school to school. Virtually all of the winning schools, however, offer programs designed to help families launch their children into colleges and/or careers with confidence that options have been carefully considered and choices made on the basis of reason rather than whim.

A secondary school cannot and should not make the ultimate decision for any student. The school's role is to facilitate the decision making by providing necessary information and helping young people learn to know themselves, their abilities, and their limitations. Then students can make choices based on solid knowledge and realistic, yet challenging, goals.

CHAPTER 12

Students at Risk

Are there special programs or procedures to identify, counsel, and assist potential dropouts or other high-risk students?

Caring and a commitment to working hard at helping at-risk students are central factors in preventing students from dropping out. Another common factor in successful programs is teamwork that unifies the efforts of classroom teachers, guidance counselors, and specialists in dealing with students having special needs.

This chapter describes components of programs that succeed at helping potential dropouts and other high-risk students through:

- Identifying Students at Risk
- Intervention and Support Services
- Helping Students Who Drop Out

Identifying Students at Risk

The key to successful specialized services and support groups is the early identification of students who need help. Winning schools have regular, systematic processes for identifying high-risk students. Some states, such as Wisconsin, have even established lists of specific criteria to help schools focus on young people at risk for dropping out.

Classroom teachers are critical in the identification process, because they see students on a regular basis. As the staff at Marist High School in Illinois expresses it, "Teacher awareness is a strong factor on which the counseling department and the administrator build a program of prevention."

A good example of using teamwork to identify high-risk students is the referral process at Parkway South High School, where counselors, grade level administrators, "Care Team" members, and grade-level attendance officers all participate in identifying students believed to be at risk. Students identified as needing help are assigned to a special needs counselor, who works with them both individually and in small groups to enhance self-esteem.

EARLY IDENTIFICATION

Because Cibola High School staff members believe that almost all ninth graders are potential high-risk students, their first dropout prevention program is geared to the entire freshman class. Called the Freshman Transition Program, it consists of two major components: preparing eighth graders to move to Cibola, and continuous orientation and counseling for ninth graders.

The WIN program (With Intervention Now) at Mount Notre Dame High School also provides for early identification of potential high-risk freshman students. Those identified are placed in study skills classes and receive daily assignment sheets requiring parent signatures. Because of its success, WIN has been expanded to include some upperclassmen as well.

At Central High School in South Dakota all incoming sophomores complete the Mooney High Risk Test, which identifies those students who have the potential to be at risk in high school. Then a full support program involving counselors and the school's special needs team goes into operation to provide assistance.

LONG-TERM MONITORING SYSTEMS

Capital High School

Capital does everything it can to keep students in school, starting with the sign on the vice-principal's door: "You'll drop out of this school over my dead body." Potential dropouts are identified by checking report cards for low grades, compiling a list of students who have attendance and discipline problems, and by noticing kids who tend to be overlooked in school.

When a list is compiled, the three administrators and four counselors divide it up and make regular weekly contact. Students who are not successful academically are referred to the study skills class to get extra help, and a special class, Health and Life Decisions, is targeted for troubled students who need to enhance their self-image. This class teaches theories of behavior, communication skills, and decision-making techniques in a small group setting.

The attendance system is divided so that four "Pod" attendance secretaries monitor the same students for four years. They know the students and families and are often the first to spot potential problems. When such situations arise, the counselor is immediately notified and attention is given. The staff at Capital believes that it is this personal attention and monitoring that has achieved a less than 3 percent dropout rate over the past five years, the lowest in their area.

A similar monitoring system is in place at Henderson High School, where a school home visitor or caseworker is sent to check on habitual absentees. This is complemented by the employment of a full-time attendance clerk, who prepares computerized printouts of absentee reports to help counselors identify potential dropouts.

Potential dropouts at Haverford Senior High School are also identified by poor attendance records, as well as warning notes, low grades, and referrals from teachers or parents. Students may also identify themselves as being at risk.

Private and parochial schools, which often specialize in college prep programs, frequently take a different tack. Students at these schools are not generally at risk of dropping completely out of high school, but they may be having difficulty academically or socially in the private school setting. For example, at Archbishop Keough High School any student failing three or more subjects at the end of the second quarter must appear before an academic review board to answer questions about her problems and her desire to remain at Keough. Students appearing before the review board must contract to meet certain academic performance criteria. Those who fail to meet the criteria must leave the school at the end of the academic year and continue their educations elsewhere.

Intervention and Support Services

Intervention programs provide support, counseling services, and academic assistance for students at risk. Some schools have full-service general programs; others have programs to meet specific needs.

Sheboygan South High School's full-service program for "children at risk" follows a state mandate. Following are some of the main features for each student's plan:

1. Appropriate curriculum modifications

2. Remedial instruction to deal with deficiencies

3. Notification and involvement of parents

4. Availability of support services, including guidance counseling, psychological counseling, social work, media services, and even police liaisons if necessary

5. Identification of community support services

6. Specialized courses to prepare for employment

7. Development of peer tutoring

8. Identification of alternative educational experiences

9. Interagency cooperation with adolescent treatment centers, hospitals, prenatal care units, and mental health and social service agencies

Each education plan for students identified as high risk is evaluated and updated annually.

COMBINING SPECIAL PROGRAMS

Schenley High School Teacher Center

Schenley offers a number of special programs typical of high schools with a serious commitment to reducing their dropout rate. For example, the counselors meet with all students who have failing grades and review their goals during each reporting period. Also, the school social worker reviews homeroom attendance sheets and teacher class cut referrals to identify and work with students who have poor attendance records.

Teenagers with chemical abuse problems work with an interdisciplinary team and attend special sessions on drug and alcohol abuse. A regular referral system to family-centered counseling is used for students who are dealing with unusual family problems or child abuse.

Select Employment Training (Project SET) is designed to support academically and/or economically disadvantaged students by placing them in jobs where they can learn skills and obtain academic units of credit for satisfactory performance. Finally, in severe cases

Schenley places students who need a different structure for their academic program in an alternative school.

EARLY INTERVENTION

The importance of early intervention cannot be overemphasized. At Northern Highlands Regional High School, the guidance counselor initiates a one-on-one intensive support program as soon as any student is identified as being at risk. Follow-up continues until a no-risk point is reached. In the few cases where this is not achieved, the full child study team picks up the case and works with the student and family until the optimal outcome possible is achieved. Northern Highlands reports that the few students who leave school each year are generally those with family problems the school cannot resolve.

SUPPORT GROUPS

Specialized support groups are an important component of the service to at-risk students at West Bloomfield High School. Students may participate in groups such as the following:

Insight Class offers an alternative to suspension for students who break rules related to drugs and alcohol. It is operated by a qualified full-time drug/alcohol instructor.

After Care is a weekly follow-up support group for recently sober and drug-free students.

Concerned Persons provides a safe place for students to discuss sensitive problems such as physical or sexual abuse.

New Student Groups are small group sessions designed to assist smooth transition into a new school.

The Death of a Friend Group helps students deal with the suicide of a fellow student.

The Parent Support Group provides an opportunity for parents and students to get together to discuss mutual problems and concerns, and for parents to obtain specialized information.

ALTERNATIVE PROGRAMS

Schools offer a variety of alternative programs enabling students who are having difficulty with the regular curriculum to complete their educations and earn diplomas. Following are a number of different examples.

Tottenville High School
Freshmen at Tottenville may participate in the Academy for Progress, a special interdisciplinary program with four components:

Stay, a two-year self-contained minischool

BBQ, a program to train students in business-related skills

ABQ, a specialized course in automotive training

Career Institute, a program for students 17 or older

In all of these programs the attendance rate has risen dramatically, a real mark of success.

O'Fallon Township High School
O'Fallon cooperates with a neighboring district in a night school diploma program, which provides an alternative school setting for those students who need it.

Yarmouth Junior-Senior High School
Yarmouth has recently implemented a program at the ninth- and tenth-grade levels called Student Support. The program is designed to deal specifically with the needs of high-risk students who are not learning-disabled but have histories of very poor academic performance, some behavior problems, and frequently poor attitudes toward themselves and school. Separate classes— Student Support 9 and Student Support 10—are scheduled for these students once a day. The program also incorporates group counseling and a variety of other services.

Clovis High School
Clovis' feeder elementary schools identify high-risk students and complete educational profiles of them, which are forwarded to the high school counselors prior to enrollment. A Saturday School program allows students to make up instructional time lost due to

truancy or excessive absences and tardies. A variety of other special programs and services, similar to many already mentioned in conjunction with other schools, are also offered at Clovis.

Palo Alto High School

Palo Alto reports that very few of its students drop out. The school attributes its success to extensive early intervention services and to specific programs such as Opportunity School, Continuation School, or Contract Learning.

Denbigh High School

Denbigh offers a number of programs aimed at the high-risk student:

Project Stay, a work incentive program

Project Care, an alternative learning program for pregnant girls

Education for Employment, a one-year course to help students develop goals and values

Point Option, an alternative school for those functioning below their potential

Dooley School

Dooley's entire program is geared to serving high-risk students. A school-wide behavior management system gives daily written feedback to every student, and programs provide for rewarding successes in many ways.

Moanalua High School

A comprehensive screening procedure is used to identify possible dropouts at Moanalua, and the CSAP (Comprehensive School Alienation Program) is planned specifically to help the alienated student. A full-time counselor is in charge of the program.

Adlai E. Stevenson High School

Pilot Study is a small study hall for high-risk freshmen and sophomores who do not qualify for special education programs at Stevenson. Each day the students attend a study hall with no more than eight other students and a teacher who takes a personal interest in them. The goal of Pilot Study is to raise students' grade point averages by assisting them in organizing their work, encouraging them when they are failing, monitoring their progress, and insisting that they are engaged in constructive work each day.

Alfred Bonnabel High School

The principal at Alfred Bonnabel selects twelve students each nine weeks on the basis of poor academic performance. This "Dirty Dozen" must provide him with weekly progress reports, and study sessions are conducted after school. Just like Lee Marvin in the Dirty Dozen movies, the principal's insistence on performance builds self-esteem and proves that somebody cares.

Midwood High School at Brooklyn College

Midwood employs a Hold Power Coordinator, who works with high-risk students, their parents, and counselors as early as the freshman year. The school has also established a Collegiate Seminar Program, in which 60 targeted at-risk tenth graders attend a special seminar class to receive tutoring, homework assistance, and study skills instruction.

Lamphere High School

Teachers at Lamphere have begun an Adopt-a-Student program to give individual attention to students experiencing difficulties.

Helping Students Who Drop Out

Despite the best efforts of school personnel, there will still be a few students who elect to drop out of school. However, even then the schools do not necessarily give up on these young people. For example, the school may provide information that will help a student to continue education at some future date or in an alternative setting. For students who decide to leave Ridgewood High School after various in-school efforts have failed, there is always an exit conference that includes an invitation to return the following term as well as specific information on how to obtain the equivalency diploma.

Jackson Hole High School has developed an Exit Aid Handbook which is reviewed with all potential dropouts. Reasons, alternatives, consequences, and available services are part of this publication.

In the true never-give-up spirit, the staff members of Wenatchee High School contact all dropouts from the previous semester by phone or by mail prior to the start of a new semester, to suggest that they return to school and to help them set up a reasonable schedule for success.

To summarize, programs for high-risk students require early identification of potential candidates, specially designed intervention and support services, personnel trained to assist students and their parents, an administration willing to support and budget for the programs, and an attitude on everyone's part that these efforts are important.

PART
FOUR

Teachers

CHAPTER 13

Teacher Input

What opportunities exist for teacher input in decisions about instruction, curriculum, disciplinary policy, teacher evaluation, and other activities?

> The philosophy of the administration is that teachers teach better and students learn more when they have the opportunity and the responsibility to determine the policies and decisions by which they are affected.
> —Rock Bridge Senior High School

Many of the recognition schools display a strong commitment to providing opportunities for input by both faculty and students. This chapter describes how schools encourage teacher participation in the decision-making process through:

- Faculty Committees
- Departmental Structure
- Participatory Management
- Other Input Methods

Faculty Committees

The committee approach is a common one in schools. Many have standing committees to deal with in-service and staff development, teacher evaluation, curriculum development, and discipline. Some schools go well beyond these basics. As Brighton High School notes, "At the source of nearly every policy or procedure is a committee of teachers who met to help solve a problem or a concern." Centennial Senior High School has had numerous faculty committees—Technology, Wellness, Assessment, Improvement of Instruction, Effective Education, and Comprehensive Arts Planning are some of the recent ones.

Two committees have regular input at Sycamore Junior High School. The Faculty Advisory Council makes recommendations to the administration on policies and general matters. The School Improvement Committee undertakes long-term goals. Additionally, all teachers serve on curriculum committees whenever their subject areas are revised.

At West Bloomfield High School, change and improvement in the area of instruction is generally managed by cooperative committee work under the school's leadership team, which is composed of representatives from every department. An interesting committee, the Professional Studies Committee, functions at Parkway Central High School. It is charged with researching the latest instructional techniques data on an ongoing basis. And a solid program of teacher enrichment grant funds is available at South Salem High School. The funds and their dispersement are handled by a faculty committee.

ELECTED REPRESENTATIVES

Coupled with faculty committees in many schools is an elected group of teachers who serve as formal representatives to speak for faculty. These are usually called "representative councils" or "representative committees." The purpose of such a group is generally to act as a liaison between teachers and the administration with respect to issues of concern to teachers.

At St. Mark's School of Texas, six elected teachers comprise the Faculty Affairs Committee. This group may address any area of faculty interest.

Departmental Structure

Most high schools function in a fairly structured departmental mode. Consequently, considerable teacher input is channeled through the departmental structure. In larger districts, the departmental structure or curricular subject areas also form the basis for district-wide committees.

Just as the school's effectiveness is largely determined by the leadership of the principal, a department is generally as effective as the leadership provided by its designated chairperson. In most cases, department heads are appointed by the administrative staff, following guidelines set out in teacher association contracts.

Several schools, however, have gone a step further in granting input to teachers. The selection of a yearly department head at Cardinal Gibbons High School is based on faculty recommendations. The recommendations and the reasons for them are submitted, in writing, to the administration, which makes the final selection. Teachers may also recommend themselves.

Jackson Hole High School goes the final step—each year teachers elect their own department chairpersons. The department structure at Jackson Hole helps ensure important faculty input on significant issues.

Participatory Management

Lip service is often paid to the principle of shared management. Many of the winning schools, however, cite specific examples of ways in which they are opening the door to empowering teachers. They appear to agree with Woodbridge High School that "We function in a highly decentralized district where most decisions are made at the level closest to the action."

The mechanism used at Ridge High School is the leadership team, made up of representatives from each department along with at-large faculty representatives. Ridge's application states:

> Minutes of the weekly meetings of this body are published and given to all faculty members. Each teacher has a representative who can speak at the leadership team meetings. The purpose of the team is to identify and solve problems and to act as a sounding board for change and to assist in the implementation of effective teacher-centered change.

Whenever a major change in school policy is contemplated at James Logan High School, a study group or task force is formed. The majority of the task force members are teachers.

Champaign Middle School at Columbia involves a teacher team in interviews for teaching positions as well as in building administration. The principal has breakfast each Friday with the counseling staff, conducts a weekly building inspection with the head custodian, and meets regularly with the learning coordinator and the teaching staff.

TEACHER/ADMINISTRATION TEAMS

Gladstone High School's Dream Team allows teachers to identify school problems, brainstorm for solutions, and carry them out. The school reports, "While in existence for only one and one-half years, this Dream Team has made significant progress."

Quality Circles are also being tried in education. Many suggestions for improvement come from the Quality Circle at Oak Grove High School. This group is comprised of teachers and other staff members who isolate problems in the school and formulate possible solutions, with considerable success.

Burns Union High School features Quality Education through Quality Circles, which was initiated to develop procedures for applying Quality Circle techniques to educational decision making. Currently each Quality Circle consists of four staff members, one clerical employee, three students, and one parent. Circle members identify problems, select those to be analyzed, and make recommendations to the administration. A recent topic was staff evaluation procedures.

There is real power in the structure of the Staff Senate at Narragansett High School. The Staff Senate, which is made up of teachers and staff members, has the power to generate new policies and implement change within certain guidelines. The unique feature of this structure is that the Staff Senate members can, if desired, override the principal's veto with a two-thirds majority vote.

Other Input Methods

One of the most obvious and yet effective ways teachers have input is through the informal interchanges that occur in faculty lounges, dining rooms, and hallways, and at school social functions. In schools with small faculties, these are highly effective for the day-to-day input most teachers desire. At larger schools, slightly more formal methods are used.

SPECIAL INPUT FORMS

At S. S. Murphy High School, annual input forms give teachers the chance to provide information and suggestions to the administration. Bimonthly feedback forms give teachers at Flowing Wells High School a regular mechanism for channeling issues to the principal.

Woodstock Union High School provides a staff idea memorandum sheet, asking teachers to point out concerns and support solutions for general discussion. At monthly faculty meetings these issues take precedence over other items.

MEETINGS

Cayucos School's principal believes a planned program for instructional growth cannot work successfully in a world of written memos alone. He practices face-to-face meetings and visits, working with all staff members to hear their concerns and address their goals.

Because the major policy-making body for schools is generally a board of education or board of trustees, some efforts are being made to establish regular forums for faculty ideas at board meetings. Two teachers at the Cate School are elected by their peers to serve as nonvoting faculty members of their Board of Trustees, representing the faculty on both subcommittees and to the full board.

SPECIAL EFFORTS

Time to meet and time to think are hard to come by in most schools. To make that time, Gretchen Whitney High School has established monthly "late start" in-service days for brainstorming and policy development.

In another effort to give people with common concerns an opportunity to work together, the schedule makers at Moanalua High School have allotted special assignment-free periods to department chairpersons and other teachers. These periods are used to work on instruction and curriculum. Additionally, department members are assigned a common preparation period, allowing them to get together to discuss instruction and curriculum.

Encouraging Participation

Schools that encourage teacher participation foster a sense of openness and teamwork in the spirit described by the staff at William H. Atwell Fundamental Academy (a self-proclaimed "closely-knit school") as one in which "Everyone feels as though they have input and everyone is approachable." A similar philosophy is expressed by the staff at Lansing Catholic Central High School: "Open verbal communication has its painful moments, but it is essential in an organization committed to growth and improvement."

As the administration at Sheboygan South High School explains, "Staff input is extremely important and effective open communication is a must." And the Holy Trinity Diocesan High School staff writes, "Faculty input has had a vital impact on the life of the school."

Winning schools not only encourage teachers to speak their minds, they listen to what they say and act on it.

CHAPTER 14

Staff Development for Teachers

Does your school have an ongoing staff development program? Please describe it and how it is planned.

Virtually every American school has some kind of staff development program. In fact, it is possible to describe a generic staff development program that would be applicable for many schools, so common and widespread have some of the development practices become. This chapter describes how the recognition schools foster staff devclopment through:

- Basic Elements
- Special Programs
- Staffing for Development
- Other Efforts
- Development Incentives

Basic Elements

Most staff development programs include various forms of some or all of the following:

1. A pattern of released time during the regular school day. This might be a "late start" or "early dismissal"

147

schedule for students. In some schools, departments use these released segments to work on their own development issues.

2. Full-day in-service institutes or professional growth days. Usually planned by an institute committee, these often focus on current instructional issues or educational research. Some are held at the building level; others are district-wide programs.

3. In many school districts, a series of staff development courses offered on a regular basis through district-level staff assigned to this responsibility. Many of these are late-afternoon or Saturday courses, and teachers can sometimes use them for advancement on salary schedules or to fulfill requirements for professional growth.

4. Encouragement for staff members to enroll in college courses relating to their field of instruction. Incentives, in addition to salary schedule advancement, include partial or total tuition reimbursement.

5. Individual visits to other schools, either in the district or outside the district. Teachers can avoid an inbred attitude by learning what is happening in the next district, town, or county. Sometimes a written summary is expected upon the teacher's return so that observations can be shared with peers.

6. Trips to off-site workshops and conferences, particularly statewide and occasionally national meetings of professional associations. Time away is usually granted, with the school picking up the cost of a substitute. Since travel money is often tight, reimbursement for expenses is generally negotiated, based on allotments to each staff member and to each department.

7. Allocation of funds—sometimes a fixed percentage of the educational budget—for staff development. To help support in-service, some states rebate funds to schools from the fees paid by teachers to register their teaching certificates. Occasionally schools can apply for competitive grants if they have a special need that matches the funder's overall goals. Some state funds may also be available for such grants. Finally, some school districts are establishing nonprofit educational

foundations as mechanisms to raise money through gifts and grants. Many of these foundations will focus on educational mini-grants for teachers to pursue specialized training.

TOPICS FOR DEVELOPMENT

A good picture of hot issues in American education can be obtained by scrutinizing a list of staff development topics offered by these schools. Great Valley High School, for example, offers such programs as Effective Instruction Research, Lesson Design, Task Analysis, Time on Task, Classroom Management, Teacher Feedback, Learning Theory, Learning Styles, Thinking Skills, and Clinical Supervision.

Courses selected for staff development at Central Catholic High School have included Stress Management for Students and Faculty, Single Parenting, Drug and Alcohol Abuse, Student Suicide, Crisis Intervention, CPR, and Emergency Care.

One or two areas of the educational program are selected each year at Philadelphia High School for Girls for concentration in staff development. Some recent choices have been Improvement of the PSAT Scores and Extension of the Writing-across-the-Curriculum Program. Speakers, workshops, curriculum focus, and committee work have all been part of staff development on the selected area of concentration.

Dr. Roland N. Patterson Intermediate School 229 is the only school in its area that has trained its entire staff in the Mastery Learning approach to instruction. An 11-day intensive staff development program was followed up with sessions for new staff members, led by experienced staff. Patterson has also trained all teachers in a special writing program and increased their awareness of "Black" English.

At Saint Bernard-Elmwood Place High School, in-services are planned to coincide with the courses of study being written or revised by the teachers. Thus, when the emphasis was on increasing efforts in student writing, the school selected a special consultant to present a two-day in-service program on writing.

Special Programs

Many recognition schools have gone well beyond the generic model described above. The in-service day at Scarborough Senior High School has been transformed into a professional growth day with an individual approach. Each teacher may ask the principal to approve absence from duty for one day each semester for professional activity. The teacher is obliged only to suggest the manner in which he or she might share the growth activity with fellow teachers.

For years, the school district to which Haverford Senior High School belongs has conducted an extensive summer workshop schedule of curriculum and staff development. From 30 to 50 workshops are held each summer, ranging in length from one day to three weeks. The district budgets $40,000 for the activity and usually an average of 150 staff members participate in the summer.

North Salem Middle School also conducts summer workshops to allow teachers to enrich curriculum and develop areas of specialization. During one summer there was 100 percent participation by the staff. North Salem also utilizes peer coaching and Teacher Centers.

Staffing for Development

The staff development program at Villa Angela Academy is coordinated by the principal and assistant principal and planned in cooperation with staff development coordinators. This group has established six action plans, in varying states of implementation, which are tied in to the school's long-range goals. Each spring the group meets for a lengthy period to review the goals and make specific suggestions for the following year's program.

Schools that are serious about staff development often make special provisions to give one or more staff members some released time to coordinate a development program. At the Dooley School, for example, one treatment specialist has as half of her job duties the responsibility for coordinating training for the school.

Several years ago, Archbishop Molloy High School created the position of administrative assistant for faculty development. Responsibilities included working with teachers new to the school, helping them to develop their teaching skills and enabling them to fit more easily into the larger school community. Recently, these duties have been transferred to two newly created positions of assistant principals for academics.

TEACHER-DEVELOPED PROGRAMS

The tendency to encourage staff to plan their own development is growing. At S. S. Murphy High School, each professional develops his or her own development plan each fall as a way to focus on needs and interests.

Ogden Junior High School teachers have cooperatively set seven areas of in-service training. Each year teachers assess needs and brainstorm for ideas and techniques to meet those needs. The teachers are in charge of their own experiences, and they are determined to make them worthwhile.

Adlai E. Stevenson High School's staff development plan is another example of the key role teachers play in shaping school programs. A committee of teachers polls the entire faculty to determine topics of interest. Teachers with special interest or ability in those topics then plan and prepare an ongoing program on the subject. They become, in other words, the implementers as well as the initiators.

Teacher-initiated staff development is an important feature at White Plains High School. Teams of three or four teachers and an administrator work on improving instructional practices by observing each other and providing objective feedback, confidentially and apart from the supervisory framework.

A real grassroots staff development approach exists at Shoreham-Wading River High School. Any teacher wishing to offer a workshop or any group of teachers wanting one offered by an outsider group may have it as long as 12 to 15 teachers sign up. Teachers are offered either compensation or in-service credit for these programs.

Other Efforts

The following widely divergent approaches offer interesting insights into what is happening in staff development across the country.

Sycamore Junior High School
Sycamore holds brief morning informational sessions to keep the staff apprised of issues in health and safety.

Blind Brook High School
Blind Brook is training its staff in Madeline Hunter's Modes of Effective Teaching, using a teacher who has received advanced training in the approach. The teacher has an extra unassigned period each day, allocated for instructional coaching of other staff members.

Lakeridge High School
Lakeridge showcases peer teaching each spring at its Peer Teaching Conference. For this conference, teachers select some of their best lessons and teach them to small groups of faculty from other departments. The purpose is to spread knowledge of teaching practices across departments and to focus on the common elements of the school's instructional model.

Dobson High School
"Teaching with Class" is what Dobson calls its program. A staff member designated as master teacher visits classrooms upon request to observe and help teachers improve instruction.

University High School
University High uses a staff development newsletter to keep faculty informed about possible activities for in-service.

Benjamin Elijah Mays School
Staff development doesn't always have to be formal; sometimes the best learning happens in less structured settings. At a designated time during each semester, the faculty at Benjamin Elijah Mays engages in an informal Brag Session, relating unique and noteworthy professional growth experiences. Reports on local, state, national, and international professional meetings attended by personnel are also presented in both faculty and grade-level meetings.

Brookwood High School
Each year the school sponsors a Staff Development Night and invites a noted speaker to challenge and motivate the faculty.

St. Rita High School
"Common sense has shown us time and time again that the first four weeks of any school year pretty well determine the effectiveness of a classroom teacher as a manager or disciplinarian within that class." That's why St. Rita's designs its program to assist new people during the first month. School officials do not stand idly by, hoping that these professional men and women will discover techniques that have proven effective at the school. Individual staff development focuses initially on classroom management and disciplinary skills. Later visits cover content, testing, and motivation.

Gretchen Whitney High School
A buddy system is used at Whitney. New teachers are adopted by at least one experienced "buddy" teacher at the beginning of the school year, and special times are set aside for the important task of helping to orient new teachers.

Marist School in Georgia
Teachers new to the profession at Marist are involved in a formal internship program directed by a college education professor and coordinated by one of his peers. In regular sessions throughout the year, new teachers learn the school philosophy, improve their teaching skills, and receive guidance from a mentor.

Brother Martin High School
At Brother Martin, a differentiated staff development program offers one sequence for new teachers, a different one for second-year staff, and a third for veterans. These seminars are held approximately six times each year.

Palo Alto High School
Schools employ many people in addition to teaching staff members; secretaries, support staff, custodians, teacher aides, and other employees also need staff development. At Palo Alto, a 14-member staff development committee includes representatives from all departments and from classified support staff as well.

Development Incentives

What motivates teachers to continue to grow and learn? Following are some examples of incentives for development.

FINANCIAL INCENTIVES

Teacher incentives at William H. Atwell Fundamental Academy, in the Dallas School District, center on the existence of the statewide Career Ladder program. Career Ladder placement is based on performance, experience, job-related education, advanced academic training, and job assignments. Salary differentials can range from $1,500 to $4,500 annually, depending on level placement.

As indicated earlier, some schools have available funding for teacher mini-grants. At McQuaid Jesuit High School, this fund is designed to encourage faculty to continue professional development. The school pays tuition costs for graduate courses and fees and related expenses for seminars, conferences, and workshops. The Teacher Incentive Program at Crest Senior High School offers grants to be used for creative and unique programs not otherwise available to teachers.

State money is often available, if a school's staff is willing to write the necessary grant application to secure it. Ferndale High School staff members have successfully authored five Practitioners' Workshop Grants from the state of Washington. The grants have provided opportunities to do in-depth work in conjunction with specialists in the identified areas.

The Flowing Wells High School District's strong commitment to staff development includes a Career Development Program, which has been recognized nationally as outstanding. Over 90 percent of the high school faculty are involved in the voluntary program, even though a teacher on the plan receives as many as 27 observations by administrators, staff development personnel, and mentor teachers during the course of each year.

TUITION AND FEE REIMBURSEMENT

All certified teachers at Northern Highlands Regional High School electing to continue professional studies at an accredited school, college, or university will have their tuition reimbursed at the rate of 100 percent, as long the course has the prior approval of the superintendent and the teacher receives a grade of B or better.

As an incentive for teachers to take advantage of the programs and services offered by professional associations, Mars Hill Bible School pays one professional membership fee for each faculty member. Parents at Menlo-Atherton High School raise money for a principal's fund, to be used for teachers wishing to go to workshops or attend professional association conferences. And Mahomet-Seymour High School pays for a subscription to professional literature for each staff member, to help teachers stay current in their field and in education.

Salaries for personnel, particularly teaching staff, are always the major portion of a school budget. Resources and funds used to hone teacher skills and increase both their productivity and sense of worth are well invested.

For a personal viewpoint on this issue, see Appendix D, page 274.

CHAPTER 15

Rewards and Incentives for Teachers

Are there formal procedures for recognizing excellent teachers? Are there special rewards or incentives available for them?

The concept that human beings thrive when they feel valued is an easy one to understand, but this does not mean that all schools are uniformly guided by it. The administrators of the recognition schools, however, pay close attention to the climate in their buildings and communicate a sense of worth to their teachers. Consequently, they also communicate to students, parents, and the community at large the knowledge that their schools are staffed by the best kinds of teachers.

Many schools follow a central core of accepted practices to encourage, recognize, and reward their best faculty members. These include:

- Honors and Awards
- Teacher of the Month or Year Programs
- Master or Mentor Teacher Programs
- Monetary Rewards

Honors and Awards

Most schools, as a matter of course, send out news releases highlighting the accomplishments of teachers and other staff members. Generally, the school or district newsletter will also carry items related to faculty news. Principals frequently send formal letters of commendation to faculty members, which also become a part of the teachers' files.

Hines Middle School rewards teacher accomplishments through certificates presented monthly at faculty meetings. Often parent and student groups cooperate with teacher organizations to honor faculty members.

An Opening-of-School Breakfast and an End-of-Year Luncheon are occasions used by Bradley Central High School to pay tribute to deserving teachers. At the Academy of Mount St. Ursula an official Teacher Recognition Day allows the student body to thank and honor teachers and other staff members for a job well done. The annual celebration at Myers Park High School extends for a full week. Among the varied activities is a Faculty Honor Luncheon cosponsored by the Parent-Teacher-Student Association.

The Student Council at Franklin High School conducts a vote whereby students elect top teachers. The top three teachers receive awards at a Teacher Appreciation Breakfast sponsored by the Student Council.

The ten top seniors at Valley High School select the outstanding teachers to be honored by their Board of Education. This incorporates another typical component of a well-planned appreciation program—the recognition accorded by school boards. At many board meetings a special place is reserved on the agenda each month for announcements of awards, including faculty and staff honors. These become a part of the official board records.

Teachers involved in innovative programs at Westbury Senior High School are invited to teach demonstration lessons during their Board of Education meetings. This has a twofold value: first, the teacher receives recognition; second, the board and public learn firsthand about a program in the school.

Commencement ceremonies are also frequently an occasion for honoring and recognizing faculty as well as the graduating class. That is true at Henderson High School and at Gladstone High School, where honored teachers are selected by the class as "honorary seniors." Some schools, such as South Kingstown High School, recognize and honor teachers who have earned distinction during the year at the traditional all-school Honors/Awards Assembly.

Community support for recognition programs is also frequent. Organizations such as the Jaycees and other service clubs are often involved, and if a school has been adopted by a business partner, that partner will generally participate. Harrah's at Reno, the adopter of Proctor Hug High School, gives a Teacher Recognition Banquet for the Hug staff.

TYPES OF AWARDS

Plaques are traditional awards. Haverford Senior High School provides plaques of commendation to Teachers of the Year. Distinguished Service Award plaques are presented by Saint Bernard-Elmwood Place High School to teachers cited for providing outstanding service. A bronze honor roll recognizing all faculty who have served the district 25 or more years is prominently displayed in the hallway of Mount Vernon High School.

Some schools show a remarkable level of creativity in planning specific awards. For example, the superintendent of Parkway South High School's district makes personal presentations of "Whale Awards" to faculty who are doing a "whale of a good job." There's a nice touch of humor, too, in the approach at Torrey Pines High School, where the principal "mugs" teachers (presents them with a school mug) in front of their classes.

A teacher who has accomplished something special at South Salem High School is presented with a Saxon Mug of the Month award at a staff meeting. On a more serious note, the administrators at Salem have commented that their most significant way of recognizing teachers is through regular written evaluations: "By taking great pride and care in the evaluation process, we are able to give teachers much appreciated feedback and recognition."

Apples have become a common symbol for education all over the country. Therefore it is not a surprise that some schools are using apples as a theme in their award programs. Recipients of the Good Apple Award at Newburgh Free Academy receive a shiny styrofoam apple with an attached thank-you card stating, "You're a good apple." The principal always adds personal comments and commendations on the card. At Los Gatos High School the idea is the same, but the award is called the Golden Apple.

Sycamore Junior High School gives teachers coupons as rewards for extra effort and energy. The coupons can be redeemed for items for their classes. Also, the administration rewards positive deeds by taking over a teacher's duty.

One final interesting and creative form of recognition is accorded to outstanding teachers at Cibola High School. In addition to Cougar pins, they receive designated parking spaces!

OTHER KINDS OF HONORS

Following are some of the other ways schools have found to recognize outstanding faculty members:

Lakeridge High School

The purpose of the annual spring Celebration of Accomplishment at Lakeridge is to review and highlight staff activities and achievements for the year. District administrators, school board and parent advisory committee members, and the local press are invited to participate in recognizing teaching excellence.

Villa Angela Academy

Villa Angela recognizes an outstanding teacher in each issue of its newsletter, which is mailed to 6,000 alumnae, parents, and benefactors. Called "Feature a Teacher," this recently added column has received very positive feedback.

White Plains High School

Students at White Plains dedicate the yearbook to one teacher, award an honorary membership in the National Honor Society to another teacher, and, as seniors, vote for faculty marshalls for the graduation procession.

Petersburg High School

Modesty might prevent most faculty from posting their professional diplomas and credentials in their classrooms. But at Petersburg the practice is strongly encouraged so that students, parents, and community members can see visible evidence of their teachers' professional training.

D. Russell Parks Junior High School

Although the staff at Parks prefers not to single out individual teachers as outstanding, the administration frequently uses notes, letters, and verbal approval to recognize extra effort. In addition, many civic groups recognize outstanding teachers.

Washington Middle School in New Mexico

The administration at Washington feels all their teacher are excellent and any special rewards would be divisive. They prefer to foster sharing, unity, and commitment. Morale boosters such as family breakfasts, secret pals, and social activities assist in making the faculty feel good about the quality of their work.

Teacher of the Month or Year Programs

Many schools have chosen to participate in a Teacher of the Year recognition program on either an informal or formal basis. Some of these programs have intriguing variations.

A example of one kind of formal program is found at Orange Glen High School. The principal and a committee select a Teacher of the Month, who receives $50. The teacher selected District Teacher of the Month receives $100, and the District Teacher of the Year receives $500. Related recognition is given to all nominees through luncheons, press releases, and photo displays.

At Newburgh Free Academy the designated Teacher of the Year receives a $1,000 award, which is sponsored by a local business partner. Ferndale Elementary School elects a Teacher of the Year, who receives an engraved golden bell. Ferndale also utilizes mentor teachers, and has awarded over $16,000 in the last four years.

Alumni associations also participate in annual teacher recognition programs. The Alumnae Appreciation Award at Cranbrook Kingswood School is given to a faculty member who exhibits a special friendliness and interest in others and in all aspects of school life, along with a willingness to cooperate and always do more than the task at hand entails. A stipend is attached to the award.

A unique Teacher of the Month program at Valley High School allows students to reward their teachers with a raffle card. One card is chosen in a monthly drawing and the winning teacher receives a day off from school.

The Teacher of the Year at Moanalua High School receives trophies, flower leis, and is asked to serve as the Grand Marshall of the Homecoming parade. And an interesting bonus for the Teacher of the Year at Providence Day School is a one-week summer vacation at the beach.

Sheboygan South High School

The Sheboygan South High School district has a very detailed and thorough program for selecting and honoring Teachers of the Year. Teachers may be nominated by parents, community members, educators, and peers. Criteria used to determine the recipients include evidence of professional commitment, attitude toward students, relationships with school families and the community, outstanding professional achievement over the previous three years, extracurricular activities, and community involvement.

Students play an important part in the nomination process—they are asked to nominate one individual who best fulfills the specific classroom-based criteria and must sign their ballots in order to have them recorded. Staff members who receive 3 percent of the student vote are placed on a staff ballot, and staff in turn vote for the candidate that best meets the teaching peer criteria.

All candidates who received at least 3 percent of the student vote and 10 percent of the faculty vote are honored as outstanding and receive special plaques at the final faculty meeting of the year. Winners are selected by a committee that evaluates the outstanding candidates on the basis of listed criteria. The overall winner receives a plaque and a $100 savings bond.

Master or Mentor Teacher Programs

A growing trend is to recognize and reward outstanding teachers by appointing them as lead, or curriculum, teachers. This practice rewards good teaching and allows teachers to gain a sense of advancement and increased influence without having to leave the classroom. Mentor or master teacher programs view teaching not as a stepping stone to school administration (unless that career change is desired) but as a profession in and of itself.

California state law now permits the designation of mentor teachers, who may earn up to $4,000 extra each year serving as master teachers, helping with staff development, or working on curriculum. Los Gatos High School has had three or four mentor teachers in each of the past few years, and Milton High School seeks applications for positions as lead teachers and curriculum teachers from faculty members who receive outstanding evaluations.

Monetary Rewards

Many of the awards already described offer some financial reward as well as recognition. Another whole category of incentives or rewards, however, is centered on financial remuneration. A typical example is the distribution of professional development funds. Lakeridge High School rewards and encourages individual teachers and teacher teams for conference or seminar attendance through such funding.

Endowed chairs and teaching excellence awards are a special feature at some private schools. St. Mark's School of Texas gives three annual awards of $5,000 each for excellent teaching. The school has also endowed four Master Teacher Chairs, providing substantial advantages in compensation for recognition as well as recruitment of top teachers. The Madeira School also has a fully endowed program of master teacherships and one history chair fully endowed with $500,000.

Each year an excellent teacher at Shulamith High School for Girls receives a $10,000 award sponsored by a private benefactor of the school. Special financial bonuses are also given throughout the year for deserving accomplishments. A trust fund set up by a former president of the school board at Rock Bridge Senior High provides annual $500 awards to recognize outstanding teachers. And every teacher at Greely High School can earn a $100 award for perfect attendance for the school year.

Irving A. Robbins Junior High School is part of a district-wide teacher incentive pay program. Teachers apply for incentive pay, propose projects, and are judged at the district level for monetary awards. Only teaching excellence is rewarded.

A number of schools have instituted sabbatical leaves as part of their services to faculty. Such is the case at Loyola High School of Baltimore, Inc., where valued teachers are encouraged to hone their skills by taking advantage of this program.

The Real Rewards

Financial awards are certainly a significant way to recognize excellence in teaching. Most teachers, however, would probably say that the spirit of recognition is what is truly important. This spirit was well expressed in the application from Alexander Hamilton High School:

> Although we are not able to financially reward our excellent teachers, we support them through superior evaluations, utilize them as model teachers, recognize them in the school, feature information about them in display cases, place letters of commendation in their files, and encourage staff application for student fellowships. We recognize their accomplishments via public address announcements and recognition at staff meetings.

Even more revealing is the viewpoint expressed in the site visitation report of Williams Bay High School: "Teachers here feel rewarded by the total success of the school and of the students."

PART
FIVE

Parents and
the Community

CHAPTER 16

Schools and Parents

Please describe specific opportunities for parent participation in school activities and in the education of their own children.

Parent cooperation is essential if students are to reach their greatest potential. Winning schools actively seek parents' opinions and advice. They encourage parents to assume significant roles in the life of the school and in the education of their children.

Many of the methods and activities used to accomplish these ends are traditional—chaperoning school events, volunteering for school projects, or raising money for needed equipment. Increasingly, however, schools are finding new ways to reach out to the parents in their communities. This chapter describes how winning schools get parents involved through:

- Meetings and Open Houses
- Newsletters, Mailings, and Surveys
- Parent Committees and Advisory Groups
- Volunteer Programs
- Booster Groups
- Special Events
- Parent Education Programs

Meetings and Open Houses

Parent meetings and open houses offer parents an opportunity to experience their children's school and teachers firsthand. Many schools make these face-to-face meetings a regular occurrence.

Adlai E. Stevenson High School offers luncheons with the principal to encourage parents to visit school while it is in session. All parents are also invited to coffee and counseling sessions to discuss college selection and the application process.

Morning curriculum coffees at Great Valley High School are open to the entire community. Information about new courses and demonstrations of new equipment are provided at these sessions. And parents are personally invited to *Kaffeeklatsch* meetings held during the school day at Wheeling High School.

Once a month parents of students at William Fremd High School are invited to join the principal in a "walk-through" to see education in progress. Conversely, the principal of Garden City Senior High School goes out into the community to speak to residents at what have been dubbed "principal forums." These are held in homes throughout the district.

"Lunch with the bunch at the bridge" is held each spring at Rock Bridge Senior High School. Parents, community and civic groups, and interested citizens are invited to tour the school and enjoy special luncheon programs. These provide insights into school activities and give the visitors an opportunity to see Rock Bridge in action.

Mission San Jose High School is committed to the belief that education is a community function. Before classrooms open on the first day of school, the staff hosts a Back-to-School Night to introduce parents and the community to the staff and the program of instruction. More than 1,000 parents and community people usually attend this event.

A highly successful parent open house at Flowing Wells High School is also the occasion for forming the Parent Advisory Committee for the year. This group, which meets once a month, enables parents to play a major role in formulating school policy and revising current practices.

The staff at Mother Cabrini High School publishes a bilingual newsletter five times a year, as well as making efforts to meet and talk directly with parents. These efforts include parent meetings by grade level, semiannual individual parent-teacher conferences, and evening parent discussion groups, which are held weekly during October. Events are held in both Spanish and English so that all parents can be included. In addition, meeting times are planned to be convenient for single, working parents, who are in a majority at this school.

Newsletters, Mailings, and Surveys

Newsletters and mailings help parents keep current with school affairs, while surveys give them a chance to make their own opinions and feelings known. Several years ago, as the first step in increasing positive relationships with parents, Southside High School conducted a telephone survey with the help of the Parent-Teacher Association. A number of activities have resulted, including a specialized survey of parents willing to serve as volunteers, teacher aides, or resource people, sharing expertise in their fields of knowledge with students in the classroom.

Parents of students at Dobson High School receive 11 mailings each year, including grade and progress reports as well as three newsletters. Villa Angela Academy mails its quarterly newsletter not only to 6,000 parents, but to alumnae, benefactors, and area businesses.

Parent Committees and Advisory Groups

Parent committees and advisory groups give parents the opportunity to have a significant impact on the policies and practices of a school. Schools committed to creating such partnerships actively seek parent advice and counsel, recognizing that parents and schools share a mutual interest and concern for students.

Although the formats or mechanisms of such groups may vary, they share a common element: parents have a regular forum in a formal structure and are given a significant role to play in advising school officials. Following are examples of schools that allow parents to play active advisory roles:

Clovis High School
With an enrollment of more than 2,600, Clovis works continuously to cultivate its relationship with parents and the community. A primary component of this relationship is a school committee composed of parents and other local community residents. The role of this group is to examine and discuss school policies, practices, and programs and make recommendations. Each spring, the school committee distributes and collects opinion

surveys. Members also serve as a sounding board for parent issues, which are then addressed at monthly meetings with the school's administrators. A special hotline allows parents to communicate immediate concerns to the committee.

Daniel Wright Middle School
An assortment of committee roles awaits parents at Wright. Besides the Parent Advisory Committee, there are the Parent Teacher Conference Committee, the Eighth-Grade Parent Committee for Graduation, the After-School Advisory Committee, and a variety of social and program assignments.

Jesuit High School
At Jesuit High School, the Parents' Club appoints a Parent Advisory Board, with individual parents assigned to each area of school life.

Claremont High School
At this California school a variety of groups have been established to involve parents (and interested community members) in the decision-making process. These include the Tri-Advisory Committee, the District Advisory Committee, the School Curriculum Committee, the School Site Council, and the Affirmative Action Advisory Committee.

Irving A. Robbins Junior High School
The formal Parent Advisory Board (P.A.B.) at Robbins consists of ten parents who respond on major issues and work to improve overall school services. At present the P.A.B. is assuming a major leadership role in educating parents on chemical substance abuse, along with establishing a parenting network to ensure safe homes for parties and other student social activities.

Novi High School
Officials at Novi report that parents vie for positions on the various task force groups that are continuously being created to deal with school issues. It is obvious that these parents recognize and appreciate the importance of their active advisory role.

South Kingstown High School
"Parents as partners" is more than an empty phrase in Wakefield, Rhode Island. An active Parent Advisory Group regularly

brings issues of community concern to the principal's attention. A special Concern for Youth committee sponsors forums on significant issues. Additionally, the screening committees for all teaching, administrative, and coaching vacancies contain at least one parent, and are open to anyone interested in volunteering.

Metairie Park Country Day School

The staff at Metairie Park reports the successful implementation of another level of "parents as partners." A Parents' Council, composed of the heads of all parent groups from all of the area's independent schools, allows for cooperative programs within the broader community of greater metropolitan New Orleans.

Volunteer Programs

Volunteers have played significant roles in many aspects of American life for decades, and in schools their role has often assumed life-sustaining proportions. In sheer person-hours, volunteer hands are important, but even more important may be the hearts won through such up-close-and-personal encounters. People tend to value what they work for, which is why volunteer programs are an effective way to build a core of rock-solid support for schools.

This sampling illustrates the diversity and occasionally unique qualities of school parent volunteer programs.

Southside High School

Parent volunteers operate Southside's copy machine and handle all of the copying for teachers. Currently two parents operate the copier each day, turning out an average of over 230,000 copies per month.

James Logan High School

At Logan parents are involved in several volunteer programs. They assist in office work, tutor in the classrooms, help teachers in the production of materials, and even provide translations of school communications into various languages.

Los Gatos High School

Recognizing that the school would be forced to curtail many services after the passage of Proposition 13, the principal called

upon the Parent-Teacher-Student Association for parent volunteers
to take up the slack. More than 100 volunteers each serve a minimum of three hours a week in the attendance and main offices, the
guidance office, the textbook office, the library, and the computer
labs. The school reports that "without these volunteers, the student center would be open only half-days and the library closed
during lunch, and guidance and attendance services curtailed."

Paul J. Gelinas Junior High School

Parent volunteers not only work in the library and chaperone
field trips, they also sponsor the Teacher Recognition Luncheon
and help Gelinas put on a Holiday Tree Lighting ceremony for the
whole community.

Orange Glen High School

Each year approximately 80 parents work with the Orange
Glen staff to register more than 2,000 students by the arena registration process. Another 15 parents help the library staff distribute
books to students who have completed registration. The Parents'
Club has implemented a tutoring program that has had a significant impact on the education of many students. And parent volunteers—250 of them—have chaperoned dances, performed clerical
tasks, served as guest speakers, or assisted in classrooms.

Darien High School

Darien enjoys an extremely high level of parent participation.
Parent volunteers are recruited and directed by a paid volunteer
coordinator. In a recent year the volunteers logged over 8,000
hours. Working in virtually every department of the school, parents monitored computer use, repaired and shelved library books,
processed forms, graded placement tests, chaperoned trips, and
judged debates. One of the special services they provide is a jobs
office that coordinates student employment opportunities.

Our Lady of Lourdes Academy

Parents are asked to fill out a volunteer form at the beginning
of the school year and to pledge their support and assistance in
activities such as teacher substitution, career days, and school festivals and teas.

Benjamin Elijah Mays School

Mays' Volunteer Services Directory contains the names of
parents and community persons interested in contributing their

time and services during the school day. These volunteers serve as classroom consultants, chaperones, and clerical assistants. Approximately 280 parents are available to serve in these paraprofessional capacities when needed.

Sycamore Junior High School
Parents at Sycamore have initiated an after-school program that uses school facilities to involve students in such activities as racquetball, Spanish, creative cooking, and bowling.

Mother McAuley Liberal Arts High School
Volunteer mothers and alumnae staff the school's bookstore as an ongoing project; proceeds go to the school's development fund. The health room is also staffed by volunteer mothers.

O'Fallon Township High School
Parents visit classrooms to discuss their own career fields, talking about education or training requirements as well as prospects for future employment in their specific areas. They also serve as volunteer teacher assistants in vocational classes such as woodworking.

Parkway Central High School
The Volunteer Corps at Parkway lists 14 specific areas for which a parent can volunteer; for example, as a computer/mathematics tutor.

Charlotte Latin School
Each day parent volunteers can be found at Charlotte Latin helping in the offices, the bookstore, and the library. Other volunteers serve on the Gardening and Grounds Committee to enhance the school's landscaping.

Edgewood High School of the Sacred Heart
Volunteers have provided over 16,000 hours of service to Edgewood, assisting with supervision, tutoring, typing, and other clerical duties. Parents also assist in supervising resource centers and the typing lab, run a one-on-one tutoring center, and produce and mail to community residents a monthly newsletter about school events and programs.

Scarborough Senior High School
The Student Council at Scarborough has developed a very special way to honor outstanding parent contributions. Each month the students name a Parent of the Month.

McQuaid Jesuit High School
By being involved in special and fundraising events, religious programs for spiritual renewal, and volunteer functions such as chaperones at dances and helpers at athletic events, "parents provide adult models of service to others," according to the application submitted by the staff at McQuaid.

Cayucos School
Cayucos' Student Council determined a need for handball courts on the playgrounds, and a three-prong partnership of students, parents, and local businesses brought it into being. Students created projects that the Parent-Teacher Association (PTA) marketed. The students also sold food goods and recruited parents to provide the labor to build the courts. The local business community donated the materials.

CHAPERONES

Parents of students in many American high schools are asked to chaperone school activities such as field trips and class outings. Several of the cited schools, however, have expanded this traditional role.

At Northern Highlands Regional High School, parents chaperone all dances. Similarly, the Student Activity Program at Mission San Jose High School recently instituted a requirement that some parents be present at all school dances, not just as chaperones but as a visible example of parent and community concern for young people. This program has been so successful that community organizations such as Young Life have freely offered their services to further stress the ties that bind the school to the community.

Since the early 1970s, parents of seniors at North Bend High School have organized and been responsible for an all-night party following the graduation ceremony in June. The tradition is strongly supported by all segments of the community, and more than 200 of the graduating seniors attend each year.

Booster Groups

Virtually all of the schools report that parents participate in parent-teacher associations and various booster groups, most often in support of sports and music programs.

The Parent-Teacher Association (PTA) program at Ballard High School demonstrates the kind of impact an organization with an interested and involved membership can have. Headed by a large executive board that plans many activities for the school, the PTA organizes an annual Career Day for students, bringing many community members into the school. In addition, the PTA provides scholarships, supports clothing drives, and organizes the art fair, as well as organizing parent volunteers to work in the school offices.

University High School not only has the All-School Athletic Boosters, Band Boosters, Pep Squad Boosters, and boosters for other individual sports, but also Academic Boosters and Latin Boosters.

Typical of the contributions made by support groups is the Dads' Club program at Gladstone High School. Twenty years ago the community and parents created and shaped a high school for their children. Since then, parents have been visible and active in and around the school. Many of them continue to support the school long after their children have graduated. One-third of the members of the Dads' Club are parents of alumni. Along with parents of current students, they contribute time, money, and energy to projects such as the installation and maintenance of athletic facilities, including the fields, turf, various outbuildings, and bleachers, dugouts, and the scoreboard. Gladstone Dads also staff the snack shack, the fall football "chain gangs," and spring field events, or help as one of a dozen volunteer coaches. In addition to boosting athletics, the Dads' Club supports fine arts, band, language study, foreign exchange programs, and "nearly any reasonable request." They have provided the school with light tables in the art room, stairs to the stage, a well-equipped weight room, and a discretionary fund to help needy students.

Wayland High School boasts a very active specialized booster group, the Committee for the Advancement of the Performing Arts. This fine arts support group makes suggestions about drama selections and performances. They also choose students to be recognized at the end of the year. Another active Wayland group, the Athletic Boosters, runs a store located in the school cafeteria, organizes nine athletic banquets each year, and plans various pep rallies for students.

Seven different support groups offer parents of students at Wheeling High School a chance to become personally involved: the American Field Service Club, the NJROTC parent group, the Spur Club for athletics, the Teacher-Parent Council, the Wheeling Instrumental League, the Choral League, and the Wheeling Scholarship Fund.

Encouraged by the open and diverse opportunities for participation, parents at Lakeridge High School take an active role. Examples of the 15 parent groups currently active at Lakeridge are volunteer tutors, the Merit Awards Committee, the Parent Awareness Group (drug and alcohol abuse prevention), and the Pacer Athletic Club. Lakeridge estimates that, in a typical year, 300 parents are directly involved in school-related support activities.

Fundraising by parent organizations frequently helps provide the cushion that makes possible the enrichment of educational and co-curricular programs. The principal at Miramonte High School, however, works closely with the Parents' Club, encouraging them to support the curriculum itself through fundraising. Last year the club raised $35,000 for the school curriculum—more than half the instructional budget supplied by the district.

An important new trend is the formalization of the fundraising process through the creation of an educational foundation. Parents established a nonprofit foundation at Gretchen Whitney High School and raised $10,000 for a desktop publishing system. Appropriately, the Parent-Teacher-Student Association uses the system to produce an outstanding parent newsletter.

Special Events

A special event can provide a focus for the relationship among the school, parents, and other groups. School calendars of the winning secondary schools list a wide variety of such events.

Mars Hill Bible School
Grandparents' Day and Visitors' Day provide opportunities to bring "the extended family" to the Mars Hill campus.

Mount Vernon High School
A Martin Luther King Breakfast and a Hall of Fame Luncheon are special events that occur annually at Mount Vernon.

Archbishop Chapelle High School
Mother-Daughter Luncheons and Father-Daughter Cruises are popular events at Archbishop Chapelle: more than 1,100 generally attend the luncheon and about 800 the cruise each year.

Kinston High School
Kinston offers a Dinner Theater, where 150 drama club members donate and prepare the food. Typically they serve 200 guests

on each of three successive nights in conjunction with a drama production. More than 100 senior citizens also are invited to attend a Sunday night performance, at the expense of civic clubs, businesses, and individuals.

Midwood High School at Brooklyn College
A special College Night Dinner for all college representatives and faculty members is hosted by the PTA before the school's College Night.

Parent Education Programs

Increasing numbers of schools are offering educational programs designed to help parents. The trend toward parent in-service programs includes topics that go far beyond the typical sessions on school success, college admissions, or career planning (although these are certainly important). Here is a sampling of programs mentioned by the winning schools:

Shulamith High School for Girls
A Parent-Student Learn-In seminar is a well-planned and successful annual program at Shulamith.

Archbishop Molloy High School
Molloy sponsors discussion groups for parents who are divorced or separated, as well as workshops on parenting.

Academy of Mount St. Ursula
This school sponsors lectures on families and adolescence, in addition to programs on college selection and financial aid.

Brother Martin High School
Parent education seminars on adolescent issues are sponsored by the Brother Martin guidance department.

Stephens County High School
Parents are included in the school-sponsored student skills seminars so that they can be involved in their children's learning processes.

James Logan High School
Workshops on topics related to parent effectiveness training are held regularly at night throughout the year by the School Community Program Council.

Oliver Wendell Holmes Junior High School

In the fall Holmes holds a three-part series of programs aimed at improving parenting skills. In the spring the school sponsors another three-part series, this time on drug prevention and intervention.

Gretchen Whitney High School

A school-wide survey to determine parent in-service needs was conducted by the Parent-Teacher-Student Association Council at Whitney. As a result, the school now offers programs on topics such as how to get accepted by highly selective colleges, as well as career and financial aid information.

Putting It All Together

Citing bits and pieces from many school-parent programs tends to suggest a fragmented approach, whereas for most of these schools parent participation is a composite of various programs. Parents act as volunteers and chaperones; serve on boards, committees, and all kinds of advisory councils; and raise money and plan special events. Parents at these schools value listening, learning, helping, and sharing in their children's education. The following examples illustrate the full range and diversity of parental involvement possible at a single school.

Clear Lake High School

At Clear Lake, parents serve as volunteers, speak to classes about their careers, operate ten different booster clubs, serve on school committees designed to promote educational excellence, judge debates and science fairs, and offer "living history" presentations to social studies classes by recounting their own experiences during World War II, the Cuban missile crisis, and other important events and times.

Central High School in South Dakota

Central's main parent group, the Big Birds, is a nonprofit association whose main purposes are to assist the school staff and facilitate communication among administration, faculty, staff, and parents. Scholarships, staff appreciation activities, drug and alcohol prevention programs, facility improvement, Homecoming and graduation activities, and other student programs have all been part of the Big Birds' contribution. Parents also supervise and are responsible for both the postgraduation and postprom activities.

It is obvious that these and the other schools cited in this chapter agree with the administration of Middletown High School: "Parental influence is the single most important factor in determining the educational success of students."

CHAPTER 17

Schools and the Community

Are there opportunities for participation in the school by other groups in the community, e.g., civic and business associations and nonprofit groups? If so, please describe them.

> The school recognizes its role within the community; and more importantly, the community considers the school an active participant in community life.
> —Narragansett High School

Ideally, schools and communities have a symbiotic relationship in which the community supports the schools and the schools enrich the community. This chapter describes how winning schools encourage community participation and what they receive from and contribute to their communities, including:

- Financial Support
- Human Resources
- Jobs and Career Programs
- Business and University Partnerships
- Cooperative Efforts
- Outreach Activities

Financial Support

Although community support takes many forms, the contribution of dollars as well as services is central. In addition to their dependence on local taxes, schools also rely on community efforts to fund special projects.

The school district of which Greely High School is a part sends a copy of the annual school budget to every resident in the district. When the budget is presented, a public meeting and two public workshops are held. Even though the communities served by Greely lack an industrial tax base, the financial support for this school district has been above the state average. Involving the community has paid off for the schools in this district.

Each month, more than 25 businesses contribute services and products to an incentive program for students who have maintained perfect attendance at Dobson High School during that month. Dobson also receives donations for its incentive programs directly from service organizations. Similarly, merchants in Chandler, Arizona (home of Chandler High School), advertise in school publications, employ students, and provide discounts for honor students and students who have perfect attendance.

Groups of civic associations have formed a coalition to work with Westbury Senior High School to foster educational excellence. Coalition members visit the principal to discuss issues related to students and the community. On Senior Class Night, the coalition groups join with private businesses to honor the achievements of senior class members. The awards and scholarships given total hundreds of thousands of dollars, and a significant number of these are derived from the local community.

Because of the community's strong and continuing support for Los Gatos High School, local service clubs conduct fundraisers to provide thousands of dollars in scholarships for graduates. One service club donated computers and provided $100,000 worth of remodeling to a school building for the Telecommunications Center. Foreign language aides and financial help for athletics are two of the other projects supported by outside funding efforts.

Human Resources

One of the major resources a community has to offer is the expertise of its residents. Many schools take advantage of this resource to improve their educational programs.

Representatives of community organizations participate at Dobson High School in most areas of the curriculum, but particularly in the school's Career Center. The center books an average of two or three outside resource speakers each week. Other regular community participants include the Mesa Police Force, which sponsors an officer to be on campus one day a week to speak in classes and act as a resource person for student concerns.

The local Rotary Club has been very helpful in providing speakers for Career Day at Episcopal High School. Another program that has proved beneficial for both students and teachers is the Lawyer in the Classroom program, sponsored by the Youth Education Committee of the Baton Rouge Bar Association. Through this program, local attorneys are assigned to serve as resource persons for classroom teachers throughout the school year. The program has been especially helpful for civics and American history teachers.

Local lawyers also help at Garger High School, by sponsoring Law Days for social studies classes. The Bay Area Arts Council also helps the school access community human resources by scheduling traveling artists and performers for assemblies and classroom seminars.

A Businessmen's Open House is an annual event at Alfred Bonnabel High School, during which the business and civic community is invited to tour the school campus. Many civic and business groups also participate in Bonnabel's annual Career Day and career awareness programs. Guest speakers are sought after and welcomed by the school, participating in an annual awards ceremony as well as in classrooms and at assemblies.

Jobs and Career Programs

A kind of symbiosis operates as a result of these human resource efforts. Businesses may find that employee recruitment is a logical outgrowth of Career Day speaking engagements. Related activities instituted by some schools include programs such as internships and job shadowing.

At Orange Glen High School, for example, guest speakers from local businesses speak to students in many vocation classes, and a Youth Opportunity Day provides a way for local businesses to meet, interview, and even hire seniors interested in careers in their business area. The Rotary and Kiwanis clubs also provide leadership training programs for Orange Glen students.

A variety of approaches is employed at Shoreham-Wading River High School. For Awareness Day and Global Studies Day, members of community groups serve as speakers and workshop leaders. A local science facility has set up a science research internship program, and a new business department program has parents and other community members speaking to business students on a weekly basis about their occupations and workplaces.

For the last several years, Wheeling High School has sponsored Career Expo 214. This is a large-scale career fair for all District 214 students and parents. More than 100 community organizations and businesses are represented at the activity. Additionally, area Rotary Clubs and Lions Clubs meet weekly with school administrators, and the Wheeling Career Advisory Council meets on a monthly basis to help build positive relationships between the school and various public and private enterprises.

The volunteer coordinator at Darien High School recruits guest speakers to serve as instructional resource persons. In addition, local businesses actively support the Junior Achievement groups and varsity clubs, as well as other specific efforts. One local corporation supports a summer project for able math students, and other local businesses supply personnel for Junior Achievement's daytime programs, for Project Business, and for Applied Economics classes.

The job-shadowing program at West Bloomfield High School allows students to spend a day with business, civic, and other community professionals. School officials report that this maximizes community support and participation. An extensive cooperative program also grants students numerous opportunities to share common knowledge with community groups and organizations. Michigan Week and career explorations bring together leaders from businesses and civic associations, parents, and citizens. The West Bloomfield High Technology Committee creates yet another forum for students, community leaders, and professionals to discuss and plan for the future in education.

The Madeira School features one of the most extensive internship programs for students. Last year, Madeira sophomores worked at 19 different community service placements and 98 congressional offices. Seniors worked in 90 different business and nonprofit placements, including a public radio station, the Smithsonian Institution, newspapers, an animal hospital, law firms, a securities company, a cable television station, an interior design studio, and a local rescue squad.

Business and University Partnerships

Business partnerships with schools often go beyond providing Career Day speakers, job shadowing opportunities, and internship sites. Schools can also derive valuable benefits through special working relationships or partnerships with business, industry, and higher education.

Most of the schools cite examples of various informal and formal arrangements with local businesses and industries. For example, a community input group called SCORE (School and Community Organized to Reinforce Education) has been created at Lincoln County High School to help bring together resources of the community to assist with identified needs of the school.

Palo Alto High School has formed mutually beneficial relationships with IBM, the University of California at Berkeley, and Stanford University. IBM field tests mathematical software at the school, where teachers and students evaluate the software and provide suggestions. In return, the corporation has aided the school in setting up a computer-assisted instruction program in geometry, including donating the software and hardware. The UC Berkeley program involves students in a study of autonomous learning as it relates to learning the computer language PASCAL. And Stanford provides invaluable resources through its Bechtel International Center and the Stanford Intern Education Program.

A cooperative program with the National Science Foundation has enabled two science teachers at A. Philip Randolph Campus High School to earn free Master's degrees. A Saturday College enrichment program in math and science benefits many students each semester. The Josiah Macy, Jr., Foundation provides private funding and program evaluation in support of the school's medical professions program. The engineering department of a local university has helped develop the new Randolph engineering program, and a program through that university's education department has enabled high school students to take tuition-free courses at the university.

John Adams Middle School's Student Council worked out a partnership with a local restaurant. In exchange for complimentary dinners for cafeteria and custodial employees, the students painted a wall at the restaurant.

Parkway South High School is involved in numerous partnerships involving over 50 businesses, 18 teachers, and more than 850 students. The business and cooperative education departments regularly invite speakers to tell students about the business community, and they have often hosted the local Chamber of Commerce Business Fair. Applied Economics in the business department is a partnership involving Junior Achievement and a business consultant who meets once a week with the class to discuss realistic business situations.

Myers Park High School welcomes the participation of community groups. Each of the Applied Economics classes has its own adult consultant from the business community. The Academic Internship Program provides opportunities for students to explore areas of academic or career interest as they work in the community with government and civic agencies, businesses, industries, or individual professionals.

FORMAL PARTNERSHIPS

Formal "adoptions" of schools by businesses are becoming a common way to link schools with commerce and industry.

Eight local businesses have adopted Torrey Pines High School, providing direct support for various aspects of the instructional program. For example, the owner of the Art Loft provides instruction and tours of his facility to commercial art students. He also donates art supplies for students' use in creating unique projects.

Local businesses also take an active role in specific curricular advisory groups at Torrey Pines. These groups provide expertise and advice in maintaining up-to-date curricula and training geared to meeting the needs of potential employers. Local businesses also offer considerable support to a number of annual special events presented by the school. For example, one large corporation provided a sponsorship grant of $15,000 to help the school stage a five-kilometer run for the entire community to enjoy.

University High School reports, "Bridges between school, community and business have grown during the last few years. The TIE program—Together Industry and Education—has brought many opportunities for students to interact with business members of the community." The Irvine, California, partnership program is an active group working to further the interaction between businesses and schools. One of the school's partners, the Newport Sheraton Hotel, provided free lodging for the school's accreditation team during their stay in the area. In turn, University High has shared samples of student art work and performances by student performing arts groups with the Sheraton.

Working with the Chamber of Commerce and business, industry, and civic organizations, Newton County High School initiated an Adopt-a-School program several years ago. To date, ten adoptions have been finalized, including those by Mobil Corporation, Hercules, Inc., and Oxford College of Emory University.

Proctor Hug High School has been adopted by Harrah's, which has had considerable impact on the school. The adoption concept will be expanded to other schools by the Reno Chamber of Commerce in the near future.

A partnership with Procter and Gamble has provided a consultant one day a week to teach the Applied Economics class at Saint Bernard-Elmwood Place High School. The company also underwrites the course by providing books, software, and a computer.

Partnering is also alive and well at Rock Bridge Senior High School. During its several years in the Partner-in-Education program, Rock Bridge has received funds for journalism students to attend a national convention, instructional materials, guest speakers, and housing for the sponsorship of a state-wide Student Council convention. State Farm Insurance Company and KOMU-TV, two of the school's partners, recently instituted a monthly program recognizing faculty and students for their accomplishments at school and in the community. Banks, cooperatives, and the Chamber of Commerce have furnished the school with instructional materials for classrooms and have hosted student field trips.

SPECIAL PARTNERSHIPS

A number of the award-winning schools have found different kinds of partners who have enriched school programs and provided special opportunities for students. An excellent example of a partnership between a school and a hospital exists at Cibola High School, which has a business relationship with St. Joseph's Hospital through the Adopt-a-School program. The following list details how each supports the other with services and personnel.

The Cibola fine arts department performs at the hospital

Students in agriculture classes provide some labor for landscaping the hospital

Several work students are placed at St. Joseph's

Mentorship students also work at the hospital

St. Joseph's participates in Cibola's spring Career Day

St. Joseph's offers a Shadow Day in various departments of the hospital for juniors and seniors

St. Joseph's offers a scholarship for a Cibola senior interested in a medical profession

St. Joseph's provides guest speakers for classroom teachers

Through an Academy of Finance, Tottenville High School is connected to Shearson, Lehman and other large brokerage firms. The firms supply advice, give lectures, mentor, and provide job opportunities. Through an Executive Intern program, Tottenville is allied to over 20 business firms, which provide work experience to students. A major alliance exists with Brooklyn Union Gas Company, which subsidizes the printing of the school's course book. Another major partner is Citicorp, which has set up a complete bank in the school and helps train students via lectures, mentors, and job experiences. Tottenville is also the major school allied to the Institute for Basic Research at Willowbrook, where 16 advanced science students do high-level research, working one-to-one with doctors.

These comments made by officials from White Plains High School illustrate what schools can do with business partnerships:

> We are proud of the many special links we have established with business organizations. To date, 115 businesses, corporations, and foundations have provided jobs, vocational counseling, lectures, and tours for our students. Many of these jobs are provided through our highly effective work-study programs. Thousands of dollars in scholarships have been provided by neighboring business organizations, and local merchants advertise in many of our school publications and game programs. Retired business executives often lend their expertise, and students participate in a monthly foreign policy consortium involving major corporate leaders, students, and teachers.

Cooperative Efforts

Many of the schools describe unusual and special types of cooperative efforts that they have successfully implemented in their own locales. The following examples illustrate the range of cooperation occurring across the country.

SPECIAL EVENTS

Each fall, Novi High School sets aside one football game day as Community Appreciation Day and provides more than 2,000 flowers to all women attending the game, as a symbol of appreciation. A Parent Club at Alfred Bonnabel High School once collaborated with the local community in putting on a huge flea market, which was held on the school campus.

The annual Yarmouth Clam Festival, organized by the Chamber of Commerce, is truly a community affair. Yarmouth Junior-Senior High School plays an active role in the festival. Student groups operate concession booths, the bands march in the parade, and the Playmakers (a drama group) perform on the green. Students also work in other groups' concession booths. Boyland Central Catholic High School also sponsors a food festival, Fest Italiana, each year. More than 150,000 people generally attend this hugely successful event.

At St. Louise de Marillac High School the student carnival Nuf Yad (Fun Day) provides an opportunity for young children from the inner city to come to Marillac and be "adopted" by a student for a day of enjoyment. Student musical groups also perform for nursing homes and other community-based organizations.

SPECIAL PROJECTS

The art and music departments at Milton High School are major contributors to programs of the Milton Arts Council, and faculty members serve on the Council's Board of Directors. The local Art Club dedicated the New Visions Gallery, which is housed in the high school and displays the work of students, teachers, parents, and citizens. Club members work in town for funds to operate the gallery. One community member who is a prominent patron of the arts underwrote the cost of lights and remodeling for the gallery, to which he has donated a substantial collection of his own books. This person also donated a valuable art collection, which is displayed at the high school. These facilities and the art history course made possible by these donations are open to any citizen in the community, and on a reservation basis to members of surrounding communities. Several citizens enrolled in the art history course have volunteered their time to keep the New Visions Gallery open after school hours.

Brighton High School is cooperating with the local Historical Society in a joint project to refurbish and rebuild a very old school for use by the community and the school district. The building trades classes are providing the work, and the Historical Society is providing the materials. And the local Building Contractors' Association has worked in cooperation with the Londonderry High School building trades program to assist students in the construction of a complete house.

Project 85 + 15 is a futuristic project at St. Louis Park High School aimed at preparing students to live in the twenty-first century. More than 500 community citizens and school staff have been involved.

ONGOING PARTNERSHIPS

A number of Stephens County High School's recognition programs are sponsored by local civic clubs and businesses. For example, a consortium of civic clubs sponsors the recognition for the top 5 percent of the graduating class, and one company gives a special wristwatch to the graduating senior having the highest average in mathematics. The Chamber of Commerce conducts tours of the school for businesses considering locating in the county and cooperates with the vocational director in planning programs to train local citizens for employment in new plants—"one of our strong suits," according to the school's staff.

A diverse array of opportunities for community-school cooperation exists at Ballard High School. For example, "real world" experts from various sectors of the economy help students prepare for an economic analysis and policymaking project at a three-week seminar. In other areas, professional and business representatives serve as consultants to students developing projects for the science fair, and also act as judges for the fair. And museums and historic homes present training clinics for student guides who are then offered opportunities to apply their training as volunteers.

Oldham County High School representatives serve as board members for a variety of community organizations, including the Youth Development Committee; the County Office for Juvenile Justice; the County Task Force for Missing, Exploited, and Abused Children; the Red Cross; the United Way; the Chamber of Commerce; and the Park Board.

Woodstock Union High School's annual Alumni Weekend has become known all over New England. Thousands return for a weekend of conviviality and fond memories, with the high school serving as the focal point of activities. Woodstock Union also sponsors a Shakespeare Festival developed by its English teachers. This is a special competition involving more than 100 students at Woodstock Union High School and an equal number from eight other New England high schools. Parents help with costumes, banners, programs, chaperoning, lodging, and meals. The Woodstock Foundation has awarded one of the teachers a grant for materials, T-shirts, judges' fees, and awards. The festival has resulted in a fellowship award for one teacher to attend a summer program at the Folger Institute in Washington, D.C.

Outreach Activities

Many schools make special efforts to reach out to segments of the community, either by offering desired services to community residents or by offering the use of their extensive physical facilities. An amazing variety of activities benefiting community members takes place in school buildings. It is common for local school districts to offer community education classes and for local community colleges to offer credit courses in evening school. Community recreation programs are often centered in high schools, including youth programs and special offerings for senior citizens, as well as open use of jogging, tennis, and gym facilities. A sampling of other common uses of school buildings includes art fairs, literacy programs, meeting sites for crisis groups, and drama and musical productions.

James Madison Junior High School has received a grant funded by the Lewis-Gale Foundation to install a fitness court. The court will be used by the entire community. As a spin-off from this project, a group of local doctors will provide free physicals to students in exchange for use of the gymnasium.

Considering the "greying" of America, it is not surprising that schools are providing special outreach and building use programs for senior citizens. Golden Opportunities is the name given to the cooperative program for senior citizens being started at Blind Brook High School. Other typical offerings for older citizens include hot lunch programs and special daytime fitness programs.

THE COMMUNITY SCHOOL

The term *community school* is becoming more and more common. The concept of a community school embraces these elements:

Parents have a variety of opportunities to share in the education of their children

The school makes special efforts to keep parents informed about programs and the progress of their children

Cooperative efforts with business and industry are extensive and mutually beneficial

Students and staff provide solid support for community projects and issues of concern to citizens

The "lighted" school house is evident, with many classes for adults and special programs for senior citizens available

There is extensive use of school facilities by individuals and groups—for dramatic and musical presentations, for civic affairs, and for recreational programs for residents of all ages

Where a community school is in place, school, parents, and community form a kind of triangle, a solid structure on which school programs are built. In the words of the winning schools:

- Mission San Jose High "is deeply committed to the belief that education is a community function."

- Stanton College Preparatory School believes that "the keys to success are communication and involvement in maintaining an excellent relationship with the local neighborhood."

- Lawton Community High School reports that its school district "aggressively pursues a close, continuous relationship with the community."

- Centennial Senior High School believes that the school is the central unifying force in all of the communities it serves.

For a personal viewpoint on this issue, see Appendix D, page 277.

PART
SIX

In Their Own Words

CHAPTER 18

Success Stories

In concluding, please describe elements of your school's program, policies, and practices which, in your judgment, are important in understanding the success of your school.

The descriptions written in response to this question cover an impressive range of topics and approaches to educational issues. Many offer potential for creative adaptations by other schools.

Following is a sampler of the interesting, unusual, practical, and inspirational ways winning schools describe their own success, quoted directly from their applications. The answers fall into several categories, including:

- Philosophy, Atmosphere, and Spirit
- Facilities and Services
- Course Offerings
- People
- Programs
- Special Events and Projects
- Alumni
- Special Challenges

Philosophy, Atmosphere, and Spirit

Oneida Middle School
Our success is due to four basic characteristics: diversity, flexibility, spontaneity, and opportunity.

Dublin Middle School
We attribute our success to a clear sense of purpose with an emphasis on unity and high academic expectations which are articulated and promoted by staff and students. A noticeable dedication to excellence creates an atmosphere conducive to high achievement.

James Madison Junior High School
We can sum up the devotion and dedication of our students and staff to quality education by recalling a special work of art, carefully prepared by multiply-handicapped children, which graces the school's lobby. It proclaims, "Madison Matadors, be the best that you can be." The tapestry adds aesthetic beauty while both challenging and encouraging all students. It is part of the positive display throughout our building.

Narragansett High School
Perhaps the single element most important in understanding the success of Narragansett is the "family" nature of the school and community. The small size of the school (530+) is an asset in many ways. First, students are recognized and known by their teachers. There is a sense of identity, of belonging, in our school. Students are also recognized as individual learners to the extent possible, and counselors provide individual counseling on the "human" matters as well. Also size is never an excuse for lack of programs and activities. Almost every teacher sponsors an activity or club or coaches an academic team or sport. There is a spirit of camaraderie and cooperation that creates an environment of pride, success, and excellence.

CAL High School
The community's support and financial commitment in education is at an all-time high. A pupil-teacher ratio of 8:1 enables students to receive maximum individualized classroom attention. The combination of factors—that students like school, that teachers enjoy their work, and that parents get involved in their children's education—enables the school to have a pleasant and highly productive learning environment.

John Adams Middle School
There is a "special friendliness" here that is an important element in our success. Students approach visitors to introduce themselves, welcome them, and offer assistance. Teachers are close

friends with each other, forming a support group for themselves and their students.

Academy of Our Lady of Good Counsel
Good Counsel's small school environment binds us together in a strong sense of community that seeks to satisfy needs both within the school itself and in the larger community. The real magic of GCA is its ability to personally touch the lives of its students. The warmth and caring engendered by this community provides stability in the frequently unstable lives of our girls. Most students graduate from Good Counsel not only with a diploma but with a sense of self-esteem.

Facilities and Services

South Salem High School
The library is the hub of South High. Each year our library is getting more use. Last year more than 1,200 classes were scheduled into the library, an average of seven a day. A very strong reference core and overall collection of 38,000 volumes supports the curriculum. Over 200 magazines, numerous newspapers and AV materials are maintained. South was the first high school in the state to have an online computerized data based system. It is also hooked up with the city and state library systems. The library is an essential research center for students and staff.

Myers Park High School
Myers Park is blessed with a beautiful campus which possesses several streams and naturally wooded areas. Approximately ten years ago, one of our graduating classes left money to the school so that work could be started to develop our entire campus as an arboretum. Since then various clubs and graduating classes and the Parent-Teacher-Student Association have donated money periodically for the purchase of additional specimens. We are presently contracting with a landscape architect to locate and identify all specimens and to make any final recommendations for specimens that are still needed. We plan to work with two naturalists to develop instructional packets that can be used by the biology teachers.

Our visual arts program has dominated local, regional, and state competitions for years. In an attempt to capture this rich heritage and to communicate it to our school community, the teachers are contacting former students and asking them to contribute a piece of work to a Myers Park Art Gallery. To date over 50 pieces of work have been collected.

Course Offerings

Lakeridge High School
Offerings in international studies prepare students for participation in a world of linked economics and culture. We provide instruction in five languages, including Japanese. We have a very active American Field Service program and also have an exchange program with a sister school in Wolverhampton, England.

Bradley Central High School
We have an outstanding vocational education program which is one of the top programs in the South. It serves over 1,200 students in many areas of instruction including home economics, agriculture, distributive education, drafting, building trades, general metals/tool and die, woodworking, electronics, welding, auto body, auto mechanics, food services, health occupations, etc.

Scranton Preparatory School
Students can be graduated from Scranton Prep and the University of Scranton or Marywood College in a seven year period. Senior year courses at Prep in American history, English, Greek, Latin, mathematics, modern foreign language and physics will be accepted for credit at both institutions of higher learning. Because of work done by Prep seniors in these advanced courses, a cumulative total of 1,234 college credits were granted to a recent graduating class.

Parkway South High School
There is a building-wide focus on global education. South has been the leader in the metro-wide International Education Consortium, which is funded in part by the Danforth and Rockefeller Foundations. This project has made possible year-long, across the curriculum studies of China, Latin America, and Africa which have touched all of our students. School-wide assemblies and festivals have been held, and scholars from Mainland China and Brazil have worked and taught in the building. Two global perspective courses have been added to the curriculum, including spoken Japanese.

West Bloomfield High School

In our new approach to physical education, classes will be integrated with the concepts of health maintenance and will concentrate on a healthy lifestyle, emphasizing diet, nutrition information, and scientifically designed exercises. Students will be tested for blood pressure, cardio-respiratory endurance, and cholesterol levels. Our program is enhanced through periodic lectures by consultants from the University of Michigan and area physicians.

O'Fallon Township High School

Geology Is, a secondary level geology program, was developed at O'Fallon under a Title IVC grant. It has since been validated by the Illinois State Board of Education as an innovative educational program and funded as part of the Illinois diffusion network. It was also validated by the U.S. Department of Education and is now on the National Diffusion Network as well. In addition, the program was selected by the National Science Teacher's Association as one of the 12 outstanding earth science programs in the United States.

Metairie Park Country Day School

We are proud of the human development component of our curriculum. Through required courses, through electives, through voluntary programs in community service and the peer support program we work to educate our students to their responsibility toward society as a whole.

Newton County High School

Astronomy is taught by an instructor who, with his students and students from vocational classes, designed and built an observatory and telescope. Within the vocational department Newton has a livestock teaching facility and show arena as well as a full scale greenhouse.

The Madeira School

An unusual feature of the school is our naturalist program under the leadership of John Trott, a professional ornithologist photographer whose pictures are widely published. Mr. Trott not only teaches courses in ornithology and field botany, using our campus of nearly four hundred acres; he conducts studies and projects for the enhancement of the environment and invites other groups and individuals to the campus.

People

Loyola High School of Baltimore, Inc.
The tools which Loyola has chosen to nurture student growth are not new nor are they unique to Loyola. They are, however, well conceived and finely honed by a care for the individual student—the hallmark of every Jesuit school. At Loyola, students find in their teachers experienced guides who are themselves fellow learners. Teachers and students are friends who last a lifetime. A tradition that spans more than 130 years in the Baltimore area, a religious and philosophical commitment to service, and the example of teachers—men and women—who are intelligent, insightful, and compassionate, all help to make a teenage boy a "man for others."

South Burlington Middle School
South Burlington Middle School has respect for the dignity of each individual as a fundamental value all teachers and students share. Our environment is safe and orderly. With an atmosphere of caring, encouraging and challenging high expectations for all students to succeed is well evidenced in all classrooms.

Central High School in South Dakota
The most important factor in the success of the education program is, without question, the faculty commitment and dedication to the education of the young people. Their main focus is on student welfare, and they are constantly searching for opportunities to better provide for our students.

Sycamore Junior High School
A portion of our success is due to the closeness of spirit, perhaps best exemplified by our "phantom" cartoonist who periodically posts a sample of his/her work in the faculty lounge, gently and humorously exposing faculty foibles.

Academy of Notre Dame de Namur
In the last 25 years Notre Dame has undergone a gradual yet purposeful transition from a highly structured institution controlled by the office of principal, held by a sister of Notre Dame, to a collaborative venture of both lay and religious persons. On every level of organization from the Board of Trustees through administration, faculty, and parent groups, decisions on matters pertinent

to the group are made in a collegial manner. The success and progress of Notre Dame flows from this vital integration within the school community.

Ferndale High School
The success of many of our programs can be directly attributed to the spirit of cooperation and mutual respect demonstrated by the faculty. In a recent self-study survey, one faculty member stated, "Our major strength and greatest asset is our faculty. Of course there are exceptions but, by and large, Ferndale High School's teachers are knowledgeable, dedicated, professional people, willing to grow and change as necessary to meet changing needs of our students. I am proud to be among them."

Lincoln High School
The people of Lincoln High School are what really makes it successful. No club could generate high levels of participation without an enthusiastic teacher/advisor. No team could demonstrate leadership and teamwork without a dedicated coach. No student could get that extra measure of attention without the willing staff members who spend extra time at helping students. The bus drivers, janitors, maintenance people, teacher aides, supervisory aides, cooks, and secretaries take pride in what they do and focus their efforts on students. Their work complements the efforts of parents, teachers, and administrators in a total educational enterprise. People, working together, make the difference at Lincoln.

Programs

Londonderry High School
Our Operation Venture program has been recognized as an exemplary physical education program in New Hampshire and New England, regularly drawing observers from other schools.

Schenley High School Teacher Center
The unique program which has brought national attention to the school is the Teacher Center component, a landmark in staff development and educational reform. For eight weeks throughout the school year, approximately fifty secondary school teachers come to Schenley for seminars on relevant education issues, update in curriculum, and refinement and expansion of instructional skills.

Resident teachers at Schenley, therefore, assume a differentiated role as they work with the adult learners, their peers, as well as the students. Reduced teaching loads enable them to devote adequate time and energy to both roles.

Petoskey Middle School
Petoskey Middle School is proud of its Adventure Education program which helps to develop the whole person by building on skills to which the regular academic structure may not lend itself. Students confront their physical and emotional fears, learning trust through activities and group problem-solving.

St. Mark's School of Texas
The Pecos Wilderness Experience, an eight-day backpacking trip to northern New Mexico, is required of upper schoolers preceding their freshman year. The trip is led by teachers and other students who are members of the Sherpa Club, a student organization for students with a keen interest in outdoor activities. The wilderness trip is intended to build class spirit and confidence, to foster love of the outdoors and respect for the environment, and to develop self-reliance.

Parkway Central High School
The Professional Studies Group is unique to Central. This group of 20 teachers has met monthly for three years to read all current literature pertaining to the profession. Many innovative teaching practices have been given birth in the group.

McQuaid Jesuit High School
There are six counselors on the school staff and they are freed from responsibility for the administrative details of student scheduling or course transfer requests. In this way they are able to concentrate on developing counseling based on students' personal, developmental needs.

They are also able to provide intensive assistance in student preparation for college information and application processes.

Centennial Senior High School
As part of a grant from the United Way, Centennial has a working arrangement with the Wilder Foundation in which they provide counseling for our "families in need" at minimal costs to those families. In return, we provide the clinic with space in our building and all utility costs. This program along with the teachers

and counselors on our staff allows us to respond to the crises that confront our students and their families.

Saint John's School

The school is particularly sensitive to the needs of our students in an era of increased societal changes and has developed programs to assist our youngsters in their development. Individual counseling and seminars focus on topics such as understanding one's place in a non-traditional family, adolescent stress, drugs, sexuality, and peer pressure. Emphasis is placed on current research and national statistics. The programs have proven to be extremely effective within our student population.

South Kingstown High School

Like many other high schools, this past spring we were faced with the suicide of one of our students. The way in which the school and the community responded reflects the spirit that lies at our core. Upon learning of our tragedy at 5 P.M. on a dreary Friday in April, school administrators decided to go on with a school dance that night that had already been scheduled. In the two hours before the dance, all available faculty members were contacted and asked to attend; local counselors and therapists were asked to come; and plans were made to set up crisis intervention centers in the school. Teachers, students, and community members came together and mourned the loss of a popular classmate.

In the days that followed the faculty room was set up as a crisis intervention center, manned by community and school counselors, and students were allowed to work through the many personal issues that developed. Many teachers took this time as an opportunity to move away from the prescribed curriculum and deal with an issue that was foremost in the minds of all our young people. This tragic incident could have done much to destroy the spirit of the school; instead, the process of learning to deal with grief and tragedy has made us stronger and has reinforced our feeling that we belong to a special community of people.

Special Events and Projects

Woodstock Union High School

Our special qualities are illustrated by events such as our Shakespeare Festival. Our English teachers have developed a Shakespeare conference and competition which involves over 100 students at Woodstock and an equal number from other New England High Schools. Parents help with costumes, banners, programs, chaperoning, lodging and meals. The Woodstock Foundation awarded one of our teachers a $2,000 grant for materials, T-shirts, judges' fees, and awards. The program was a huge success and resulted in our lead teacher being awarded a fellowship at the Folger Institute.

William Fremd High School
Since 1982 Fremd students have enjoyed our spring Arts and Activities Festival. Student groups and professional artists combine to present a variety of popular programs. A recent month-long Festival included a student musical, student synchronized swim show, and concerts by student bands and orchestra; student art and photography exhibits; the home economics student fashion show; a dance group, steel band, and a chamber music trio; a multimedia presentation on the reenactment of French explorer LaSalle's voyage through North America; a weaver, a graphic artist, a cartoonist, and a journalist. Many of the artists provided workshops for our students. All but two of the events were free. The Festival is organized each year by a committee of faculty, students, and parents.

Scarborough Senior High School
This year planned school promotion activities are being launched so that Scarborough might get a chance to tell the Scarborough story more often. SHS has given out copies of SHS InfoPac, Scarborough A+ tee shirts, and "Scarborough is Number 1 because of Me" bumper stickers.

Lansing Catholic Central High School
Spectrum 87 was a celebration and display of student achievements, including a Science Fair (all science students complete a project), art fair, spring musical concert, sampling of foreign food (French pastry, Spanish dishes, etc.), and book fair. Parents, relatives, and community members visit this open house to view over 600 student displays, enjoy food, attend the concert, and socialize.

Wayland High School
We continue to set as a goal being on the cutting edge of educational advancements. We were recently funded by the state ($100,000) for a child care center which serves as a lab setting for other courses.

Kinston High School

The Kinston City Schools operate a fleet of 27 buses manned by teenage drivers. Their routes cover a total of 6,500 miles per week. Never in the history of the school has there been a major accident. Bus driving classes and a superior Director of Transportation fortify the program. Manning a bus teaches responsibility, punctuality, and concentration as probably no other assignment.

Alumni

Central High School in Pennsylvania

The tradition of academic excellence permeates the very essence of our school. Alumni of the school feel deeper about Central than they do about their college or professional schools. The alumni also contribute financially to the school. Approximately $100,000 in scholarship prizes are awarded each year at graduation. The alumni also help administer a trust fund which generates $50,000 a year for the improvement of education at Central. The alumni also contribute by having a career conference each year during which 30–40 men return to the school to share their experiences and advise students.

Mount Notre Dame High School

The Alumnae-Development Office, established in 1982, now has a staff of two full-time professionals and one secretary. Through the efforts of this office, alumnae spirit and loyalty have been revitalized and our public image enhanced by the publication of Mount Notre Dame Developments, which gives appropriate recognition to our achievements and programs and to those students and teams who have won honors and awards. Such recognition undoubtedly encourages others to "go for it" and gives the entire school community a sense of pride in their school.

Special Challenges

Dr. Ronald N. Patterson Intermediate School 229

With over half of our students from families below the poverty line—with crime, drugs and alcohol abuse frighteningly familiar, Dr. Ronald N. Patterson Intermediate School still has many students who excel. The school as a center of learning is a priority, supported by innovative ideas, teacher training, staff cooperation and administrative backbone. We strive for excellence; we reach it.

Maryhurst High School

At Maryhurst, we have labeled some girls as "Maryhurst miracles" because there is truly a transformation that is evident in their stay with us. When girls first arrive at Maryhurst, they are placed in a locked dorm to prevent them from running away. Within a few months, they stabilize and move to the open dorms. The educational process at Maryhurst is structured around six levels of performance, each with varying privileges and responsibilities. Students are challenged to progress and supported when they fail. Maryhurst is often the last resort for kids who have not responded to counseling, foster homes and other special education services. We believe Maryhurst gives them hope and courage to believe in themselves and their ability to succeed.

Mother Cabrini High School

The success of Mother Cabrini High School must be understood against its larger environment. Our immediate neighborhood is known as the drug capital of New York. Our students must face daily the harsh realities of city life with all its attendant neighborhood and home problems. Facing this (in the words of the Educational Philosophy of the Missionary Sisters of the Sacred Heart), we attempt to provide:

> an atmosphere of love, understanding and commitment; of acceptance and appreciation of the diversity within the community; conducive to proper exercise of freedom and of personal and social responsibility.

> We strive to respect the dignity and uniqueness of each individual; foster the development of the total person. . . .

A final element in our success is that, in large part, we do provide an environment of order, safety, and hope in the midst of much chaos and disruption in our students' lives.

CHAPTER 19

Portrait of a Principal

In what ways does the principal demonstrate instructional and administrative leadership?

If there is one theme that stands out above all others in the applications received from these schools, it is that the principal is critical to the success of the institution—the linchpin that holds both programs and people in place.

The quotations provided here form a composite portrait of a multitalented, dedicated, and visionary person, a true leader. Individual statements are not matched with individual schools; however, the schools whose descriptions are included are listed at the end of the chapter.

The epitaph on architect Sir Christopher Wren's tomb in St. Paul's Cathedral reads, "If you would see his monument, look around." To find a detailed portrait of these principals, one has only to look at what has been created in the 271 buildings of the award-winning schools. They are all that has been described in the preceding chapters, and much more.

The Principal as Effective Manager

Our principal is certainly attuned to the best practices in providing everyone an opportunity to "buy into" the action and in employing ways to create a healthy school climate in which people flourish.

A genius at juggling all of the roles, from financial planner to public relations professional, this headliner relates to kids and earns their respect.

He employs well qualified teachers and then expects them to teach well and grow professionally.

He has established a climate of mutual trust and respect. He listens attentively to faculty input, is receptive to new ideas, and is flexible and willing to compromise when prudent.

He is responsible for the preparation and maintenance of the budget.

She is an organized person with agendas for all meetings and clearly established expectations.

The principal delegates well.

Administrative and leadership qualities are demonstrated through his planning and organizational skills.

The principal spends a great deal of time with the staff and encourages them to discuss ideas and concerns with him.

This principal is not a "desk" principal.

He maintains up-to-date information on instruction, staff development opportunities, and other administrative concerns.

The principal interprets state mandates, district goals, community sentiment and the school mission to the staff.

Problem-solving is a shared effort with him, the other administrators, and the teachers.

She is committed to the training of key personnel.

He involves himself in professional associations.

He measures the effectiveness of the school's program by how well the priceless hours of a school day are spent.

The principal delegates authority without delegating responsibility.

She is responsible for "making it happen if it's going to happen."

He serves as a conduit of information and as a facilitator to teachers.

Democratic in dealings with faculty and staff.

Faculty are treated as professionals whose hard work is appreciated.

He values communal more than hierarchical relationships.

She meets regularly with custodians, secretaries, guidance staff, student officers and their sponsors, coaches, as well as the school's many standing committees.

He handles difficult issues calmly and professionally.

Her administration philosophy stresses a "hands-on" approach.

The Principal as Role Model

Hard working? You bet. Days start early, to get the desk work out of the way, and include all those evening and week-end activities too.

He begins his day early and serves as an excellent role model for the staff.

He is flexible and a risk-taker. Our principal is a visionary.

He sets very high expectations for himself.

He is visible every day to students and staff, and is in the cafeteria almost every day to be available.

She practices a policy of high visibility. She visits every classroom during the first days of school and thereafter conducts regular visits.

He helps set the tone of the school. He is honest, hard-working, and places people in higher priority than procedures or paper.

He sets the example of "standard of excellence" for the school.

He appears to have unlimited energy.

With his arrival a new vitality pervaded the school. An important bond with teachers is established through his willingness to step into the classroom to teach lessons throughout the school year.

The principal models desired behavior.

His actions dictate the tone of the school.

He writes well and speaks well.

He sets a tone of professionalism in dress and manner.

The principal sets a positive and up-beat tone for all school activities.

The principal also leads by example and is sincere; his philosophy is mirrored by all.

The Principal as Friend and Advocate

He is an empathetic listener.

As one student put it, "He's a friend to every kid."

Open to change. Well known to students.

He is a facilitator and an advocate of both student and teacher leadership activities.

The principal provides support for special programs to expand student and faculty experiences by coordinating the initial efforts, encouraging participants, and monitoring progress.

A sense of trust has been fostered by the principal.

He promotes a family atmosphere that is unique in a school as large as ours.

He makes the faculty feel special and cared for.

His use of humor in appropriate ways has helped develop a high degree of staff morale and a nice way to relieve the pressures and stresses that can be a part of any school day.

The Principal as Teacher and Learner

First, the principal is a teacher, not necessarily in the classroom but by example and by direction provided to the students and the teaching staff.

Her professional enthusiasm for learning and professional development is contagious.

He has never stopped being a learner.

He teaches a class and in this way he maintains a teacher's eye view and remains in contact with students.

He views classroom visitations as an important part of his instructional leadership role.

She demonstrates intense interest in instruction research.

He welcomes new ideas.

She gives demonstration lessons for the benefit of new teachers.

The Principal as Leader

The principal has a specific vision about where the school is and where it can go.

The principal is a leader in an effective teaching program.

The principal works with instructional chairpersons to facilitate the growth of leadership abilities.

The principal fulfills the role of instructional leader.

He keeps the faculty abreast of the latest educational findings pertinent to different areas.

One full day every four to six weeks he schedules a teacher input day.

He visits with other staff members daily, visiting each teacher at least once a month informally.

The principal schedules at least two formal conferences with each staff member during the year for the purposes of performance review and assessment/feedback.

He initiated the writing component of the annual school plan and has provided support and leadership for a schoolwide approach to writing.

He encourages leadership in all staff.

He encourages those with leadership potential and provides them with opportunities to demonstrate their leadership skills.

The principal represents the school to the community.

She is a valued resource to staff.

He fulfills the role of catalyst for the staff and for the development of the school.

He has encouraged and supported every innovation which has been adopted since he became principal.

The most frequently asked question by the principal is, "How can we help the teachers become more effective?"

Provides strong leadership in support of the arts.

Allows everyone to take risks for students.

She is readily available, well read, and flexible to the concerns of her teachers.

His leadership has brought a vision of growth and change to the school.

He participates actively in district activities.

He leads by example.

She constantly encourages teachers to pursue higher degrees.

He is sensitive to specific concerns of the community.

He recognizes that people are at the center of education.

He has a tolerance for ambiguity.

Has made teachers feel that they have a personal and professional stake in the school.

He has demonstrated over and over again his willingness to take risks, especially when there is evidence of educational success.

He is an inspirator.

In Their Own Words from

Academy of Mount St. Ursula
Academy of Our Lady of Good Counsel
Adlai E. Stevenson High School
Alfred Bonnabel High School
Archbishop Keough High School
Archbishop Molloy High School
Baboquivari Junior High School
Ballard High School
Blind Brook High School
Bradley Central High School
Brighton High School
CAL High School
Cayucos School
Centennial Senior High School
Central High School in Pennsylvania
Central High School in South Dakota
Central High School in Tennessee
Cibola High School
Claremont High School
Denbigh High School
Dooley School
Dr. Roland N. Patterson Intermediate School 229

East High School
Edgewood High School of the Sacred Heart
Garden City Senior High School
Garger High School
Great Valley High School
Greely High School
Gretchen Whitney High School
Harold S. Vincent High School
Haverford Senior High School
Haywood High School
Henderson High School
Holy Trinity Diocesan High School
James Logan High School
Kinston High School
Lakeridge High School
Lansing Catholic Central High School
Lincoln High School
Los Gatos High School
Maryhurst High School
Menlo-Atherton High School
Metairie Park Country Day School
Middletown High School
Mission San Jose High School
Moanalua High School
Mount Vernon High School
Myers Park High School
North Olmsted High School
Northern Highlands Regional High School
Oak Grove High School
Ogden Junior High School
Oldham County High School
Orange Glen High School
Our Lady of Lourdes Academy
Palo Alto High School
Parkway Central High School
Parkway South High School
Petersburg High School
Pompton Lakes High School
Poolesville Junior-Senior High School
Proctor Hug High School
Rock Bridge Senior High School
S. S. Murphy High School
Saint Bernard-Elmwood Place High School

Saint John's School
Scarborough Senior High School
Schenley High School Teacher Center
Sheboygan South High School
Shoreham-Wading River High School
Shulamith High School for Girls
South Salem High School
South Winnishiek Senior High School
Southwest High School
St. Mark's School of Texas
Stanton College Preparatory School
Vacaville High School
West Bloomfield High School
Westbury Senior High School
William Fremd High School
William H. Atwell Fundamental Academy
Woodbridge High School
Woodstock Union High School
Xavier Preparatory School
Yarmouth Junior-Senior High School

Appendixes

Alphabetical List of Recognized Schools: 1987

A. Philip Randolph Campus High School (New York, NY)
Academy of Mount St. Ursula (Bronx, NY)
Academy of Notre Dame de Namur (Villanova, PA)
Academy of Our Lady of Good Counsel (White Plains, NY)
Adlai E. Stevenson High School (Prairie View, IL)
Admiral Akers School (Nas Lemoore, CA)
Alexander Hamilton High School (Milwaukee, WI)
Alfred Bonnabel High School (Metairie, LA)
Amherst Middle School (Amherst, NH)
Archbishop Chapelle High School (Metairie, LA)
Archbishop Keough High School (Baltimore, MD)
Archbishop Molloy High School (Briarwood, NY)
Audubon Junior High School (Los Angeles, CA)
Baboquivari Junior High School (Sells, AZ)
Ballard High School (Louisville, KY)
Ben Davis Junior High School (Indianapolis, IN)
Benjamin Elijah Mays School (Atlanta, GA)
Blind Brook High School (Rye Brook, NY)
Blue Springs Junior High School (Blue Springs, MO)
Blue Valley Middle School (Overland Park, KS)
Bonn American High School (West Germany) (APO, NY)
Boyland Central Catholic High School (Rockford, IL)
Bradley Central High School (Cleveland, TN)
Bradley Middle School (San Antonio, TX)
Brighton High School (Brighton, MI)
Broadmoor Middle Laboratory School (Shreveport, LA)
Brookwood High School (Snellville, GA)
Brother Martin High School (New Orleans, LA)
Brown Middle School (Harrison, TN)
Burns Union High School (Burns, OR)

Butte des Morts Junior High School (Menasha, WI)
CAL High School (Latimer, IA)
Capital High School (Olympia, WA)
Cardinal Gibbons High School (Fort Lauderdale, FL)
Cate School (Carpinteria, CA)
Cayucos School (Cayucos, CA)
Centennial Senior High School (Circle Pines, MN)
Central Catholic High School (Pittsburgh, PA)
Central High School (Philadelphia, PA)
Central High School (Aberdeen, SD)
Central High School (Harrison, TN)
Champaign Middle School at Columbia (Champaign, IL)
Chandler High School (Chandler, AZ)
Charlotte Latin School (Charlotte, NC)
Cibola High School (Albuquerque, NM)
Claremont High School (Claremont, CA)
Clear Lake High School (Houston, TX)
Clear Lake Intermediate School (Houston, TX)
Clovis High School (Clovis, CA)
Cranbrook Kingswood School (Bloomfield Hills, MI)
Creighton Preparatory School (Omaha, NE)
Crest Senior High School (Shelby, NC)
D. Russell Parks Junior High School (Fullerton, CA)
Dalton Junior High School (Dalton, GA)
Daniel Wright Middle School (Lake Forest, IL)
Darien High School (Darien, CT)
Deer Path Junior High School (Lake Forest, IL)
Denbigh High School (Newport News, VA)
Desert Shadows Middle School (Scottsdale, AZ)
Dobson High School (Mesa, AZ)
Dooley School (Richmond, VA)
Dover High School (Dover, DE)
Dr. Roland N. Patterson Intermediate School 229 (Bronx, NY)
Dublin Middle School (Dublin, OH)
Dwight-Englewood School (Englewood, NJ)
Dzilth-na-o-dith-hle Community School (Bloomfield, NM)
East High School (West Chester, PA)
Edgar Martin Middle School (Lafayette, LA)
Edgewood High School of the Sacred Heart (Madison, WI)
Episcopal High School (Baton Rouge, LA)
Episcopal School of Acadiana (Cade, LA)
Evergreen Junior High School (Evergreen, CO)
Fairfield College Preparatory School (Fairfield, CT)

Farragut Middle School (Knoxville, TN)
Ferndale Elementary School (Ferndale, CA)
Ferndale High School (Ferndale, WA)
Flowing Wells High School (Tucson, AZ)
Fort Couch Middle School (Upper St. Clair, PA)
Franklin High School (Franklin, WI)
Fremont Senior High School (Fremont, NE)
Garden City Senior High School (Garden City, NY)
Garger High School (Essexville, MI)
Garrison Junior High School (Walla Walla, WA)
Gatesville Elementary School (Gatesville, NC)
Georgetown Visitation Preparatory School (Washington, DC)
Geyser Public School (Geyser, MT)
Gladstone High School (Gladstone, OR)
Granby Memorial Middle School (Granby, CT)
Great Valley High School (Malvern, PA)
Greely High School (Cumberland, ME)
Greenway Middle School (Phoenix, AZ)
Gretchen Whitney High School (Cerritos, CA)
Harold S. Vincent High School (Milwaukee, WI)
Harwood Junior High School (Bedford, TX)
Haverford Senior High School (Havertown, PA)
Haywood High School (Brownsville, TN)
Henderson High School (West Chester, PA)
Hines Middle School (Newport News, VA)
Holy Trinity Diocesan High School (Hicksville, NY)
Homestead High School (Cupertino, CA)
Horace Mann Academic Middle School (San Francisco, CA)
Irving A. Robbins Junior High School (Farmington, CT)
Irvington Middle School (Irvington, NY)
Jackson Hole High School (Jackson, WY)
James Logan High School (Union City, CA)
James Madison Junior High School (Roanoke,VA)
Jefferson Junior High School (Washington, DC)
Jesuit High School (Tampa, FL)
Jesuit High School New Orleans (New Orleans, LA)
John Adams Middle School (Albuquerque, NM)
Kate Griffin Junior High School (Meridian, MS)
Kesling Middle School (LePorte, IN)
King Philip Middle School (West Hartford, CT)
Kinston High School (Kinston, NC)
Kirby-Smith Junior High School (Jacksonville, FL)
Koda Junior High School (Clifton Park, NY)

Lakeridge High School (Lake Oswego, OR)
Lamphere High School (Madison Heights, MI)
Lansing Catholic Central High School (Lansing, MI)
Larson Middle School (Troy, MI)
LaSalle Institute (Troy, NY)
Lawton Community High School (Lawton, MI)
Lincoln County High School (Lincolnton, GA)
Lincoln High School (Wisconsin Rapids, WI)
Londonderry High School (Londonderry, NH)
Los Altos Intermediate School (Camarillo, CA)
Los Gatos High School (Los Gatos, CA)
Loyola High School of Baltimore, Inc. (Towson, MD)
Lutheran High School North (Mount Clemens, MI)
Lutheran High School West (Detroit, MI)
Lynnhaven Junior High School (Virginia Beach, VA)
McQuaid Jesuit High School (Rochester, NY)
Madeira School (Greenway, VA)
Mahomet-Seymour High School (Mahomet, IL)
Marian Heights Academy (Ferdinand, IN)
Marist High School (Chicago, IL)
Marist School (Atlanta, GA)
Mars Hill Bible School (Florence, AL)
Martin Kellogg Middle School (Newington, CT)
Maryhurst High School (Louisville, KY)
Meany Middle School (Seattle, WA)
Menlo-Atherton High School (Atherton, CA)
Mentor Shore Junior High School (Mentor, OH)
Mesa Union School (Somis, CA)
Metairie Park Country Day School (Metairie, LA)
Middletown High School (Middletown, MD)
Midwood High School at Brooklyn College (Brooklyn, NY)
Millard North Junior High School (Omaha, NE)
Miller Junior High School (San Jose, CA)
Milton High School (Milton, MA)
Miramonte High School (Orinda, CA)
Mission San Jose High School (Fremont, CA)
Moanalua High School (Honolulu, HI)
Mooresville Junior High School (Mooresville, NC)
Mother Cabrini High School (New York, NY)
Mother McAuley Liberal Arts High School (Chicago, IL)
Mount Notre Dame High School (Cincinnati, OH)
Mount Vernon High School (Mount Vernon, NY)
Myers Park High School (Charlotte, NC)

Narragansett High School (Narragansett, RI)
Nether Providence Middle School (Wallingford, PA)
Newburgh Free Academy (Newburgh, NY)
Newton County High School (Covington, GA)
Norland Middle School (Miami, FL)
North Bend High School (North Bend, OR)
North Olmsted High School (North Olmsted, OH)
North Salem Middle School (North Salem, NY)
Northern Highlands Regional High School (Allendale, NJ)
Northfield Mount Hermon School (Northfield, MA)
Novi High School (Novi, MI)
Oak Grove High School (Oak Grove, MS)
Oak Grove Junior High School (Bloomington, MN)
O'Fallon Township High School (O'Fallon, IL)
Ogden Junior High School (Oregon City, OR)
Oldham County High School (Buckner, KY)
Oliver Wendell Holmes Junior High School (Wheeling, IL)
Olympus Junior High School (Salt Lake City, UT)
Oneida Middle School (Schnectady, NY)
Orange Glen High School (Escondido, CA)
Our Lady of Lourdes Academy (Miami, FL)
Palmer Junior High School (Independence, MO)
Palms Junior High School (Los Angeles, CA)
Palo Alto High School (Palo Alto, CA)
Parcells Middle School (Grosse Pointe Woods, MI)
Parkway Central High School (Chesterfield, MO)
Parkway East Junior High School (Creve Coeur, MO)
Parkway South High School (Manchester, MO)
Paul J. Gelinas Junior High School (Setauket, NY)
Petersburg High School (Petersburg, AK)
Petoskey Middle School (Petoskey, MI)
Philadelphia High School for Girls (Philadelphia, PA)
Pittsford Middle School (Pittsford, NY)
Polk Middle School (Albuquerque, NM)
Pompton Lakes High School (Pompton Lakes, NJ)
Poolesville Junior-Senior High School (Poolesville, MD)
Port Jefferson Junior High School (New York, NY)
Proctor Hug High School (Reno, NV)
Providence Day School (Charlotte, NC)
Ridge High School (Basking Ridge, NJ)
Ridgewood High School (Ridgewood, NJ)
Robert G. Cole Junior/Senior High School (San Antonio, TX)
Rock Bridge Senior High School (Columbia, MO)

Romeville Elementary School (Convent, LA)
S. S. Murphy High School (Mobile, AL)
Sage Valley Junior High School (Gillette, WY)
Saint Bernard-Elmwood Place High School (Saint Bernard, OH)
Saint John's School (Santurce, PR)
Santa Fe Indian School (Santa Fe, NM)
Scarborough Senior High School (Houston, TX)
Schenley High School Teacher Center (Pittsburgh, PA)
Scotia-Glenville High School (Scotia, NY)
Scranton Preparatory School (Scranton, PA)
Seth Low Intermediate School 96 (Brooklyn, NY)
Shaker Heights Middle School (Shaker Heights, OH)
Sheboygan South High School (Sheboygan, WI)
Shiloh Middle School (Lithonia, GA)
Shoreham-Wading River High School (Shoreham, NY)
Shulamith High School for Girls (Brooklyn, NY)
Skowhegan Area High School (Skowhegen, ME)
South Burlington Middle School (South Burlington, VT)
South Kingstown High School (Wakefield, RI)
South Salem High School (Salem, OR)
South View Junior High School (Edina, MN)
South Winnishiek Senior High School (Calmar, IA)
Southside High School (Fort Smith, AR)
Southside Junior High School (Jacksonville, FL)
Southwest High School (San Diego, CA)
St. Louis Park High School (St. Louis Park, MN)
St. Louise de Marillac High School (Northfield, IL)
St. Mark's School of Texas (Dallas, TX)
St. Rita High School (Chicago, IL)
St. Thomas More Catholic High School (Lafayette, LA)
Stanton College Preparatory School (Jacksonville, FL)
Stephens County High School (Toccoa, GA)
Stone Ridge Country Day School of the Sacred Heart
      (Bethesda, MD)
Sycamore Junior High School (Cincinnati, OH)
Thompkins Middle School (Evansville, IN)
Torrey Pines High School (Leucadia, CA)
Tottenville High School (Staten Island, NY)
Tredyffrin/Easttown Junior High School (Berwyn, PA)
University High School (Irvine, CA)
University of Chicago Laboratory High School (Chicago, IL)
Vacaville High School (Vacaville, CA)
Valley High School (Sacramento, CA)

Valley View Junior High School (Edina, MN)
Van Hise Middle School (Madison, WI)
Villa Angela Academy (Cleveland, OH)
Washington Middle School (Albuquerque, NM)
Washington Middle School (Glendive, MT)
Wayland High School (Wayland, MA)
Weiser High School (Weiser, ID)
Wenatchee High School (Wenatchee, WA)
West Bloomfield High School (West Bloomfield, MI)
West Hills Middle School (West Bloomfield, MI)
Westbury Senior High School (Westbury, NY)
Wheeling High School (Wheeling, IL)
White Plains High School (White Plains, NY)
White Plains Middle School (White Plains, NY)
Whitmore Union Elementary School (Whitmore, CA)
Wilbur Rowe Junior High School (Milwaukee, OR)
William Fremd High School (Palatine, IL)
William H. Atwell Fundamental Academy (Dallas, TX)
William H. Farquhar Middle School (Olney, MD)
Williams Bay High School (Williams Bay, WI)
Woodbridge High School (Irvine, CA)
Woodmere Middle School (Hewlett, NY)
Woodstock Union High School (Woodstock, VT)
Worthingway Middle School (Worthington, OH)
Xavier Preparatory School (New Orleans, LA)
Yankton Senior High School (Yankton, SD)
Yarmouth Junior-Senior High School (Yarmouth, ME)

High Schools Recognized: 1986–1987 Secondary School Recognition Program

School	Principal
ALABAMA	

Mars Hill Bible School
698 Cox Creek Parkway
Florence, AL 35630

Mr. Lawrence Williams
(205) 767-1203

S. S. Murphy High School
100 South Carlen Street
Mobile, AL 36606

Mr. Paul J. Sousa
(205) 479-4526

ALASKA

Petersburg High School
Post Office Box 289
Petersburg, AK 99833

Mr. Leigh S. Wright
(907) 772-3861

ARIZONA

Chandler High School
350 North Arizona Avenue
Chandler, AZ 85224

Mr. Robert Caccamo
(602) 963-4537

Dobson High School
1501 W. Guadalupe Road
Mesa, AZ 85202

Mr. Paul L. Walsh
(602) 898-2902

Flowing Wells High School
3725 N. Flowing Wells Road
Tucson, AZ 85705

Dr. John J. Pedicone
(602) 887-1100

School	Principal

ARKANSAS

Southside High School   Mr. Wayne Haver
4100 Gary   (501) 646-7371
Fort Smith, AR 72903

BUREAU OF INDIAN AFFAIRS

Santa Fe Indian School   Dr. Robbilyn Plummer
1501 Cerrillos Road   (505) 988-6263
Santa Fe, NM 87501

CALIFORNIA

Cate School   Dr. John P. McLeod
Post Office Box 68   (805) 684-4127
1960 Cate Mesa Road
Carpinteria, CA 93013

Claremont High School   Dr. Bertrand J. Raiche
1601 North Indian Hill Boulevard   (714) 624-9053
Claremont, CA 91711

Clovis High School   Mr. Rene M. Errotabere
1055 Fowler Avenue   (209) 299-7211
Clovis, CA 93612

Gretchen Whitney High School   Mr. Robert S. Beall
16800 Shoemaker   (213) 926-5566, ext. 2401
Cerritos, CA 90701

Homestead High School   Dr. Edmond D. Bangle
21370 Homestead Road   (408) 735-6271
Cupertino, CA 95014

James Logan High School   Mrs. Judy Bender
1800 H Street   (415) 471-2520
Union City, CA 94587

Los Gatos High School   Mr. Ted Simonson
20 High School Court   (408) 354-2730
Los Gatos, CA 95030-6973

Menlo-Atherton High School   Mrs. Joyce B. Rosenstiel
555 Middlefield Avenue   (415) 322-5311
Atherton, CA 94026

School	Principal
Miramonte High School 750 Moraga Way Orinda, CA 94563	Mr. Robert W. Gilbert (415) 376-4423
Mission San Jose High School 41717 Palm Avenue Fremont, CA 94539	Mrs. Sharon Belshaw-Jones (415) 657-3600
Orange Glen High School 2200 Glen Ridge Road Escondido, CA 92027	Dr. Ed Brand (619) 480-3070
Palo Alto High School 50 Embarcadero Road Palo Alto, CA 94301	Mr. James Shroyer (415) 329-3831
Southwest High School 1685 Hollister Street San Diego, CA 92154	Ms. Elizabeth W. Cogdill (619) 691-5465
Torrey Pines High School 625 N. Vulcan Avenue Leucadia, CA 92024	Mr. Robert Sanchez (619) 755-0125
University High School 4771 Campus Drive Irvine, CA 92715	Mr. Robert Bruce (714) 854-7500
Vacaville High School 100 W. Monte Vista Avenue Vacaville, CA 95688	Mrs. Grace B. Powell (707) 446-6789
Valley High School 6300 Ehrhardt Avenue Sacramento, CA 95823	Mrs. Giannina Santangelo (916) 689-6500
Woodbridge High School 2 Meadowbrook Irvine, CA 92714	Mr. Greg Cops (714) 786-1104

CONNECTICUT

School	Principal
Darien High School High School Lane Darien, CT 06820	Dr. Velma B. Saire (203) 655-3981

School	Principal

CONNECTICUT (continued)

Fairfield College Preparatory School
North Benson Road
Fairfield, CT 06430

Reverend Charles H. Allen
(203) 254-4000

DELAWARE

Dover High School
625 Walker Road
Dover, DE 19901

Mr. Patrick H. Lynn
(302) 736-5571

DEPARTMENT OF DEFENSE DEPENDENTS SCHOOLS

Bonn American High School
Box 390, American Embassy
APO New York 09080

Dr. Lowell T. Jacobson
228-379234
(West Germany)

DISTRICT OF COLUMBIA

Georgetown Visitation Preparatory
School
1524 35th Street NW
Washington, DC 20007

Sister Mary Berchmans
Hannan
(202) 337-3350

FLORIDA

Cardinal Gibbons High School
4601 Bayview Drive
Fort Lauderdale, FL 33308

Reverend Joseph J.
Kershner
(305) 491-2900

Jesuit High School
4701 N. Himes Avenue
Tampa, FL 33614

Reverend Albert C. Louapre
(813) 877-5344

Our Lady of Lourdes Academy
5525 S. W. 84th Street
Miami, FL 33143

Sister Peter Mary Birster
(305) 667-1623

Stanton College Preparatory School
1149 West 13th Street
Jacksonville, FL 32209

Dr. Veronica W. Valentine
(904) 633-3394

School	Principal

GEORGIA

Benjamin Elijah Mays School
3450 Benjamin Mays Drive S.W.
Atlanta, GA 30331

Mrs. Rubye D. McClendon
(404) 696-0900

Brookwood High School
1255 Dogwood Road
Snellville, GA 30278

Mr. Emmitt M. Lawson, Jr.
(404) 972-7642

Lincoln County High School
Ward Avenue
Post Office Box 579
Lincolnton, GA 30817

Mr. W. Andrew Henderson
(404) 359-3121

Marist School
3790 Ashford-Dunwoody Road N.E.
Atlanta, GA 30319

Reverend Joel M. Konzen
(404) 457-7201

Newton County High School
140 Ram Drive
Covington, GA 30209

Mr. Truman T. Atkins
(404) 787-2250

Stephens County High School
Route 5, White Pine Road
Toccoa, GA 30577

Mr. Marion E. Smith
(404) 886-6825

HAWAII

Moanalua High School
2825 Ala Ilima Street
Honolulu, HI 96818

Mr. Edward C. Jim
(808) 833-1836

IDAHO

Weiser High School
Route 1, Box 22
Weiser, ID 83672

Mr. James A. Reed
(208) 549-2595

ILLINOIS

Adlai E. Stevenson High School
16070 West Highway 22
Prairie View, IL 60096

Dr. Richard P. DuFour
(312) 634-4000

School	Principal

ILLINOIS (continued)

Boylan Central Catholic High School
4000 Saint Francis Drive
Rockford, IL 61105

Sister Anthony Marelli
(815) 877-2513

Mahomet-Seymour High School
302 West State Street
Mahomet, IL 61853

Mr. John W. Wilkinson
(217) 586-4962

Marist High School
4200 West 115th Street
Chicago, IL 60655

Brother Anthony M.
Iazzetti
(312) 881-6360

Mother McAuley Liberal Arts
High School
3737 West 99th Street
Chicago, IL 60642

Sister Cathleen M. Cahill
(312) 881-6500

O'Fallon Township High School
600 South Smiley Street
O'Fallon, IL 62269

Mr. Robert H. Bellina
(618) 632-3507

St. Louise de Marillac High School
315 Waukegan Road
Northfield, IL 60093

Sister Anne Marie Butler
(312) 446-9106

St. Rita High School
6310 South Claremont Avenue
Chicago, IL 60636

Reverend Patrick E.
Murphy
(312) 925-6600

University of Chicago Laboratory
High School
1362 East 59th Street
Chicago, IL 60616

Mr. Wendell R.
McConnaha
(312) 962-9446

Wheeling High School
900 South Elmhurst Road
Wheeling, IL 60090

Dr. Thomas W. Shirley
(312) 537-6500

William Fremd High School
1000 South Quentin Road
Palatine, IL 60067

Mr. Thomas G. Howard
(312) 358-6222

School	Principal

INDIANA

Marian Heights Academy
R.R. 3, Box 202
Ferdinand, IN 47532

Sister Mary Dominic
Frederick
(812) 367-1431

IOWA

CAL High School
Post Office Box 458
Latimer, IA 50452

Mr. John Robbins
(515) 579-6085

South Winneshiek Senior High School
303 South Washington
Calmar, IA 52132

Mr. Jon David Trotter
(319) 562-3226

KENTUCKY

Ballard High School
6000 Brownsboro Road
Louisville, KY 40218

Mrs. Alexandra Allen
(502) 454-8206

Maryhurst School
1015 Dorsey Lane
Louisville, KY 40223

Ms. Janet McWilliams
Calvert
(502) 245-1576

Oldham County High School
Post Office Box 187
Buckner, KY 40010

Mr. Blake Haselton
(502) 222-9461

LOUISIANA

Alfred Bonnabel High School
8800 Bruin Drive
Metairie, LA 70003

Mr. Paul F. Vitrano
(504) 443-4564

Archbishop Chapelle High School
8800 Veterans Boulevard
Metairie, LA 70003

Mr. Alvin L. Murphy
(504) 467-3105

Brother Martin High School
4401 Elysian Fields Avenue
New Orleans, LA 70122

Brother Ivy LeBlanc
(504) 283-1561

Episcopal High School
3200 Woodland Ridge Boulevard
Baton Rouge, LA 70816

Reverend Paul B. Hancock
(504) 293-3180

School	Principal

LOUISIANA (continued)

Episcopal School of Acadiana
Post Office Box 380
Cade, LA 70519

Reverend Robert Nielsen
(318) 365-1416

Jesuit High School New Orleans
4133 Banks Street
New Orleans, LA 70119

Reverend Harry W.
Tompson
(504) 486-6631

Metairie Park Country Day School
300 Park Road
Metairie, LA 70005

Mrs. Sally P. Janvier
(504) 837-5204

St. Thomas More Catholic
    High School
450 East Farrel Road
Lafayette, LA 70508

Mrs. Yvonne B. Jumonville
(318) 988-3700

Xavier Preparatory School
5116 Magazine Street
New Orleans, LA 70115

Sister Eileen Sullivan
(504) 899-6061

MAINE

Greely High School
Cumberland Center
Cumberland, ME 04021

Mr. Warren G. Galway
(207) 829-5534

Skowhegan Area High School
West Front Street
Skowhegan, ME 04976

Mr. Thomas H. Farrell
(207) 474-5511

Yarmouth Junior-Senior High School
West Elm Street
Yarmouth, ME 04096

Dr. Kenneth P. Nye
(207) 846-5535

MARYLAND

Archbishop Keough High School
1201 Caton Avenue
Baltimore, MD 21227

Sister Joan Elias
(310) 646-2878

Loyola High School of Baltimore, Inc.
Chestnut Avenue and Charles Street
Towson, MD 21204

Dr. Donald W. Urbancic
(301) 823-0601

School	Principal

Middletown High School
200 High Street
Middletown, MD 21769

Dr. Michael N. Riley
(301) 371-5000

Poolesville Junior-Senior High School
17501 Willard Road
Poolesville, MD 20837

Mrs. Terrill R. Meyer
(301) 972-7410

Stone Ridge Country Day School
   of the Sacred Heart
9101 Rockville Pike
Bethesda, MD 20814

Sister Anne Dyer
(301) 657-4322

MASSACHUSETTS

Milton High School
Central Avenue
Milton, MA 02186

Mr. Allen G. Adams
(617) 696-7220, ext. 300

Northfield Mount Hermon School
Main Street
Northfield, MA 01360

Reverend Richard P.
   Unsworth
(413) 498-5311

Wayland High School
Old Connecticut Path
Wayland, MA 01778

Dr. Sharon D. Hennessy
(617) 358-7746

MICHIGAN

Brighton High School
7878 Brighton Road
Brighton, MI 48116

Mr. Thomas Mikolajczyk
(313) 229-1400

Cranbrook Kingswood School
Box 801
Bloomfield Hills, MI 48013

Mr. Samuel A. Salas
(313) 645-3602

Garger High School
213 Pine Street
Essexville, MI 48732

Mr. Dan Harfst
(517) 894-9710

Lamphere High School
610 West 13 Mile Road
Madison Heights, MI 48071

Mr. Richard Yaroch
(313) 589-3943

School   **Principal**

MICHIGAN (continued)

Lansing Catholic Central High School   Mr. James B. Miner
501 N. Marshall Street   (517) 484-4465
Lansing, MI 48912

Lawton Community High School   Mr. Gail W. Persons
Post Office Box 430, 2nd Street   (616) 624-4191
Lawton, MI 49065

Lutheran High School North   Mr. Dale E. Cooper
16825 Twenty Four Mile Road   (313) 781-9151
Mount Clemens, MI 48044

Lutheran High School West   Mr. Kenneth Palmreuter
8181 Greenfield   (313) 584-3621
Detroit, MI 48228

Novi High School   Dr. Robert S. Youngberg
24062 Taft Road   (313) 344-8300
Novi, MI 48050

West Bloomfield High School   Dr. Gary A. Faber
4925 Orchard Lake Road   (313) 851-6100
West Bloomfield, MI 48033

MINNESOTA

Centennial Senior High School   Mr. Lawrence H. Biehn
4707 North Road   (612) 780-7620
Circle Pines, MN 55014

St. Louis Park High School   Mr. Richard L. Wainio
6425 West 33rd Street   (612) 925-4300
Saint Louis Park, MN 55426

MISSISSIPPI

Oak Grove High School   Mrs. Carolyn C. Lott
Route 4, Box 1121   (601) 264-8309
Hattiesburg, MS 39402

MISSOURI

Parkway Central High School   Dr. Gary M. Chesley
369 North Woods Mill Road   (314) 851-8220
Chesterfield, MO 63017

School	Principal
Parkway South High School 801 Hanna Road Manchester, MO 63021	Mr. Craig H. Larson (314) 394-8300
Rock Bridge Senior High School 4303 South Providence Road Columbia, MO 65203	Dr. W. Wayne Walker (314) 449-3731

MONTANA

Geyser Public School Post Office Box 70 Geyser, MT 59447	Mr. Richard Moe (406) 735-4368

NEBRASKA

Creighton Preparatory School 7400 Western Avenue Omaha, NE 68114	Mr. James W. Rouse (402) 393-1190
Fremont Senior High School 1750 North Lincoln Fremont, NE 68025	Dr. Ken Thomson (402) 721-6720, ext. 241

NEVADA

Proctor Hug High School 2880 Sutro Street Reno, NV 89520	Dr. John Genasci (702) 786-7766

NEW HAMPSHIRE

Londonderry High School 295 Mammoth Road Londonderry, NH 03053	Mr. Edmond Thibodeau (603) 432-6941

NEW JERSEY

Dwight-Englewood School 315 East Palisade Avenue Englewood, NJ 07631	Ms. Gene Wojtyla (201) 569-9500
Northern Highlands Regional High School Hillside Avenue Allendale, NJ 07401-1498	Mr. John Mintzer (201) 327-8700, ext. 20

School   Principal

NEW JERSEY (continued)

Pompton Lakes High School   Mr. Joel B. McKenzie
Lakeside Avenue   (201) 835-7100
Pompton Lakes, NJ 07442

Ridge High School   Dr. Michael A. Pinnella
South Finley Avenue   (201) 766-3070
Basking Ridge, NJ 07920

Ridgewood High School   Mr. Robert W. Honsinger
627 East Ridgewood Avenue   (201) 670-2821
Ridgewood, NJ 07451

NEW MEXICO

Cibola High School   Mrs. Linda M. Taylor
1510 Ellison Drive N.W.   (505) 897-0110
Albuquerque, NM 87114

NEW YORK

A. Philip Randolph Campus   Mrs. Lottie L. Taylor
   High School   (212) 926-0113
Convent Avenue at 135th Street
New York, NY 10031

Academy of Mount Saint Ursula   Sister Barbara Calamari
330 Bedford Park Boulevard   (212) 364-5353
Bronx, NY 10458

Academy of Our Lady of   Sister Ellen Curry
   Good Counsel   (914) 949-0178
52 North Broadway
White Plains, NY 10603

Archbishop Molloy High School   Brother John Klein
83-53 Manton Street   (718) 441-2100
Briarwood, NY 11435

Blind Brook High School   Mr. Ronald Wilson
King Street   (914) 937-3600
Rye Brook, NY 10573

Garden City Senior High School   Mr. Joseph L. Prusan
170 Rockaway Avenue   (516) 294-3030
Garden City, NY 11530

School	Principal
Holy Trinity Diocesan High School 98 Cherry Lane Hicksville, NY 11801	Reverend John C. Seidenschwang (516) 433-2900
LaSalle Institute 174 Williams Road Troy, NY 12180	Brother James Romond (518) 283-2500
McQuaid Jesuit High School 1800 Clinton Avenue South Rochester, NY 14618	Father Paul Nochelski (716) 473-1130
Midwood High School at Brooklyn College Bedford Avenue and Glenwood Road Brooklyn, NY 11210	Mr. Leonard J. Harrison (718) 859-9200
Mother Cabrini High School 701 Fort Washington Avenue New York, NY 10040	Sister Sharon Morano (212) 923-3540
Mount Vernon High School 100 California Road Mount Vernon, NY 10552	Mr. Richard A. Capozzola (914) 668-6580
Newburgh Free Academy 201 Fullerton Avenue Newburgh, NY 12550	Mr. Ronald F. Shapiro (914) 561-8500
Scotia-Glenville High School Sacandaga Road Scotia, NY 12302	Mr. Richard J. McGuire (518) 382-1231
Shoreham-Wading River High School Route 25A Shoreham, NY 11786	Mr. Norman L. Bussiere (516) 929-8500
Shulamith High School for Girls 1277 East 14th Street Brooklyn, NY 11230	Dr. Susan R. Katz (718) 338-7154
Tottenville High School 100 Luten Avenue Staten Island, NY 10312	Mr. Herbert Balish (718) 356-2220

School	Principal

NEW YORK (continued)

Westbury Senior High School
Post Road
Westbury, NY 11590

Mr. Pless Dickerson
(516) 997-8034

White Plains High School
550 North Street
White Plains, NY 10605

Dr. Donald Kusel
(914) 997-2198

NORTH CAROLINA

Charlotte Latin School
Post Office Box 6143
Charlotte, NC 28207

Dr. E. J. Fox, Jr.
(704) 846-1100

Crest Senior High School
Route 3
Shelby, NC 28150

Mr. George Litton
(704) 482-5354

Kinston High School
2601 North Queen Street
Kinston, NC 28501

Mr. William L. Peedin, Jr.
(919) 527-8067

Myers Park High School
2400 Colony Road
Charlotte, NC 28209

Mr. Joseph W. Peel
(704) 525-2821

Providence Day School
5800 Sardis Road
Charlotte, NC 28226

Mr. Eugene A. Bratek
(704) 364-6848

OHIO

Mount Notre Dame High School
711 East Columbia Avenue
Cincinnati, OH 45215

Sister Carol Diemunsch
(513) 821-3044

North Olmsted High School
5755 Burns Road
North Olmsted, OH 44070

Dr. Dianna M. Lindsay
(216) 777-7700, ext. 266

Saint Bernard-Elmwood Place
    High School
4615 Tower Avenue
Saint Bernard, OH 45217

Mr. Larry Irwin
(513) 641-2020

School	Principal

Villa Angela Academy
17001 Lake Shore Boulevard
Cleveland, OH 44110

Sister Virginia De Vinne
(216) 692-3950

OREGON

Burns Union High School
1100 Oregon Avenue
Burns, OR 97720

Mr. Charles D. "Chuck"
Vawter
(503) 573-2044

Gladstone High School
18800 Portland Avenue
Gladstone, OR 97027

Mr. Richard B. Baker
(503) 655-2544

Lakeridge High School
1235 Overlook Drive
Lake Oswego, OR 97034

Dr. Thomas S. Lindersmith
(503) 635-0319

North Bend High School
14th and Pacific
North Bend, OR 97459

Mr. Ken Stobie
(503) 756-2521, ext. 319

South Salem High School
1910 Church Street
Salem, OR 97302

Mr. Daniel N. Johnson
(503) 399-3252

PENNSYLVANIA

Academy of Notre Dame de Namur
560 Sproul Road
Villanova, PA 19085

Sister Regina Finnegan
(215) 687-0650

Central Catholic High School
4720 Fifth Avenue
Pittsburgh, PA 15213

Brother Edward Sheehy
(412) 621-8189

Central High School
Ogontz and Olney Avenues
Philadelphia, PA 19141

Dr. Sheldon S. Pavel
(215) 224-6015

East High School
450 Ellis Lane
West Chester, PA 19380

Dr. David E. Cox
(215) 436-7200

Great Valley High School
Route 401 and Phoenixville Pike
Malvern, PA 19355

Mr. James A. Kase, III
(215) 644-6610

School	Principal

PENNSYLVANIA (continued)

Haverford Senior High School
200 Mill Road
Havertown, PA 19083

Mr. Mel Drukin
(215) 446-4570

Henderson High School
Lincoln and Montgomery Avenues
West Chester, PA 19380

Dr. Eliot W. Larson
(215) 436-7221

Philadelphia High School for Girls
Broad Street and Olney Avenue
Philadelphia, PA 19141

Mrs. Marion L. Steet
(215) 927-4500

Schenley High School Teacher Center
Center Avenue and Bigelow Boulevard
Pittsburgh, PA 15213

Dr. John R. Young
(412) 622-8240

Scranton Preparatory School
1000 Wyoming Avenue
Scranton, PA 18509

Reverend Herbert B. Keller
(717) 961-7737

PUERTO RICO

Saint John's School
1466 Ashford Avenue
Santurce, PR 00907

Mrs. Maria M. Guardiola
(809) 728-5343

RHODE ISLAND

Narragansett High School
245 South Pier Road
Narragansett, RI 02882

Dr. Todd D. Flaherty
(401) 792-9400

South Kingstown High School
81 Columbia Street
Wakefield, RI 02879

Mr. Eric D. Wertheimer
(401) 792-9611

SOUTH DAKOTA

Central High School
225 Third Avenue SE
Aberdeen, SD 57401

Mr. Richard Engler
(605) 225-3822

Yankton Senior High School
2000 Mulberry Street
Yankton, SD 57078

Mr. David M. Bitter
(605) 665-2073

School	Principal

TENNESSEE

Bradley Central High School
1000 South Lee Highway
Cleveland, TN 37311

Mr. Dale R. Hughes
(615) 479-5436

Central High School
5728 Highway 58
Harrison, TN 37341

Mr. Charles H. Preston
(615) 344-8336

Haywood High School
1175 East College
Brownsville, TN 38012

Mr. Gordon Perry
(901) 772-1845

TEXAS

Clear Lake High School
2929 Bay Area Boulevard
Houston, TX 77058

Mr. Edgar B. Taylor, III
(713) 488-6670

Robert G. Cole Junior/Senior
    High School
1900 Winans
San Antonio, TX 78234

Mr. Clinton E. Compton
(512) 824-7535

Scarborough Senior High School
4141 Costa Rica
Houston, TX 77092

Mr. Peter J. Ferrara
(713) 681-4618

St. Mark's School of Texas
10600 Preston Road
Dallas, TX 75230-4047

Mr. David V. Hicks
(214) 363-6491

VERMONT

Woodstock Union High School
Route 4
Woodstock, VT 05091

Mr. Leo P. Corriveau
(802) 457-1317

VIRGINIA

Denbigh High School
259 Denbigh Boulevard
Newport News, VA 23602

Mr. Stanley Lovett, Jr.
(804) 877-9278

School	Principal

Dooley School
8000 Washington Highway
Richmond, VA 23227

Mrs. Pamela G. Alterescu
(804) 262-1663

Madeira School
8328 Georgetown Pike
Greenway, VA 22067

Mr. Charles McK. Saltzman
(703) 556-8200

WASHINGTON

Capital High School
2707 Conger Avenue
Olympia, WA 98502

Mr. Douglas Heay
(206) 753-8880

Ferndale High School
Post Office Box 425
Ferndale, WA 98248

Mr. Daniel P. Farrell
(206) 384-9210

Wenatchee High School
1101 Millerdale Street
Wenatchee, WA 98801

Mr. John W. Gordon
(509) 663-8117

WISCONSIN

Alexander Hamilton High School
6215 West Warnimont Avenue
Milwaukee, WI 53208

Mrs. Janie R. Hatton
(414) 541-7720

Edgewood High School of
    the Sacred Heart
2219 Monroe Street
Madison, WI 53711

Sister Kathleen Phelan
(608) 257-1023

Franklin High School
8222 South 51st Street
Franklin, WI 53132

Mr. Romuald A. Kucinski
(414) 421-3000

Harold S. Vincent High School
7501 North Granville Road
Milwaukee, WI 53224

Mrs. Kery Kafka
(414) 354-4144

Lincoln High School
1801 16th Street South
Wisconsin Rapids, WI 54494

Mr. Timothy E. Laatsch
(715) 423-1520

School	Principal
Sheboygan South High School 3128 South 12th Street Sheboygan, WI 53081	Mr. Gerald K. Freitag (414) 459-3636
Williams Bay High School 139 Congress Street Post Office Box 259 Williams Bay, WI 53191	Dr. Arnold Frank (414) 245-6224

WYOMING

Jackson Hole High School Post Office Box 568 Jackson, WY 83001	Mr. Jay S. Cason (307) 733-7475

APPENDIX C

Junior High/Middle Schools Recognized: 1986–1987 Secondary School Recognition Program

School	Principal

ARIZONA

Baboquivari Junior High School
Post Office Box 248
Sells, AZ 85634

Mr. Sharron Walker
(602) 383-2601

Desert Shadows Middle School
5858 East Sweetwater
Scottsdale, AZ 85254

Mr. William W. Cooper
(602) 996-1823

Greenway Middle School
3003 E. Greenway Road
Phoenix, AZ 85032

Mr. Donald Skawski
(602) 992-8860

BUREAU OF INDIAN AFFAIRS

Dzilth-na-o-dith-hle Community
    School
Star Route 4, Box 5003
Bloomfield, NM 87413

Mr. D. Dwane Robinson
(505) 632-3674

CALIFORNIA

Admiral Akers School
Post Office Box 1339
NAS Lemoore, CA 93245

Mr. John A. Jones
(209) 998-5707

Audubon Junior High School
4120 Eleventh Avenue
Los Angeles, CA 90008

Mr. Gene McCallum
(213) 299-2882

School   **Principal**

CALIFORNIA (continued)

Cayucos School   Mr. William W. Wood
301 Cayucos Drive   (805) 995-3694
Cayucos, CA 93430

D. Russell Parks Junior High School   Dr. LeNelle Cittadin
1710 Rosecrans   (714) 477-7785
Fullerton, CA 92633

Ferndale Elementary School   Mr. Alan W. Jorgensen
Post Office Box 667, 164 Shaw   (707) 786-9535
Ferndale, CA 95536

Horace Mann Academic Middle   Mr. Mario Chacon
    School   (415) 826-4504
3351 23rd Street
San Francisco, CA 94110

Los Altos Intermediate School   Mr. F. J. Fuchs
700 Temple Avenue   (805) 482-4656
Camarillo, CA 93010

Mesa Union School   Dr. Dennis J. Convery
3901 North Mesa School Road   (805) 485-1411
Somis, CA 93066

Miller Junior High School   Mr. Andrew Garrido
6151 Rainbow Drive   (408) 252-3755
San Jose, CA 95129

Palms Junior High School   Mrs. Minnie W. Floyd
10860 Woodbine Street   (213) 837-5236
Los Angeles, CA 90034

Whitmore Union Elementary School   Mr. David Klasson
Post Office Box 10   (916) 472-3243
Whitmore, CA 96096

COLORADO

Evergreen Junior High School   Mr. Charles R. Horn
2052 Highway #74   (303) 674-5536
Evergreen, CO 80439

School	Principal

CONNECTICUT

Granby Memorial Middle School
309 Salmon Brook Street
Granby, CT 06035

Mr. Ralph Wallace
(203) 653-2591

Irving A. Robbins Junior High School
20 Wolf Pit Road
Farmington, CT 06032

Dr. James M. Aseltine
(203) 677-2683

King Philip Middle School
100 King Philip Drive
West Hartford, CT 06117

Mrs. Constance Beaudry
(203) 233-8236

Martin Kellogg Middle School
155 Harding Avenue
Newington, CT 06111

Mr. Robert B. Buganski
(203) 666-5418

DISTRICT OF COLUMBIA

Jefferson Junior High School
8th and H Streets S.W.
Washington, DC 20024

Ms. Vera M. White
(202) 724-4881

FLORIDA

Kirby-Smith Junior High School
2034 Hubbard Street
Jacksonville, FL 32206

Mr. Jack B. Shanklin, Jr.
(904) 633-5815

Norland Middle School
1235 Northwest 192nd Terrace
Miami, FL 33169

Mr. John F. Gilbert
(305) 653-1210

Southside Junior High School #211
2948 Knights Lane East
Jacksonville, FL 32216

Dr. Jerry R. Gugel
(904) 737-4970

GEORGIA

Dalton Junior High School
408 West Crawford Street
Dalton, GA 30720

Mr. Donald P. Amonett
(404) 278-3903

Shiloh Middle School
4285 Shiloh Road
Lithonia, GA 30058

Dr. Lowell Ensey
(404) 972-3224

School	Principal

ILLINOIS

Champaign Middle School at Columbia
    at Columbia
1103 North Neil Street
Champaign, IL 61810

Mr. Michael Cain
(217) 351-3819

Daniel Wright Middle School
1370 Riverwoods Road
Lake Forest, IL 60045

Mr. Anthony A. Baade
(312) 295-1560

Deer Path Junior High School
155 West Deerpath
Lake Forest, IL 60045

Mr. Richard A. Howell
(312) 234-6010

Oliver Wendell Holmes Junior
    High School
221 South Wolf Road
Wheeling, IL 60090

Mr. Avi Poster
(312) 520-2790

INDIANA

Ben Davis Junior High School
1155 S. High School Road
Indianapolis, IN 46241

Dr. David Shull
(317) 244-2438

Kesling Middle School
306 East 18th Street
La Porte, IN 46350

Mr. Robert E. Schmielau
(219) 362-7507

Thompkins Middle School
1300 W. Mill Road
Evansville, IN 47710

Mr. Robert B. Ahrens
(812) 425-8253

KANSAS

Blue Valley Middle School
7500 West 149th Terrace
Overland Park, KS 66223

Dr. Richard M. Seipel
(913) 681-2807

LOUISIANA

Broadmoor Middle Laboratory School
441 Atlantic
Shreveport, LA 71105

Mr. W. Edward Hearron
(318) 861-2403

School	Principal

Edgar Martin Middle School
401 Broadmoor Boulevard
Lafayette, LA 70503

Mr. Lester Duhon
(318) 984-9796

Romeville Elementary School
Route 1, Box 93
Convent, LA 70723

Mrs. Janic Vee Henderson
(504) 562-3684

MARYLAND

William H. Farquhar Middle School
16915 Batchellors Forest Road
Olney, MD 20832

Mr. J. Thomas Hickman
(301) 924-2200

MICHIGAN

Larson Middle School
2222 East Long Lake Road
Troy, MI 48098

Mr. William P. Jacka
(313) 689-8710

Parcells Middle School
20600 Mack Avenue
Grosse Pointe Woods, MI 48236

Mr. William Christofferson
(313) 343-2107

Petoskey Middle School
601 Howard Street
Petoskey, MI 49770

Mr. Carl R. Moser
(616) 347-6023, ext. 245

West Hills Middle School
2601 Lone Pine Road
West Bloomfield, MI 48033

Mrs. Beverly Stone
(313) 851-1383

MINNESOTA

Oak Grove Junior High School
1300 West 106th Street
Bloomington MN 55431

Mr. Roger W. Hahn
(612) 884-7435

South View Junior High School
4725 South View Lane
Edina, MN 55424

Dr. Kenneth Dragseth
(612) 927-9721

Valley View Junior High School
6750 Valley View Road
Edina, MN 55435

Dr. Albert J. Ogren
(612) 944-2110

School	Principal

MISSISSIPPI

Kate Griffin Junior High School
2814 Davis Street
Meridian, MS 39301

Dr. Mary Linda Guin
(601) 483-5221

MISSOURI

Blue Springs Junior High School
2103 Vesper
Blue Springs, MO 64015

Dr. Don G. Gray
(816) 229-1141

Palmer Junior High School
218 North Pleasant
Independence, MO 64050

Mr. Jerry L. Moore
(816) 254-7474

Parkway East Junior High School
181 Coeur De Ville Drive
Creve Coeur, MO 63141

Mrs. Bonnie L. Reid
(314) 878-6414

MONTANA

Washington Middle School
505 N. Meade
Glendive, MT 59330

Mr. Harry M. Darling
(406) 365-2356

NEBRASKA

Millard North Junior High School
2828 S. 139 Plaza
Omaha, NE 68144

Dr. Gary T. Barta
(402) 895-8280

NEW HAMPSHIRE

Amherst Middle School
Cross Road, Post Office Box 966
Amherst, NH 03031

Mr. Paul D. Collins
(603) 673-8944

NEW MEXICO

John Adams Middle School
5401 Glenrio Road, NW
Albuquerque, NM 87105

Mr. Richard Beattie
(505) 836-4311

School	Principal

Polk Middle School
2220 Raymac Road, SW
Albuquerque, NM 87105

Mr. William R. Gore
(505) 877-6444

Washington Middle School
1101 Park Avenue, SW
Albuquerque, NM 87102

Mrs. Dolores R. Klingbeil
(505) 764-2000

NEW YORK

Dr. Roland N. Patterson
  Intermediate School 229
275 Harlem River Park Bridge
Bronx, NY 10453

Mr. Felton M. Johnson
(212) 583-3300

Irvington Middle School
101 Main Street
Irvington, NY 19533

Dr. Andrew C. Kerfut
(914) 591-9494

Koda Junior High School
970 Route 146
Clifton Park, NY 12065

Dr. Gary Adelson
(518) 371-7392

North Salem Middle School
Old Route 124
North Salem, NY 10560

Mr. James Walker
(914) 669-5414

Oneida Middle School
Oneida Street
Schenectady, NY 12308

Mr. Walter J. LeClair
(518) 370-8260

Paul J. Gelinas Junior High School
Mud Road
Setauket, NY 11733

Mrs. Marion Gaigal
(516) 689-7200, ext. 260

Pittsford Middle School
Barker Road
Pittsford, NY 14534

Mr. Sherman L. Craig
(716) 385-6750

Port Jefferson Junior High School
Spring Street, Port Jefferson
New York, NY 11777

Mr. Larry Lazar
(516) 473-8151

Seth Low Intermediate School 96
99 Avenue P
Brooklyn, NY 11204

Mr. John L. Mancini, Jr.
(718) 236-1344

School   **Principal**

NEW YORK (continued)

White Plains Middle School   Mr. Bernard R. Cropsey
7 Amherst Place   (914) 997-2251
White Plains, NY 10605

Woodmere Middle School   Mrs. Irma Marmor
1170 Peninsula Boulevard   (516) 374-0643
Hewlett, NY 11557

NORTH CAROLINA

Gatesville Elementary School   Mr. John A. Lane
Post Office Box 187   (919) 357-0835
Gatesville, NC 27938

Mooresville Junior High School   Mr. Brady M. Guin, Jr.
160 South Magnolia Street   (704) 663-3841
Mooresville, NC 28115

OHIO

Dublin Middle School   Mr. Paul W. King
150 West Bridge Street   (614) 764-5919
Dublin, OH 43017

Mentor Shore Junior High School   Mr. Neil J. Sharp
5670 Hopkins Road   (216) 255-4444
Mentor, OH 44060

Shaker Heights Middle School   Dr. Richard Peterjohn
20600 Shaker Boulevard   (216) 921-1400
Shaker Heights, OH 44120

Sycamore Junior High School   Mr. James W. Sears
5757 Cooper Road   (513) 791-8013
Cincinnati, OH 45242

Worthingway Middle School   Mr. Paul J. Cynkar
6625 Guyer Street   (614) 431-6560
Worthington, OH 43085

OREGON

Ogden Junior High School   Dr. Robert F. Hunter
14133 S. Donovan Road   (503) 657-2425
Oregon City, OR 97045

School	Principal

Wilbur Rowe Junior High School
3606 South East Lake Road
Milwaukie, OR 97222—6999

Mr. Timothy P. Olson
(503) 653-3718

PENNSYLVANIA

Fort Couch Middle School
515 Fort Couch Road
Upper St. Clair, PA 15241

Mr. Thomas Harshman
(412) 854-3046

Nether Providence Middle School
200 S. Providence Road
Wallingford, PA 19086

Dr. Gene J. Herninko
(215) 566-9006

Tredyffrin/Easttown Junior High School
840 Old Lancaster Road
Berwyn, PA 19312

Mr. Cecil Mosenson
(215) 644-1460

TENNESSEE

Brown Middle School
5716 Highway 58
Harrison, TN 37341

Mr. Curtis Drake
(615) 344-8316

Farragut Middle School
200 West End Avenue
Knoxville, TN 37922

Dr. Donald G. Rhodes
(615) 966-9756

TEXAS

Bradley Middle School
14819 Heimer Road
San Antonio, TX 78232

Mrs. Audrey Villarreal
(512) 496-2666

Clear Lake Intermediate School
15545 El Camino Real
Houston, TX 77062

Mr. Ross McGlothlin
(713) 488-1296

Harwood Junior High School
3000 Martin Drive
Bedford, TX 76021

Mr. James Downe
(817) 283-4441

William H. Atwell
    Fundamental Academy
1303 Reynoldston Lane
Dallas, TX 75232

Mr. Robert B. Yowell
(214) 376-7321

School	Principal

UTAH

Olympus Junior High School
2217 East 4800 South
Salt Lake City UT, 84117

Dr. Maurice W. Johnson
(801) 273-2120

VERMONT

South Burlington Middle School
500 Dorset Street
South Burlington, VT 05403

Mr. Mark H. Kennedy
(802) 658-9080

VIRGINIA

Hines Middle School
6160 Jefferson Avenue
Newport News, VA 23605

Mr. Bob C. James
(802) 826-6331

James Madison Junior High School
1160 Overland Road S.W.
Roanoke, VA 24015

Dr. Elizabeth D. Lee
(703) 981-2394

Lynnhaven Junior High School
1250 Bayne Drive
Virginia Beach, VA 23454

Mr. G. E. McGovern
(804) 481-4685

WASHINGTON

Garrison Junior High School
906 Chase Street
Walla Walla, WA 99362

Mr. William I. Jordan
(509) 527-3040

Meany Middle School
301 21st Avenue East
Seattle, WA 98112

Mr. Thomas F. Lord
(206) 281-6160

WISCONSIN

Butte des Morts Junior High School
501 Tayco Street
Menasha, WI 54952

Mr. Harold I. Pelton
(414) 729-5060

Van Hise Middle School
4801 Waukesha Street
Madison, WI 53705

Dr. Marvin F. Meissen
(608) 267-4289

School	Principal

WYOMING

Sage Valley Junior High School
1000 Lakeway Drive
Gillette, WY 82716

Mr. LeRoy M. Larson
(307) 682-2225

APPENDIX D

Personal Viewpoints

The School Improvement Team:
An Organization for Effective Change

FLOWING WELLS HIGH SCHOOL

> It takes a great deal of courage to distribute one's power to others, yet quite a bit more stupidity not to.

We use a team approach for educational change utilizing the principal as a facilitator of a "school improvement team" at Flowing Wells High School. The team approach was largely responsible for our school's recognition as one of the nation's effective secondary schools.

Ultimately, any educational change, whether in purpose, program, process, procedure, or product, can result in school improvement only if the human resources in the local school are adequate for bringing about change (Lipham, 1979).

In spite of statements by some researchers (March 1978) who took a somewhat skeptical view that attempting to improve American education by changing the structure of the school or the behavior of administrators and supervisors is unlikely to produce dramatic or even perceptible results (as if one "could change the tides at Tybee Beach by splitting into the Savannah River"), evidence has clearly demonstrated that the manner in which goals and objectives are developed, and the system created for quality participation in decision making based upon a common mission and clear vision, can make a significant difference in the outcomes of the school.

Goodlad (1977), Trump (1972), Lipham and Daresh (1979), and others identified principal leadership as a major contributor to effective schools, and Griffiths as early as 1959 clearly noted that most organizations, including the school, tend to change more

Reprinted by permission of John J. Pedicone, Ph.D., Assistant Superintendent, Flowing Wells High School, Tucson, AZ 85705.

from the top down than they do from the bottom up. However, more recently a great body of research has emerged supporting that concept in light of the extent to which the leader involves others in decisions directly affecting them and actively solicits input to create goals and objectives, provided that a clear sense of the overall mission of the school has been established.

Peters and Waterman (1982) and Lewis (1986) proclaimed that effective organizations, including schools, have several common characteristics, not the least of which are that they welcome new ideas and reward the people who offer them, that such organizations have the courage to change things even when all is going well, that administrators have the courage to share power and authority with school people, and to involve all school people at all levels of the organization to improve performance and solve problems.

With this philosophy in mind, the administration at Flowing Wells High School developed a middle management team comprised of department instructional leaders. All department chairpersons were removed from their positions and rehired under a clear set of expectations which had been mutually determined by administration and faculty. These expectations required that instructional leadership be a primary qualification and that a student-centered approach exist throughout all aspects of the school program. A clear mission was created which included attention to academic, personal, and social growth of students, recognition of individual worth, efforts to satisfy individual needs and interests, and preparation of students for life after high school. A motto emerged which directed the school mission. It stated "We can make a difference."

Next, a management incentive program was created to encourage continual innovation, reinforce curricular and co-curricular programs, and reward ideas both emotionally and monetarily. The concept of the distribution of power was nurtured and delivered throughout the entire organization and on into the lives of students on campus. This philosophy was articulated frequently and an open climate which invited risks and required accountability was developed. Each year department chairpersons were provided one overall school goal and they were expected to develop several departmental goals in line with that year's direction. An annual theme was generated which supported the school motto and over time a spirit of progress and school-wide direction was experienced by each member of the educational family.

Parents had been involved throughout the process through a Parent Advisory Committee, which grew to over 40 members. Staff, faculty, students, and parents were vested in the outcomes of the school.

At the beginning of the 1986–1987 school year, a School Improvement Team was formed which consisted of faculty, staff, parents, and administrators. The goal was to identify and define all programs within the school in order to determine what existed for purposes of greater coordination and articulation. Department heads were asked not to be active members of this team so that the efforts of the organization could involve others in the next series of changes. The team was divided into four groups: an Extracurricular/Student Activities Committee, a Special Programs Committee, a Curriculum Committee, and a Home/School Committee. From their efforts emerged a blueprint of the entire school program, which led to the development of four questionnaires which have been and will be distributed to parents, students, teachers, and community members. The data collected will be used to reestablish new objectives for the next several years and become annual assessment instruments for continued program evaluation and change.

Through these efforts Flowing Wells High School has become a dynamic organization with a wide distribution of power and influence. Collaboration has increased and people respect each other's rights to disagree and resolve problems. Individuals feel that each is an integral part of the success of the school and each other. This synergy has resulted in a sense of educational wisdom which has made a difference in the lives of our members.

References

Goodlad, J. I., "Principals Are the Key to Change," *AIGE Forum,* Spring 1977.

Lewis, J., Jr., *Achieving Excellence in Our Schools* (Westbury, NY: J. L. Wilkerson, 1986).

Lipham, J. M., "Change Agentry and School Improvement: The Principal's Role," working paper, November 1979.

Lipham, J. M., and J. C. Daresh, *Administrative and Staff Relationships in Education: Research and Practice in IGE Schools* (Madison: Wisconsin Research and Development Center for Individual Schooling, 1980).

March, J. G., "American Public School Administration: A Short Analysis," unpublished paper, Stanford University, 1978.

Peters, T. J., and R. H. Waterman, Jr., *In Search of Excellence* (New York: Harper & Row, 1982).

Trump, J. L., "Principal Most Potent Factor in Determining School Excellence," *NASSP Bulletin,* March 1972.

John J. Pedicone, Ph.D.
Assistant Superintendent,
Administrative Services

Writing for Everyone

SCOTIA-GLENVILLE HIGH SCHOOL

With the firm conviction that good writing can be achieved at all academic levels, the teachers of English at Scotia-Glenville High School have constructed a writing program that blends several of the contemporary techniques recommended for the teaching of writing. The program incorporates the following components:

- Structured prewriting activities
- Peer support and evaluation through writing groups
- Revision and editing by the individual writer
- Use of writing as a prereading and transition tool
- Community interest and support of writing

For good writing to occur students must learn the importance of a serious, sensitive communal atmosphere. Teachers must write and share their writings and feelings with students. Students must see writing as a process that often begins as a struggle with words. During the prewriting sessions the teachers give the assignment a title, state the instructional objectives, present several prewriting stimuli or activities, and illustrate several approaches to the assignment by using former students' or their own drafts.

Students receive peer support through writing groups. In a cooperative atmosphere, students find writing groups helpful, encouraging, and fun. Writing groups on the high school level work best when students react in written as well as verbal form to each other's work. The writer uses these suggestions during the revision process and must react in writing to suggestions that were not

Reprinted by permission of Mary L. Hardt, Academic Head of English, Scotia-Glenville School District.

incorporated into the final draft. Although peer evaluation is an integral part of almost every assignment in the writing classes, teachers continue to give positive reinforcement and concrete suggestions for improvement by reading draft after draft and offering suggestions for clarity and improvement.

Writing can be a means of transition from student-related concerns to the literature of another time and place. Journal writing serves this purpose. For a journal assignment teachers give a topic or theme relating to a piece of literature. The students complete a journal entry on the theme or topic before reading the assigned piece of literature. After reading the selection, they compare their thoughts and ideas to the author's in another journal entry.

A few years ago, Mrs. Jean Rose taught a Creative Writing Class at the Senior Citizen Meals Center in Scotia. Several of her high school students went with her to this class. The intergenerational communication that developed inspired Mrs. Rose to invite the adults to her writing classes in the fall. She obtained permission from the superintendent of schools and began the fall semester with five senior citizens as regular class members. The adult members attended class twice a week rather than every day and participated in the assignment class and in the writing group. As members of a consistent writing group, they became well acquainted with the students. Initial skepticism on the part of all participants turned to excited enthusiasm. Thus the Interage Creative Writing Class was born. Adult membership has included parents, teachers, and community members in addition to the senior citizens. Class size allows about ten adult members per semester. Adult members receive grades and progress reports for their work. This year an adult received a prize at the Awards Assembly.

An outgrowth of the Interage Creative Writing Class is the Annual Interage Seminar. This is a one-day program held at an off-campus location. Participants include twenty individuals from each of four groups: junior high, high school, age 20–60, age 65+. The day consists of small and large group activities, each designed to help participants examine and share their values and ideas. Activities early in the day are low risk in order to establish group trust. Later activities demand a higher amount of self-disclosure. The activities illustrate similarities and differences within varying age groups. The day fosters discussion, understanding, and new recruits for the Interage Creative Writing Class.

The teachers of English at Scotia-Glenville High School view writing as a valuable process accessible to anyone. Thus, any student who is willing to write and rewrite from group and teacher suggestions will succeed and receive acclaim and reinforcement through grades, writing group support, publication in the literary magazine and yearbook, and placement in contests. Teachers view themselves as successful because they graduate students of widely varying abilities who share joy and satisfaction in writing.

Mary L. Hardt
English Department
Scotia-Glenville High School

The Role of Leadership and Citizenship Education In U.S. Secondary Schools

ST. MARK'S SCHOOL OF TEXAS

In their remarks at the presentation ceremonies for the 1987 Exemplary Secondary School Recognition Awards, both President Reagan and Education Secretary William J. Bennett acknowledged the role of schools in training the leaders of the future. The award application form in the U.S. Constitution's bicentennial year placed extraordinary emphasis on citizenship and civics education. To the extent that the recognized schools have been able to create and implement practical and sequential curricular, co-curricular, and extracurricular programs in leadership and citizenship, they can indeed serve as examples for other schools seeking effective ideas in these areas.

Most schools regard citizenship education as a significant part of their mission, and they hope to produce the "leaders of tomorrow." But when claims in this area are considered critically, they often prove to be mere lip service to the concept, and schools too frequently place students in dependent positions where what they are actually learning is docility and rote acceptance of faculty and administration directives.

The curricular components of citizenship and leadership education are familiar—they consist primarily of strong, imaginative teaching in history and civics, where governmental processes are presented and examples of decent, courageous, effective leadership in the national record are considered.

Extracurricular instruction in these areas is also familiar, consisting most often of involvement with student government and club leadership. But here there are great differences in the degree of

Reprinted by permission of Randall Holdridge, Dean of Students, St. Mark's School of Texas.

commitment schools bring to bear. While many students are restricted to planning pep rallies and proms, in exemplary schools they are engaged substantively in the governance of their institutions, serving on committees, overseeing student discipline, participating in the evaluation and planning of curriculum and other school programs, and working closely with adult leaders on matters that really count.

Some of the most exciting programs in leadership and citizenship education are co-curricular in nature. Complementing the standard curricular offerings, these programs sometimes challenge students to apply the facts and concepts they have learned in the classroom. Often they draw upon community resources not routinely exploited to the advantage of students, and bring into the schools men and women expert in one field or another who find their interactions with students to be novel and stimulating. Some of the really outstanding co-curricular programs are tailor-made, designed explicitly to address current student or institutional interests and needs.

What can be said in every case is that teaching students to be involved and effective leaders means allowing them to lead—giving them responsibilities they can take seriously. And it means running the risk that they may fail. Of course it also calls for much patience on the part of adults working with them, who could often achieve alone in a week's time the results it takes a group of students months to secure. Seeing the process rather than the product as the critical factor is the key to successful citizenship and leadership education in exemplary schools.

Randall Holdridge
Dean of Students

The Academic Coach

LINCOLN COUNTY HIGH SCHOOL

The age of educational reform brought with it numerous opportunities for creative adjustments within schools. School administrators were challenged to develop new strategies that would restore academic integrity to the classrooms. Lincoln County High School had long been recognized for athletic successes. Numerous state championships had been secured and the community has great pride in its "winning tradition." It was this strong athletic tradition that encouraged us to examine a new concept for academic development: the academic coach.

In our community the athletic coach is revered and respected. The overall development and success of our athletic program is due in a great part to his involvement and determination. He will not settle for anything less than excellence!

As a school administrator, I knew we wanted to get that same feeling of commitment and resolve in the instructional areas. My wife once said, "We need someone to coach and encourage academics as much as they do athletics." I ran with her idea.

I began to research other schools to see if an academic coach had ever been tried. I read about one or two programs, but nothing seemed to be exactly what we wanted. Finally, the assistant principal and I drew up what we considered a reasonable job description for an academic coach.

Selling the idea to the superintendent and the Board of Education was much easier than had been anticipated. They readily understood how important it was to get a good coach and how much positive influence a coach could have. (Remember, we have a *strong* tradition of excellent athletic coaches.)

Reprinted by permission of W. Andrew Henderson, Principal, Lincoln County High School, Georgia.

The next step was to find the right person for the job. I explained the position to the entire faculty and interviewed those expressing an interest. A young, enthusiastic English teacher surfaced.

A year after the program was initiated, we were able to start paying our academic coach a supplement, similar to those paid to the athletic coaches. This helped establish the credibility of the program and enabled everyone to see that the school was committed to academic as well as athletic success.

The rest of the story is history. The program has been ultra-successful and much of our academic success can be traced to the leadership and hard work of our academic coach. In 1987, Lincoln County High School won two state championships: one in football *and* one in academic competition. The record speaks for itself!

W. Andrew Henderson
Principal

An outline of the responsibilities of the academic coach at Lincoln County High School appears on the following page.

Academic Coach Responsibilities
Lincoln County High School

I. Academic Publicity
  A. Newspaper articles (minimum of two per month)
  B. Posters around school—constantly stressing academic achievement

II. Coordinating Academic Contests
  A. State Department Essay Contests
  B. U.S. Army Reserve Essay Contest
  C. Coordinating academic competition. Ensuring every discipline is involved in appropriate competition. Working with department heads to keep up-to-date. Competitions including, but not limited to: Quiz Bowl, Georgia History Quiz, Social Science Fair, Math Team, Chemistry, Physics, Science Fair, Spelling Bee, Literary, etc.

III. Record-Keeping for Honor Roll and Honorable Mention
  A. Identifying honor roll and honorable mention students each nine weeks
  B. Article for paper (Re: honor roll/honorable mention)
  C. Updating records year to year for each student making honor roll or honorable mention.
  D. Issuing sweatshirts, T-shirts, and jackets to academic winners
  E. Issuing and monitoring use of gold and white cards

IV. Liaison between School and Academic Booster Club (ABC)
  A. Heading up fund raisers for ABC
  B. Attending all ABC meetings
  C. Working with ABC projects and events

V. Setting Up and Monitoring High School Academic Contests
  A. Homeroom with the highest average
  B. Grade with the highest average
  C. Others (Quiz Bowls, Math Team, Social Science Fair, etc.)

VI. Working with Academic Banquet Committee

VII. Coordinating Honor's Day Program

VIII. Conducting "How to Study" Workshops for Eighth-Grade Minicourse

IX. Coordinating and Monitoring All Facets of the After-School Study Hall Program

X. Being responsible for Coordinating One Assembly per Year, with Emphasis on Academic Improvement, Study Skills, Motivation, etc.

Developing Self-Discipline and Self-Esteem

GEORGETOWN VISITATION PREPARATORY SCHOOL

As I began to write this essay, a student dropped by my office to thank me for a pleasant school year. While speaking with her it suddenly occurred to me that it would be more credible to hear the school's philosophy of discipline articulated by one of its students rather than by its headmistress.

The young woman in question has spent three years under the tutelage of Georgetown Visitation and, after faithful service on the school's Honor Board, has been elected its president for the next school year. Her reply to my query about discipline is interesting.

Jennifer finds discipline to be a subtle factor in school life. Rules are not multiplied and those that do exist help students to develop a sense of self-discipline. Long litanies of "do's and don'ts" are unnecessary because students are aware of the behavior expected of them. Those who risk rule infractions understand the consequences of their actions. Through her personal experience of serving on the Honor Board, Jennifer believes that participation on this and the Board of Student Conduct helps to bring discipline "down among" the students rather than having it superimposed from on high.

After speaking with Jennifer, I discovered two other dimensions of Visitation's attempts to foster self-discipline in the address given by Kate, one of our recent graduates, during the commencement exercises. Kate told her audience that the values education at Georgetown Visitation is a powerful factor in the development

Reprinted by permission of Georgetown Visitation Preparatory School, Washington, DC 20007.

271

of self-discipline. Courses such as Bioethics and Peace and Justice Studies have "readied students for the inevitable moral decisions that await them in the future." Kate also pinpointed a second all-important element in this process in these words: "The idea that service to others is an integral part of a complete education is one which Visitation has genuinely instilled in us." When pondering the words that best describe the spirit of the school, Kate mentioned "honesty, integrity, trust, understanding, depth, love, laughter, and happiness."

My third contributor of ideas on self-discipline is a graduate of the early 1980s who, in an essay for the school catalogue, zeroes in on the notion of responsibility. I quote Francine: "In the process of education perhaps nothing is more valuable than the acceptance of responsibility. Visitation's Honor Code places the burden of personal integrity squarely upon every student's shoulders, leaving the choices and inherent consequences of these choices hinging upon each one's decision. Efforts toward achieving standards of acceptable behavior strive to develop self-direction, personal character, and mutual caring."

From these student comments we may glean three primary ingredients in building self-discipline and, concurrently, self-esteem in a school community. Education is essential. The reasons behind school rules must be explained, while the rules themselves must be reduced to the minimum necessary for ensuring order. To be most effective, the rules should be centered upon a value such as respect—for oneself, for other individuals, and for the community at large.

A second important factor is to allow students an active role in the process of setting appropriate norms of discipline and in handling abuses or infractions. Participation in this manner leads to a sense of ownership, which, in turn, strengthens the process.

Finally, all efforts should be centered on creating an environment within the school community calling students forth from the narrow confines of their personal lives to an understanding of their responsibility to serve others, both within and beyond the school community. Service of others is the most effective way of nurturing self-esteem and self-discipline.

In the area of drug and alcohol abuse the same principles apply. Educating in partnership with parents through open discussion, entrusting students with responsibilities for developing guidelines for student behavior at social events, and opening the eyes of our young people to the pitfalls of selfish behavior—all contribute to a higher degree of maturity, which is founded on the solid rock of self-discipline and self-direction.

Sister Mary Berchmans Hannan
Headmistress

Empowering Teachers

ADLAI E. STEVENSON HIGH SCHOOL

"Empowerment" has been defined as "the degree to which the opportunity to use power effectively is granted or withheld from individuals" (Kanter, 1983). More simply, it is the opportunity to act upon one's ideas. The concept of empowerment has been embraced by outstanding companies. Almost without exception, these companies have shifted the concept of employee from one who carries out orders to one who takes responsibility and initiative, monitors his or her own work, and uses supervisors as facilitators and consultants. They have realized that the people who know the most about any job are those doing it. Unfortunately, the concept of empowerment has generally not been embraced by school leaders. A recent survey ("Teachers Want More Control," 1986) of 8,500 teachers revealed that only 28 percent of them could be classified as empowered. More than 85 percent of the respondents believed the quality of instruction would improve if they were allowed to increase their involvement in curriculum decisions.

If schools are to make teacher empowerment the basis of school improvement as the Carnegie Foundation has recommended, school administrators must embrace Charles Garfield's finding (1986) that "power given is power gained" and find ways to empower their teachers. Here are some specific ideas for increasing teacher involvement in key areas.

1. *Developing the Curriculum.* Teachers who will be responsible for delivering a curriculum should play a major role in its development.

Reprinted by permission of Dr. Richard P. DuFour. For more information on empowerment, see Richard DuFour and Robert Eaker, *Fulfilling the Promise of Excellence* (Westbury, NY: Wilkerson Press, 1987).

2. *Assessing Student Achievement.* If locally developed tests are to be used, teachers should work collectively to develop them. If standardized achievement tests are to be used, teachers should help select the tests that best fit the school curriculum.

3. *Selecting Instructional Materials.* Teachers who will use particular textbooks, equipment, and materials should have the major voice in their selection.

4. *Planning and Presenting Staff Development Programs.*

5. *Determining Instructional Styles and Strategies.* Although a principal can and should establish parameters for classroom instruction, those parameters should stop short of mandating particular teaching strategies. As Ted Sizer observed, "Autonomy is an essential condition for effective teaching." Day-to-day instructional decisions should remain with the teacher.

6. *Scheduling.* Scheduling is a bone of contention at all levels of public schooling. Why shouldn't teachers be invited to make these decisions collectively? Not only would they better understand the difficulties inherent in scheduling, but their collective deliberations might result in workable ways of resolving some of those difficulties.

7. *Hiring New Staff.* Teachers should play a role in the interviewing and selection of colleagues, particularly if they will be called on to work closely with the new staff members.

8. *Mentoring.* Veteran teachers can play a key role in assisting new teachers learn the procedures and culture of a school. Mentors can also serve as peer coaches who observe colleagues in the classroom and give them feedback on their teaching.

Empowerment is not simply turning teachers loose and hoping for the best. It is providing a clear structure which enables them to work within established parameters in creative and autonomous ways. The challenge confronting today's school administrator is to establish these parameters and then encourage teachers to operate within them.

References

Garfield, Charles, *Peak Performers: The New Heroes of American Business* (New York: William Morris, 1986), p. 182.

Kanter, Rosabeth Moss, *The Change Masters* (New York: Simon and Schuster, 1983), p. 18.

Sizer, Theodore, "The Student-Teacher Triad," in *In Honor of Excellence* (Reston, VA: National Association of Secondary School Principals).

"Teachers Want More Control of the Work Place ... But Only One-Fourth Are Empowered," *Education U.S.A.*, April 21, 1986, p. 4.

Dr. Richard P. DuFour
Principal/Assistant Superintendent for Instruction

Community Schools

POOLESVILLE JUNIOR-SENIOR HIGH SCHOOL

Space in Montgomery County Public Schools is available for rent to all commercial and nonprofit groups and individuals. The Community Use of Schools Program is a service provided through an Interagency Coordinating Board in cooperation with the county government and the schools. The board is composed of citizen and public agency members who coordinate policies and procedures for the community use of school facilities.

Each community school is staffed with an activities coordinator who plans and schedules building use and acts as a liaison with the school, community, and public service providers. A Community School Advisory Council is maintained in each location. The council and coordinator assess community needs to suggest activities and to seek agencies to provide service.

The Poolesville Community School serves a region located 40 miles from Washington, D.C. The school is located in a small town surrounded by rural areas. Unlike other Montgomery County communities, our location has very few public resources. The school and community share a single library facility. The Health Clinic is open only a few hours weekly, and a limited commuter bus service is the only public transportation available. There are no movie theaters, fast food restaurants, or shopping malls where students can meet their peers to enjoy leisure time. Consequently, the school campus and activities are central to the social as well as the academic life of a typical Poolesville youth.

Operating seven days a week, the community school provides civic, cultural, and recreational activities to suit many ages and interests. Agricultural and family fun fairs have attracted crowds. Recent performances by Up with People packed the auditorium.

Reprinted by permission of Terrill Meyer, Principal, Poolesville Junior-Senior High School, Montgomery County, Maryland.

Young adolescents have been drawn to an after-school drop-in center and after-school sessions in snack preparation, computer use, and fashion/cosmetics. Additional child care services for the community school cluster will be offered at the neighboring elementary school.

The benefits of serving as the community center are manifold. Not only is space utilized wisely, but a sense of belonging is established in many who might otherwise feel disassociated with the school. Operating 17 hours a day allows those with odd hours and rigorous work schedules to still find a time when the school is open to them. Photographs and displays allow all who pass through the facility to be informed about school happenings and student accomplishments. The intergenerational mixture attending many community school activities is exhilarating. Best of all, school personnel, students, and community members feel a closeness prized in a transient region such as the one we abut.

Terrill Meyer
Principal

Index

A. Philip Randolph Campus High
   School
  basic skills program at, 87
  community resources of, 182
  community service at, 71
  courses on democracy at, 50
  extra credit at, 96
  goal statement of, 8
  learning about law at, 49
  writing support staff at, 40
Academy of Mount St. Ursula
  goals of, 6
  parent education program at, 175
  teacher honors at, 157
Academy of Notre Dame de Namur
  community service at, 69
  courses on democracy at, 50
  on drugs, 113
  goals of, 5
  people as success of, 198
Academy of Our Lady of Good
   Counsel
  global view at, 46
  goal statement of, 10
  honors from, 95
  learning about law at, 54
  success of, 195
Adlai E. Stevenson High School
  goal statement of, 8
  parent participation in, 166
  on rules and policies, 101
  staff development for, 151
  students at risk at, 136
  study skills materials at, 82
  writing curriculum of, 29

Administration, high expectations of,
  93–94
After-school work (ASW), 104
Alaska Writing Consortium Project,
  32
Alcohol, students and, 113–114
Alexander Hamilton High School
  on rewards for teaching, 162
  writing curriculum of, 29
Alfred Bonnabel High School
  basic skills program at, 87
  community event at, 186
  high expectations of, 92
  human resources of, 180
  students at risk at, 137
  writing curriculum of, 30, 31
Alumni, 203
Archbishop Chapelle High School,
  parent participation in, 174
Archbishop Keough High School,
  students at risk at, 132
Archbishop Molloy High School
  communicating goals at, 15, 16
  community service at, 68
  parent education program of, 175
  staff development for, 150
  study skills courses at, 77
  writing support staff of, 40
Armed Services Vocational Aptitude
  Battery (ASVAB), 123
Assignments, writing, 30–31
Athletics, 64
Atmosphere, 193–195
At-risk students
  identifying, 130–132

At-risk students *(continued)*
  services for, 132–137
Audubon Junior High School, incentive program of, 97

Baboquivari Junior High School
  assessing writing competency at, 25
  goal statement of, 12
  incentive program of, 97
Ballard High School
  basic skills program at, 87
  community partnership with, 187
  goal statement of, 9
  parent participation in, 173
  specialized writing program at, 42
  writing lab of, 37
Basic skills, students and, 83–89
Bay Area Writing Project, 32
Ben Davis Junior High School, career
  program of, 128
Benjamin Elijah Mays High School
  basic skills program at, 88
  career program of, 128
  parent participation in, 170
  social science fairs at, 55
  staff development for, 152
Blind Brook High School
  college prep services of, 125
  on drugs, 115
  global view at, 46
  outreach activity of, 188
  rules of, 61
  staff development for, 151
  students and discipline policies of,
    100
  study skills courses at, 78
  writing across the curriculum at, 26
  writing curriculum of, 31
Blue Springs Junior High School
  honors from, 95
  writing across the curriculum at, 26
Bonn American High School
  faculty training in writing at, 32
  in foreign location, 57
Boyland Central Catholic High School
  communicating goals at, 16

writing across the curriculum at,
  24
Bradley Central High School
  communicating goals at, 18
  course offerings of, 196
  on rules and policies, 101
  teacher honors at, 157
Bradley Middle School, on drugs, 111
Brighton High School
  assessing writing competency at, 25
  community service at, 67
  faculty committees of, 141
  goals of, 5
  special projects of, 186
Broadmoor Middle Laboratory
    School, learning about law at, 48
Brookwood High School
  counseling program of, 128–129
  on drugs, 110
  specialized writing program at, 42
  staff development for, 152
Brother Martin High School
  parent education program at, 175
  staff development for, 153
  writing curriculum of, 29
Brown Middle School, high expectations of, 92
Burns Union High School
  goal statement of, 8
  progress reports of, 119
  teacher input at, 144
  teacher-developed policies of, 100
Business Partnership Board, 5
Business partnerships, 181–183
Butte des Morts Junior High School,
  18

CAL High School, success of, 194
California Writing Project, 32
Capital High School, students at risk
  at, 131–132
Cardinal Gibbons High School
  prep services of, 127
  community service at, 70
  goal monitoring at, 13
  specialized reports of, 118

Cardinal Gibbons High School
(continued)
teacher input at, 143
writing curriculum of, 28
Career days, 124
Career information, 122–129
Career programs, 180–181
Cate School
counseling at, 122
teacher input at, 145
writing across the curriculum at, 26
writing lab of, 37
Cayucos School
parent participation in, 172
teacher input at, 145
Centennial Senior High School
communicating goals at, 15
as community school, 189
on drugs, 111
faculty committees of, 142
program as success of, 200
visiting teachers at, 57
writing curriculum of, 30
Central Catholic High School
courses on democracy at, 50
staff development for, 149
Central High School (Pennsylvania)
high expectations of, 92
special event as success of, 203
Central High School (South Dakota)
basic skills program at, 84
communicating goals at, 18
on drugs, 111
goals review at, 14
parent participation in, 176
people as success of, 198
student discipline at, 104
students at risk at, 131
Central High School (Tennessee)
goals of, 6
student discipline at, 103
Champaign Middle School at
Columbia, teacher input at, 143
Chandler High School
assessing writing competency at, 25
on drugs, 110

faculty training in writing at, 33
financial support of, 179
goals review at, 14
high expectations of, 91
Character and values
co-curricular programs, 63–64
and community service, 64–71
policies and procedures, 59–63
special programs, 71–74
Charlotte Latin School
community service at, 69
economics courses at, 49
faculty training in writing at, 34
goals of, 7
parent participation in, 171
role models at, 62
Cibola High School
business partnership with, 184
peer counseling at, 72
students at risk at, 131
teacher awards from, 158
writing guide of, 35
Claremont High School
basic skills program at, 86
career center at, 125
goals of, 4
parent participation in, 168
program on self-esteem at, 72
Clear Lake High School
on character and values, 60
goal statement of, 8
parent participation in, 176
writing across the curriculum at, 26
Cleveland State University's National
Writing Project, 33
Close-Up program, 53
Clovis High School
on drugs, 114
parent participation in, 167
students at risk at, 135
study skills materials at, 82
Clubs
and community service projects, 70
and organizations, 63
Co-curricular programs, 63–64
College days, 124

College information, 122–129
Community
  business and partnerships with,
    181–185
  communicating goals to, 17–18
  cooperative efforts with, 185–188
  financial support, 178–179
  human resources from, 179–180
  involving the,
  job and career programs with,
    180–181
  learning about, 47
  outreach activities, 188–189
  service programs, 64–71
Computer labs, 36–38
Computer services, on college and
  careers, 124
Contests, writing, 31
Couch Middle School, on drugs and
  alcohol, 115
Counseling
  career, 122–123
  guidance, 81
  peer, 72–73
Courses, 196–197
Cranbrook Kingswood School
  goal statement of, 10
  teacher awards from, 160
Creighton Preparatory School
  basic skills program at, 84
  career information from, 127
  community service at, 64
  goals of, 5
Crest Senior High School
  athletics at, 64
  communicating goals at, 17
  goals review at, 14
  staff development for, 154
  teacher-developed policies of,
    100
  writing guide of, 35
Curriculum
  planning, 5
  study skills across the, 80–81
  writing, 27–32
  writing across the, 22–27

D. Russell Parks Junior High School
  teaching honors from, 159
  writing lab of, 36
Dalton Junior High School, school
  motto of, 61
Daniel Wright Middle School, parent
  participation in, 168
Darien High School
  college and career center at, 125
  incentive program of, 97
  parent participation in, 170
  resource persons at, 181
  writing program at, 30, 38, 39
Deer Path Junior High School
  basic skills testing at, 84
  study skills courses at, 79
Delphi Plan, 6
Democracy
  elective courses, 48–51
  models and simulations, 51–52
  required courses, 45–48
  special programs, 52–58
Denbigh High School
  assessing writing competency at,
    24
  students at risk at, 136
Desert Shadows Middle School, goal
  statement of, 9
Designated Vocational Instructor
  (DVI) program, at Lincoln High
  School, 128
Discipline
  expectations, consequences, and
    rewards of, 103–107
  responsibilities for, 102–103
  rules and policies for, 99–101
Dobson High School
  accelerated curriculum of, 96
  clubs and organizations of, 63
  faculty training in writing at, 34
  financial support of, 179
  human resources of, 179
  parent participation in, 167
  staff development for, 152
  writing lab at, 36
Dobson High Writing Project, 34

Dooley School
  goals of, 4
  students at risk at, 136
Dover High School
  study skills courses at, 78
  writing across the curriculum at, 23
Dr. Roland N. Patterson Intermediate School 229
  challenges of, 203
  faculty training at, 34
  progress reports of, 118
  staff development for, 149
Dropouts. *See* At-risk students
Drugs
  education on, 110–111
  parent and student participation regarding, 113–115
  program on, 109–111
  and school and community climate, 115
  staff participation and training regarding, 111–113
Dublin Middle School
  student discipline at, 106
  success of, 194
Dwight-Englewood School
  basic skills program at, 87
  clubs and organizations at, 63
  learning about law at, 48
  writing curriculum of, 29

East High School
  course in American military history at, 51
  writing across the curriculum at, 23
Economics courses, 49
Edgar Martin Middle School, incentive program of, 97
Edgewood High School of the Sacred Heart
  Close-Up program at, 53
  parent participation in, 171
  writing curriculum of, 29, 31
Education, on drugs, 110–111
Eighth-grade orientation, 123

Elective courses, on democracy, 48–51
Episcopal High School
  human resources of, 180
  students and discipline policies of, 100
  writing curriculum of, 29
Episcopal School of Acadiana
  honors from, 95
  study skills courses at, 80
  writing curriculum of, 30
Evergreen Junior High School
  honors from, 95
  writing curriculum of, 31
Expectations. *See* High expectations
Extra credit, 96

Facilities and services, 195
Faculty
  committees, 141–142
  communicating goals to, 16
  discipline policies developed by, 100
  high expectations of, 93–94
  training in teaching writing, 32–35
  See also Teachers
Fairfield College Preparatory School, community service at, 66
Ferndale Elementary School, teacher awards from, 160
Ferndale High School
  on drugs, 112
  people as success of, 199
  staff development for, 154
  study skills program at, 81
  writing across the curriculum at, 23
Financial support, 178
Firsthand experience, 47
Flowing Wells High School
  communicating goals at, 16
  community service at, 66
  global view at, 46
  goals of, 4, 10
  parent participation in, 166
  on rules and policies, 101

Flowing Wells High School
    (continued)
    staff development for, 154
    teacher input at, 144
Franklin High School
    Bicentennial celebration at, 54
    community service at, 71
    progress reports of, 120
    teacher honors at, 157
Fremont Senior High School
    basic skills program at, 86
    goal statement of, 11

Garden City Senior High School
    career program of, 127
    courses on democracy at, 51
    on drugs, 110
    extra credit at, 96
    faculty training in writing at, 32
Garger High School
    Close-Up program at, 53
    faculty training in writing at, 34
    human resources of, 180
    incentive program of, 97
    learning about law at, 48
    student discipline records of, 103
    writing across the curriculum at, 26
Gatesville Elementary School, on
        drugs, 114
Georgetown Visitation Preparatory
        School
    community service at, 65
    goals of, 4, 11
    study skills courses at, 80
Geyser Public School
    Close-Up program at, 53
    on drugs, 115
    global view at, 46
    goal statement of, 8
Gladstone High School
    career information from, 127
    communicating goals at, 17
    community service at, 71
    goals of, 6
    high expectations of, 91
    parent participation in, 173

    teacher honors at, 157
    teacher input at, 144
    writing promotion at, 44
Goals
    categories of, 11–12
    communicating, 14–18
    monitoring and revision of, 12–14
    planning, 3–7
    statement of, 7–12
    writing and school, 22–27
Granby Memorial Middle School,
        community service at, 70
Great Valley High School
    parent participation, 166
    specialized writing program at, 43
    staff development for, 149
Greater Phoenix Area Writing
        Project, 33
Greely High School
    community service at, 68
    faculty training in writing at, 32
    financial support of, 179
    progress reports of, 116
    teaching awards at, 162
Greenway Middle School, communi-
        cating goals at, 17
Gretchen Whitney High School
    college prep services of, 125
    community service at, 69
    parent participation in, 174, 176
    staff development for, 153
    teacher input at, 145
    writing across the curriculum at, 23
Guidance counselors, 81
Guides, for teaching writing, 35–36

Harold S. Vincent High School,
        study skills materials at, 82
Harvard Milton Academy, study
        skills program at, 82
Harwood Junior High School, com-
        munity service at, 66
Haverford Senior High School
    basic skills program at, 89
    communicating goals of, 17
    faculty training in writing at, 33

Haverford Senior High School
 (continued)
 learning about law at, 49
 staff development for, 150
 students at risk at, 132
 teacher honors at, 158
 writing promotions at, 43
Haywood High School
 communicating goals at, 16
 on rules and policies, 101
 writing across the curriculum at,
 26
Henderson High School
 community service at, 69
 motto of, 90
 students at risk at, 132
 teacher honors at, 157
High expectations
 as clear messages, 90–94
 as special honors and incentives,
 95–98
Hines Middle School, teacher honors
 and awards at, 157
Historical anniversaries, 54
Holy Trinity Diocesan High School
 on drugs, 112
 teacher input at, 146
 writing across the curriculum at, 23
Homestead High School
 assessing writing competency at, 25
 communicating goals at, 16
 high expectations of, 93
Honors and incentives, 95–98
Horace Mann Academic Middle
 School, basic skills program at,
 88
Human resources, 179–180

Incentives, for teachers, 156–162
Information, college and career,
 122–129
In-school suspension (ISS), 104
In-service, writing program, 33–35
Intervention
 on drugs, 110–111
 for students at risk, 134

Involvement, community, 4–6
Irving A. Robbins Junior High
 School
 parent participation in, 168
 teaching awards at, 162

Jackson Hole High School
 students at risk at, 137
 teacher input at, 143
 writing support staff of, 40
James Logan High School
 cheating policy at, 61
 goal monitoring at, 13
 parent participation in, 169, 175
 teacher input at, 143
 writing guide of, 36
James Madison Junior High School
 outreach activity of, 188
 success of, 194
Jefferson Junior High School, career
 program at, 127
Jesuit High School (Florida)
 basic skills program at, 86
 parent participation in, 168
Jesuit High School New Orleans,
 study skills courses at, 78
John Adams Middle School
 career information from, 127
 community resources of, 182
 goals of, 6
 success of, 194

Kate Griffin Junior High School,
 honors from, 95
Kesling Middle School, basic skills
 program at, 85
King Philip Middle School, firsthand
 experience at, 47
Kinston High School
 community service at, 67
 parent participation in, 174
 special event as success of, 203
Kirby-Smith Junior High School,
 rules of, 60
Koda Junior High School, clubs and
 organizations at, 63

Laboratory programs in basic skills, 85
Lakeridge High School
  on alcohol and drugs, 114
  community service at, 68
  course offerings of, 196
  goal monitoring at, 13
  parent participation in, 174
  progress reports of, 117
  staff development for, 152
  study skills materials at, 82
  teachers' monetary rewards at, 161
  teaching honors from, 159
  writing across the curriculum at, 23
  writing lab of, 37
Lamphere High School
  communicating goals at, 15
  community service at, 67
  goals of, 5
  specialized reports of, 118
  students at risk at, 137
  writing lab of, 36
Lansing Catholic Central High School
  special event as success of, 202
  teacher input at, 145
Larson Middle School
  progress reports of, 117
  tutoring writing at, 38
Law, learning about, 48–49, 53–54
Lawton Community High School
  communicating goals at, 15
  as community school, 189
  goals of, 5
  motto of, 91
  role models at, 62
  student discipline at, 105
Library media specialists, 81
Lincoln County High School
  communicating goals at, 15
  community resources of, 182
  incentive program of, 97
  progress reports of, 120
  specialized reports of, 118
  student discipline records of, 103
Lincoln High School
  basic skills program at, 88

career program of, 128
people as success of, 199
Literacy Network, 33
Londonderry High School
  Bicentennial program at, 54
  on drugs, 112
  learning about community at, 47
  program as success of, 199
  writing curriculum of, 29
Los Altos Intermediate School, learning about law at, 53
Los Gatos High School
  basic skills program at, 85
  financial support of, 179
  parent participation in, 169
  role models at, 62
  on student behavior, 102
  teacher awards from, 158, 161
Louisville Writing Project, 32
Loyola High School of Baltimore, Inc.
  goal statement of, 8, 11
  people as success of, 198
  teaching awards from, 162
  writing program at, 39
Lutheran High School North, learning about law at, 48
Lutheran High School West
  courses on democracy at, 50
  goals of, 6
  progress reports of, 117
Lynnhaven Junior High School
  basic skills program at, 86
  study skills courses at, 80

McQuaid Jesuit High School
  college and career center at, 125
  communicating goals at, 16
  community service at, 68
  incentive program of, 97
  parent participation in, 172
  program as success of, 200
  remedial writing at, 40
  staff development for, 153
  on student behavior, 102
  writing curriculum of, 30

McQuaid Jesuit High School
  (continued)
  writing program at, 39
  writing promotions at, 43
Madeira School
  community service at, 66
  course offerings of, 197
  intern program of, 57, 181
  teachers' monetary rewards at, 162
Mahomet-Seymour High School
  on drugs, 108
  staff development for, 154
  student discipline at, 107
Management, team approach to, 4
Marion Heights Academy, writing
  curriculum of, 31
Marist High School (Illinois)
  basic skills program at, 84
  students at risk at, 130
  writing lab of, 37
Marist School (Georgia)
  staff development for, 153
  writing curriculum of, 27
Mars Hill Bible School
  basic skills program at, 86
  parent participation in, 174
  staff development for, 154
  teacher-developed policies of, 100
Martin Kellogg Middle School,
  global view at, 47
Maryhurst High School
  challenges of, 204
  faculty training in writing at, 32
  student discipline at, 105
Master teacher program, 161
Materials, for teaching writing,
  35–36
Meany Middle School, study skills
  courses at, 80
Menlo-Atherton High School
  goals of, 5
  staff development for, 154
  writing and school goals at, 22
  writing support staff at, 39
Mentor Shore Junior High School,
  communicating goals at, 18

Mentor teacher program, 161
Mesa Union School, goal statement
  of, 12
Metairie Park Country Day School
  communicating goals at, 17
  course offerings of, 197
  goals of, 4
  parent participation in, 169
  study skills courses at, 80
  writing across the curriculum at, 26
Middletown High School
  basic skills program at, 88
  on character and values, 73
  college prep services of, 126
  communicating goals at, 16
  high expectations of, 94
  on monitoring attendance, 119
  progress reports of, 120
  social studies debates at, 55
Midwood High School at Brooklyn
  College
  community service at, 67
  goal monitoring at, 13
  high expectations of, 92
  learning about law at, 49
  model Congress of, 51
  parent participation in, 175
  students at risk at, 137
  writing promotion at, 43
Millard North Junior High School,
  firsthand experience at, 47
Miller Junior High School
  patriotic program at, 55
  writing promotion at, 43
Milton High School
  on drugs and alcohol, 113, 114
  eighth-grade orientation at, 123
  mentor teacher program of, 161
  special projects of, 186
  writing program at, 39
Miramonte High School
  athletics at, 64
  career center at, 125
  parent participation in, 174
Mission San Jose High School
  as community school, 189

Mission San Jose High School
  (*continued*)
  parent participation in, 166, 172
Moanalua High School
  students at risk at, 136
  teacher awards from, 160
  teacher input at, 145
  writing lab of, 37
Models, national and international,
  51–52
Montgomery County Schools, goal
  statements of, 11
Mooresville Junior High School,
  principal's role at, 62
Mother Cabrini High School
  challenges of, 204
  communicating goals at, 18
  high expectations of, 94
  parent participation in, 166
  on student behavior, 102
Mother McAuley Liberal Arts High
  School
  at History Fair, 55
  parent participation in, 171
  writing across the curriculum at, 24
Mottoes, 90–91
Mount Notre Dame High School
  at model United Nations, 51
  peer counseling at, 72
  special event as success of, 203
  students at risk at, 131
Mount Vernon High School
  clubs and organizations at, 63
  on monitoring attendance, 119
  parent participation in, 174
  study skills materials at, 82
  teacher awards at, 158
Myers Park High School
  cheating policy at, 61
  college prep services of, 126
  communicating goals at, 17
  community resources of, 183
  economics courses at, 49
  facilities and services of, 195
  student discipline at, 105
  teacher honors at, 157

  tutoring writing at, 38
  writing across the curriculum at,
    24

Narragansett High School
  college prep services of, 126
  goals of, 5
  on school's role in community, 178
  success of, 194
  teacher input at, 144
Nether Providence Middle School,
    faculty training in writing at, 32
Newburgh Free Academy
  communicating goals at, 15
  learning about law at, 49, 53
  student discipline at, 104
  study skills materials at, 82
  teacher awards from, 158, 160
Newton County High School
  business partnership with, 183
  course offerings of, 197
  faculty training in writing at, 35
  goals of, 5
  writing and school goals at, 22
  writing program at, 38
Norland Middle School, goals of, 5
North Bend High School
  on drugs, 112
  parent participation in, 172
  progress reports of, 118
  study skills materials at, 82
North Olmsted High School
  basic skills testing at, 84
  communicating goals at, 17
  faculty training in writing at, 33
  on student behavior, 102
  study skills materials at, 82
North Salem Middle School
  staff development for, 150
  writing support staff at, 40
Northern Highlands Regional High
  School
  communicating goals at, 15
  on drugs, 112
  extra credit at, 96
  parent participation in, 172

Northern Highlands Regional High
  School *(continued)*
  staff development for, 154
  students at risk at, 134
Northern Nevada Writing Project, 35
Northfield Mount Hermon School
  community service at, 71
  courses on democracy at, 50
  remedial writing at, 40
  study skills courses at, 78
Novi High School
  community event at, 186
  goals of, 5
  parent participation in, 168
  progress reports of, 119
Novi Task Force on Excellence, goals
  of, 5

Oak Grove High School
  Close-Up program at, 53
  high expectations of, 91
  learning about community at, 47
  teacher input at, 144
Oak Grove Junior High School, goal
  statement of, 12
Objectives. *See* Goals
O'Fallon Township High School
  college prep services of, 126
  course offerings of, 197
  parent participation in, 171
  students at risk at, 135
  writing across the curriculum at, 24
Ogden Junior High School, in-service
  training for, 151
Ohio Writing Project, 33
Oldham County High School
  community partnership with, 187
  goals of, 6
  learning local government at, 52
  student discipline at, 106
  writing curriculum of, 30
Oliver Wendell Holmes Junior High
  School, parent education program at, 176
Olympus Junior High School, on
  drugs, 111

Oneida Middle School
  progress reports of, 118
  remedial writing at, 41
  success of, 193
Orange Glen High School
  career program of, 180
  goals review at, 13
  incentive program of, 97
  parent participation in, 170
  study skills courses at, 78
  teaching awards from, 160
Organizations, clubs and, 63
Orientation, eighth-grade, 123
Our Lady of Lourdes Academy,
  parent participation in, 170
Outreach programs, 70–71, 181

Palmer Junior High School, near
  Human Historic District, 56
Palms Junior High School, debating
  society at, 55
Palo Alto High School
  community resources of, 182
  global view at, 46
  goal monitoring at, 13
  peer counseling at, 72
  staff development for, 153
  students at risk at, 136
  writing lab of, 37
Parcells Middle School, study skills
  program at, 81
Parents
  booster groups of, 172–174
  committees and advisory groups
    of, 166–169
  communicating goals to, 16–17
  education programs for, 175–176
  meetings and open houses with,
    165–166
  newsletters, mailings, and surveys
    for, 166
  special events for, 174–175
  and student achievement, 94
  in volunteer programs, 169–172
Parkway Central High School
  community service at, 70

Parkway Central High School
  (continued)
  faculty committees of, 142
  goal statement of, 12
  parent participation in, 171
  program as success of, 200
Parkway South High School
  community resources of, 182
  course offerings of, 196
  courses on democracy at, 50
  discipline policy of, 100
  goals of, 4
  honors from, 95
  remedial writing at, 41
  students at risk at, 131
  teacher awards at, 158
  writing lab of, 37
Paul J. Gelinas Junior High School,
  parent participation in, 170
Peer counseling, 72–73
Peer tutoring, 38
Pennsylvania Writing Project, 33
Petersburg High School
  faculty training in writing at, 32
  simulated local government at,
    52
  student discipline at, 106
  teaching honors from, 159
Petoskey Middle School
  program as success of, 200
  writing curriculum of, 30
Phi Delta Kappa, 6
Philadelphia High School for Girls
  communicating goals at, 17
  goals of, 7
  staff development for, 149
  study skills courses at, 80
Philosophy, 193–195
  statement of, 4
Pittsford Middle School
  specialized reports of, 118
  writing curriculum of, 28
Planning, and goals, 3–7
Policies
  on character and values, 59–62
  clear rules and, 99

Polk Middle School, communicating
  goals at, 17
Pompton Lakes High School
  college preparatory skills courses
    at, 79
  simulated local government at, 52
Poolesville Junior-Senior High
  School
  college prep services of, 125
  communicating goals at, 15
  community service at, 67
  goal statement of, 11
  rules of, 60
  on student behavior, 102
Principal, portrait of, 205–211
Proctor Hug High School
  business partnership with, 184
  clubs and organizations at, 63
  global view at, 46
  goals review at, 13
  incentive program of, 97
  teacher honors at, 158
  writing guide of, 35
Programs, 199–201
Promotions, 41–44
Providence Day School
  faculty training in writing at, 34
  Great Decisions program at, 56

Reports, 116–121
Resources and support, for teaching
  writing, 35–40
Rewards, for teachers, 156–162
Ridge High School
  college prep services of, 126
  goals of, 6
  study skills courses at, 78, 80
Ridgewood High School
  college prep services of, 126
  policies of, 61
  student discipline at, 105
  students at risk at, 137
  teacher input at, 143
  writing program at, 39
Rock Bridge Senior High School
  business partnership with, 184

Rock Bridge Senior High School
(continued)
on drugs and alcohol, 114
goals review at, 14
motto of, 91
parent participation in, 166
teaching awards at, 162
Role models, 62
principals as, 207–208
Rules
developing clear, 99
for teaching character and values,
60–62

S. S. Murphy High School
goals review at, 13
patriotic graduations at, 56
staff development for, 150
teacher input at, 144
writing curriculum of, 31
Sage Valley Junior High School, goal
statement of, 8
Saint Bernard-Elmwood Place High
School
basic skills program at, 88
business partnership with, 184
faculty training in writing at, 33
goals review at, 13
incentive program of, 97
staff development for, 149
teacher awards at, 158
Saint John's School
community service at, 69
goals of, 4
program as success of, 201
Santa Fe Indian School, on drugs, 111
Scarborough Senior High School
assessing writing competency at, 25
communicating goals at, 16
parent participation in, 171
progress reports of, 117
on rules and policies, 101
special event as success of, 202
staff development for, 149
Schenley High School Teacher Center
communicating goals at, 17

program as success of, 199
specialized writing program at, 41
students at risk at, 133
School Improvement Unit, 4
Scotia-Glenville High School
course in sports history at, 51
guidance course at, 81
high expectations of, 93
learning about law at, 48
writing promotion at, 43
Scranton Preparatory School
community service at, 65
course offerings of, 196
high expectations of, 91
writing guides of, 35
Seth Low Intermediate School 96,
community service at, 68
Sheboygan South High School
students at risk at, 132
teacher awards from, 160–161
teacher input at, 146
writing support staff at, 39
Shiloh Middle School, teacher-
developed policies of, 100
Shoreham-Wading River High School
career program of, 180
clubs and organizations at, 63
community service at, 68
courses on democracy at, 50
goals review at, 14
staff development for, 151
on student behavior, 103
Shulamith High School for Girls
clubs and organizations of, 63
at model United Nations, 51
moral awareness at, 72
parent education program at, 175
student discipline at, 104
teachers' financial bonuses at, 162
writing curriculum of, 31
Simulations, local government, 52
Skowhegan Area High School
assessing writing competency at, 25
on drugs, 109–110
goals of, 6
speakers' program at, 55

South Burlington Middle School
  people as success of, 198
  student discipline at, 105
South Kingstown High School
  assessing writing competency at, 25
  courses on democracy at, 50
  goal statement of, 11
  high expectations of, 92
  parent participation in, 168
  program as success of, 201
  teacher honors at, 157
  writing and school goals at, 22
South Salem High School
  on drugs and alcohol, 114
  facilities and services of, 195
  faculty committees of, 142
  goal monitoring at, 13
  progress reports of, 116
  teacher awards at, 158
South View Junior High School, goal
    statement of, 12
South Winnishiek Senior High School
  basic skills program at, 87
  Citizens of the Month at, 57
Southside High School, parent
    participation in, 167, 169
Southside Junior High School,
    advanced social studies at, 57
Southwest High School
  basic skills program at, 86
  writing across the curriculum at, 23
Special events, 201–203
Specialized programs
  for teaching democracy, 52–58
  for teaching writing, 41–44
Spirit, 193–195
St. Louis Park High School
  basic skills program at, 87
  Close-Up program at, 53
  discipline policy of, 100
  goals of, 6
  special projects of, 187
  writing curriculum of, 28
St. Louise de Marillac High School
  community event at, 186
  high expectations of, 92

on legislative action, 52
  motto of, 90
St. Mark's School of Texas
  on character and values, 60
  on drugs, 113
  Issues Day at, 56
  program as success of, 200
  study skills courses at, 79
  teacher input at, 142
  teachers' monetary rewards at,
    161
St. Rita High School, staff develop-
    ment for, 152
St. Thomas More Catholic High
    School, specialized writing pro-
    gram at, 43
Staff development, for teachers,
    147–155
Stanton College Preparatory School
  college prep services of, 125
  as community school, 189
  personal relationships at, 62
  study skills courses at, 77
  writing curriculum of, 31
  writing program at, 38
Statement of philosophy, 4
Stephens County High School
  communicating goals at, 17
  community partnership with, 187
  parent education program at, 175
Stone Ridge Country Day School of
    the Sacred Heart
  community service at, 65
  rules of, 61
Students
  and basic skills, 83–89
  college and career information for,
    122–129
  communicating goals to, 15–16
  and discipline, 99–107
  and drugs, 108–115
  participation in discipline policies,
    100–101
  reporting progress of, 116–121
  at risk, 130–138
  and study skills, 77–82

Study skills
  across the curriculum, 80–81
  and counselors and media special-
    ists, 81
  courses on, 77–79
  materials, 81–82
  students and, 77–82
Success stories, 193–204
Summer programs, in basic skills, 84
Support groups, 134
Support staff, 39–40
Sycamore Junior High School
  faculty committees of, 142
  parent participation in, 171
  people as success of, 198
  staff development for, 151
  teacher awards from, 158

Teachers
  input from, 141–146
  rewards and incentives for, 156–162
  staff development for, 147–155
  See also Faculty; Teaching
Teaching
  character and values, 59–74
  about democracy, 45–58
  writing, 22–27, 32–44
  See also Teachers
Team approach, 4
Testing, 123
Thompkins Middle School, career
  information from, 127
Torrey Pines High School
  business partnership with, 183
  teacher awards at, 158
  tutoring writing at, 38
  writing curriculum of, 29
Tottenville High School
  business partnership with, 185
  clubs and organizations at, 63
  community service at, 67
  goals review at, 13
  learning about law at, 48
  model Congress of, 51
  specialized writing program at, 42
  students at risk at, 135

Tradition, goals and, 7
Tredyffrin/Easttown Junior High
  School, principal's role at, 62

University High School
  business partnership with, 183
  communicating goals at, 18
  on drugs, 111
  faculty training in writing at, 32
  parent participation in, 173
  staff development for, 152
  writing support staff at, 39
University of Chicago Laboratory
  School
  basic skills program at, 88
  counseling at, 123
  progress reports of, 119
  students and discipline at, 101
  writing and school goals at, 22
University of New Mexico Education
  Department, 6
University of North Carolina's Charlotte Writing Project, 34
University partnerships, 181–183

Vacaville High School
  basic skills program at, 88
  communicating goals at, 15
  high expectations of, 91
  writing program at, 42
Valley High School
  study skills courses at, 78
  teacher honors at, 157, 160
  writing lab of, 36
Valley View Junior High, code of
  conduct at, 62
Van Hise Middle School
  high expectations of, 92
  writing curriculum of, 28
Vermont Writing Project, 32
Villa Angela Academy
  communicating goals at, 16
  community service at, 65
  parent participation in, 167
  staff development for, 150
  teaching honors from, 159

Wallingford-Swarthmore Writing
   Project, 33
Washington Middle School
   (Montana), career program at,
   127
Washington Middle School (New
   Mexico)
   progress reports of, 119
   student discipline at, 105
   teaching honors from, 159
Wayland High School
   athletics at, 64
   Close-Up program at, 53
   goals review at, 14
   parent participation in, 173
   special event as success of, 202
   writing lab of, 36
Wenatchee High School
   on drugs, 113
   high expectations of, 92
   students at risk at, 137
   writing and school goals at, 22
West Bloomfield High School
   career program at, 181
   clubs and organizations at, 63
   course offerings of, 197
   on drugs, 109–110
   faculty committees of, 142
   global view at, 46
   in social studies olympiad, 55
   students at risk at, 134
   writing curriculum of, 29
   writing lab of, 36
Westbury Senior High School
   financial support of, 179
   on student behavior, 103
   teacher honors at, 157
   writing across the curriculum at,
   23, 26
Wheeling High School
   basic skills program at, 89
   career program of, 181
   on drugs, 113
   high expectations of, 91
   parent participation in, 166, 173
   study skills program at, 80

White Plains High School
   business partnership with, 185
   community service at, 71
   foreign policy issues at, 56
   goals of, 6, 11
   staff development for, 151
   teaching honors from, 159
Wilbur Rowe Junior High School,
   study skills courses at, 79
William Fremd High School
   on drugs, 109–110
   high expectations of, 93
   parent participation in, 166
   special event as success of, 202
   writing lab of, 36
   writing support staff at, 40
William H. Atwell Fundamental
   Academy
   staff development for, 153
   teacher input at, 145
William H. Farquhar Middle School,
   sensitivity awareness at, 72
Williams Bay High School, on
   rewards for teaching, 162
Woodbridge High School
   global view at, 46
   goals of, 5
   goals review at, 14
   learning about community at, 47
   teacher input at, 143
   writing across the curriculum at, 26
Woodmere Middle School, citizenship policy at, 62
Woodstock Union High School
   community partnership with, 187
   faculty training in writing at, 32
   special event as success of, 201
   teacher input at, 145
   writing guide of, 35
World view, 46–47
Worthingway Middle School, on
   drugs, 113
Write Track Program, 34
Writing
   across the curriculum, 22–27
   assessing competency of, 24

Writing *(continued)*
    assignments, 30–31
    contests, 31
    curriculum, 27–32
    faculty training in teaching, 32–35
    labs, 36–38
    remedial, 40–41
    resources and support for teaching, 35–40
    and school goals, 22–27
    special needs in teaching, 40–41
    specialized courses in, 28–30
    specialized programs and promotions for, 41–44

Xavier Preparatory School
    remedial writing at, 40
    on student behavior, 107

Yankton Senior High School, high expectations of, 93
Yarmouth Junior-Senior High School
    community event at, 186
    Constitution debate at, 56
    on drugs, 114
    specialized reports of, 118
    students at risk at, 135
    writing curriculum of, 31
    writing lab of, 37